sona
BOOKS

First published in the UK by Sona Books, an imprint of Danann Media Publishing Limited

Original material reproduced by courtesy of Future Publishing/FourFourTwo 2023

CAT NO. SON0567

Cover design: Darren Grice
Book design: Paul Southcombe
Editor: Martin Corteel
Proof reader: Cameron Thurlow
Contributors: Chris Flanagan, Mark White and Ed McCambridge and Cameron Thurlow

Cover images: Getty Images
Book images: Alamy, Getty images
Additional images:
joshjdss
Jacek Stanislawek
Steindy
Soccuer.ru

Made in EU.

ISBN: 978-1-915343-30-7

PREMIER LEAGUE LEGENDS

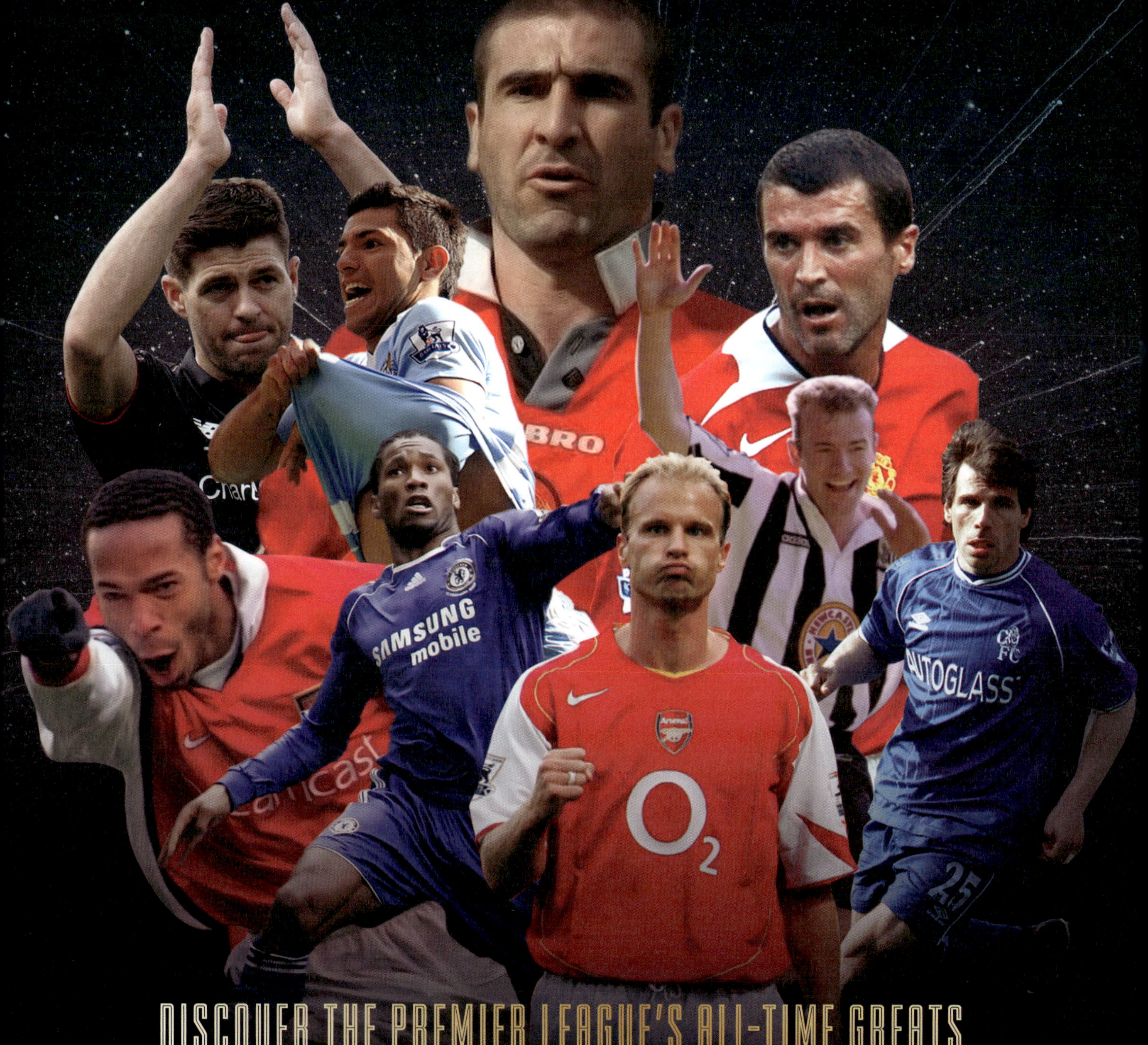

DISCOVER THE PREMIER LEAGUE'S ALL-TIME GREATS

CONTENTS

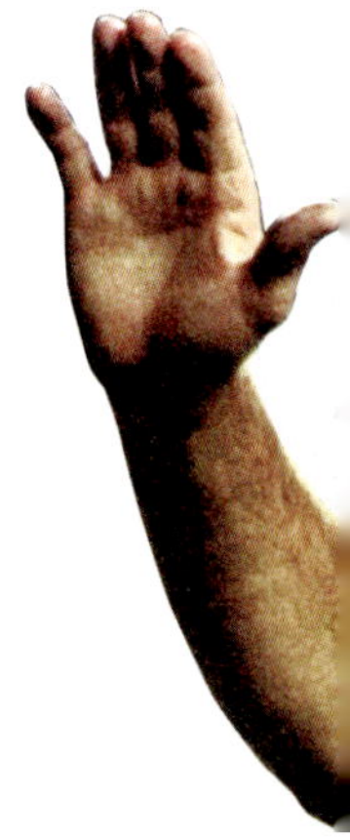

ETIHAD
AIRWAYS
THISTLE
HOTELS
Everton
Chang
NEWCASTLE
BROWN ALE

FILA
Dr. Martens
NIKE
ETIHAD AIRWAYS
125 YEARS

INTRODUCTION

On Saturday 15 August 1992, a multi-billion pound behemoth was born, as the inaugural season of the Premier League kicked off, changing the face of English football forever. Now, as well as the best players from the British Isles, English football would be able to attract some of the top talent from around the globe – from Jurgen Klinsmann and Dennis Bergkamp to Luis Suarez and Eric Cantona.

In Premier League Legends we celebrate the very best entertainers, goal-getters and deadly destroyers from the past three decades of action. We kick off with a rundown of the top 100 players and some of the most iconic names of the Premier League era, while we also dive into the FourFourTwo magazine archives to unearth in-depth features and exclusive interviews with the likes of Juninho, David Ginola and Paolo Di Canio and relive some of the glorious goals, superb skills and show-stopping saves we've been privileged to witness ever since that historic Saturday afternoon in the summer of 1992. Enjoy!

100 GREATEST PLAYERS

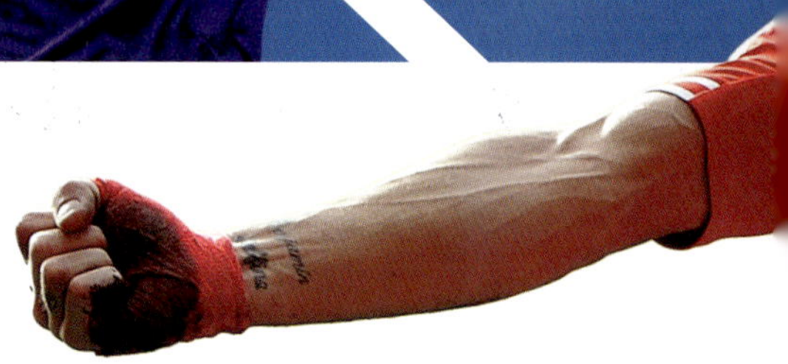

EVER

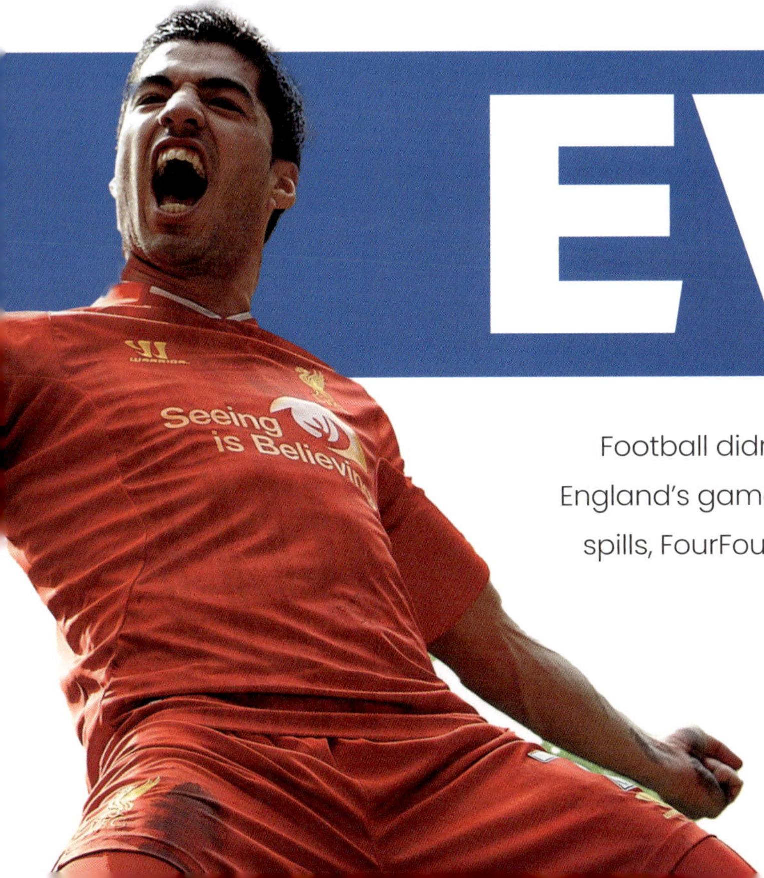

Football didn't begin in 1992, but an era that would alter England's game forever did. After three decades of thrills and spills, FourFourTwo ranks the ultimate icons who defined a generation

100 PETER CROUCH

ASTON VILLA, SOUTHAMPTON, LIVERPOOL, PORTSMOUTH, TOTTENHAM, STOKE, BURNLEY

LEGACY Crouch might be best known for his lofty stature, robotic dance moves and good-natured podcast patter – but real fans know there was sao much more to his game.

The Spurs academy graduate cut his teeth in Sweden and the second tier before finally getting his top-flight chance with Aston Villa in 2001. Graham Taylor fancied him; David O'Leary didn't.

It wasn't until Crouch was flogged to Southampton in 2004 that his Premier League career got going.
He netted only three goals before Christmas, but Harry Redknapp's arrival – and James Beattie's January sale – paved the way for nine goals in the new year. They couldn't keep the Saints up, but did earn Crouch his first England call-up and a shock transfer to Liverpool in 2005.

He promptly went 18 matches without a goal. "I really wanted to head back to Southampton as fast as possible," he told *FFT* in 2018. "I was thinking, 'What have I done?'" Finally, he broke his Reds duck with a wildly deflected effort that somehow lobbed Wigan keeper Mike Pollitt – the first of a brace that afternoon.

They accounted for two of 108 Premier League goals, of which a record 53 were headers. At each of his clubs, team-mates appreciated Crouch's all-round forward play, but the simple knowledge that hopeful crosses into the box were never futile certainly did no harm. There was more than that, of course: just rewatch that outrageous effort for Stoke against Manchester City in March 2012.

In July 2008, Crouch was reunited with Redknapp at Portsmouth in an £11 million move, then again at Spurs for £10m one year later. 'Arry made the targetman one of his first signings after landing the job in north London. The striker was often used as an impact substitute, but achieved cult status at White Hart Lane by netting the goal against Manchester City which effectively secured Spurs' spot in the Champions League/European Cup for the first time since 1962.

Crouch's languid playing style allowed him to extend his career until the ripe old age of 38. At Stoke, and later Burnley, the unmistakable sight of him warming up continued to perk up hopeful crowds until as late as 2019.

As one of just 33 players to have struck a century of Premier League goals, Crouch's place in history is assured. He is among even more exclusive company in one regard – a player universally admired by fans of every team. Those headers, loose limbs, velcro touch, occasional eye for the spectacular and happy-go-lucky personality made him impossible to dislike – unless you were a centre-back marking him at a corner, that is.

Not bad for a guy once referred to as "the 20ft chicken" by rival non-league fans at Dulwich Hamlet.

HIGHLIGHT Right foot, left foot, header: Crouch's perfect hat-trick at Anfield – the only treble in his career – guided Liverpool to a 4-1 win over Arsenal in March 2007.

99 ANDREI KANCHELSKIS

MANCHESTER UNITED, EVERTON, MANCHESTER CITY, SOUTHAMPTON

LEGACY Alex Ferguson's love of fast and skilful wingers can be traced back to Kanchelskis' £650,000 arrival from Shakhtar Donetsk. The nimble Russian helped United secure back-to-back Premier League titles from 1993, but couldn't prevent a high-profile spat with his boss. Instead, he became a cult hero at Everton before shorter stints at Manchester City and Southampton.

HIGHLIGHT A hat-trick against Man City in November 1994 and double for the Toffees at Anfield a year later. Andrei liked a derby.

98 BRAD FRIEDEL

LIVERPOOL, BLACKBURN, ASTON VILLA, TOTTENHAM

LEGACY The American stopper holds the record for the most consecutive Premier League appearances. Between August 2004 and October 2012, Friedel played 310 straight matches – comprising eight years, six managers and three clubs.A fine leader, communicator and goalkeeper.

HIGHLIGHT Friedel bagged a 90th-minute equaliser for Blackburn against Charlton in February 2004... only for the Addicks to net an even later winner to take the spoils 3-2.

97 PEPE REINA

LIVERPOOL, ASTON VILLA

LEGACY Hailed as "the best keeper in Spain" by Liverpool manager Rafael Benitez upon his 2005 arrival from Villarreal, Reina's first task was to oust Champions League final legend Jerzy Dudek. It wasn't even a fight: Reina immediately grabbed the No.1 shirt, racking up 134 clean sheets in 285 Premier League appearances for the Reds – earning him the Golden Glove award in three consecutive campaigns.

HIGHLIGHT Breaking Liverpool's record of consecutive Premier League clean sheets (eight) during his first, rock-solid season.

96 STEVE BRUCE

MANCHESTER UNITED

LEGACY Bruce's contributions to early-90s Manchester United deserve much greater credit. As one half of a formidable defensive partnership with Gary Pallister, the affable Northumbrian helped United win three of the opening four Premier Leagues – the first as skipper, via one almighty intervention...

HIGHLIGHT Brucie's brace – superb headers in the 86th and 96th minutes – gave United a fabled 2-1 win over Sheffield Wednesday in April 1993. Fergie's side never looked back, sealing the title with two matches to spare.

95 EMILE HESKEY

LEICESTER, LIVERPOOL, BIRMINGHAM, WIGAN, ASTON VILLA

LEGACY Heskey's 110 Premier League goals place him 25th in the all-time scoring chart, but the Leicester man was always valued for more than his bare numbers. His total may have been helped by longevity over innate scoring talent – only six players have exceeded Heskey's 516 top-flight appearances – but he earned every single strike through his tireless work ethic and selfless style.

The rule of thumb was very simple: pair your best striker with Heskey, sit back and enjoy the results. No matter the partner – Robbie Fowler or Michael Owen at Liverpool, Gabriel Agbonlahor at Aston Villa – the 6ft 2in frontman proved the perfect foil. "Fowler had more natural talent; Ronaldo, Shearer, Rooney [too]... but it's about how you complement each other," Owen once recalled.

Heskey may never have troubled Golden Boot lists, but his managers didn't seem to care. Neither did he.

"I never considered myself a prolific scorer, but I knew what else I brought to the table: I created a lot, could hold the ball up and understood my roles," he told *FFT*.

Nevertheless, he still smashed home 14 league goals for Liverpool during their 2000-01 treble-winning season, firing Gerard Houllier's side to a third-place league finish.

Such skills were evident early. The future 62-cap England international made his Premier League debut at just 17 for local club Leicester, who were relegated shortly after his bow but bounced back at the first attempt. Upon their return, Heskey – then a nippy wide forward – hit 10 goals in consecutive campaigns, in between coming second to David Beckham for the 1996-97 PFA Young Player of the Year award (ahead of Fowler). There was little doubting the Foxes prodigy's potential.

The goals didn't quite flow as expected from there, but Liverpool's decision to make Heskey their record signing for £11m in March 2000 – then the third-most expensive domestic transfer in English football history – sent a clear message. There always appeared to be something that only those on the inside truly appreciated.

"Heskey may be heavily criticised by some English fans, but I don't see it like that," noted former FIFA World Player of the Year Rivaldo in 2002. "I played against him a couple of times for Barcelona and realised what a quality player he is. If you ask me which Englishman I think would be able to cope with playing in my team, Brazil, I say Heskey."

HIGHLIGHT A cracker against Coventry for Leicester in November 1999 was the very best of Heskey: terrific chest control, then a brilliant finish moving away from goal.

94 JAMIE CARRAGHER
LIVERPOOL

LEGACY The one-club man willingly played anywhere he was needed in his early Reds career, moving to a permanent home at centre-back under Rafael Benitez. His strong leadership made him an Anfield pillar for 17 years. "Carragher was the most difficult opponent in terms of aggression," revealed Didier Drogba.
HIGHLIGHT An 18-year-old Carra slotted into midfield on his full Liverpool debut at home to Aston Villa in January 1997 – and headed the opening goal in a 3-0 victory.

93 JAMES MILNER
LEEDS, NEWCASTLE, ASTON VILLA, MANCHESTER CITY, LIVERPOOL

LEGACY Milner has enjoyed the career of a dozen different players. He's been the Premier League's youngest-ever scorer, a touchline-hugging wideman under Sir Bobby Robson at Newcastle, and a goal-getter with Aston Villa. Now 36, the shapeshifting Yorkshireman has settled into his final position as Liverpool's Mr Reliable in midfield… or is that right-back? A colossus.
HIGHLIGHT Sure, Millie's a three-time title winner, but that goal for Leeds in 2002 – aged 16 years, 356 days – takes some beating.

92 KASPER SCHMEICHEL
MANCHESTER CITY, LEICESTER

LEGACY Being the son of a legend didn't give Schmeichel much of a leg-up. He had to work his way up off the Manchester City bench, eventually reaching the Premier League with Leicester in 2014. Then he helped the Foxes maintain their top-flight status before the natural conclusion of, er, winning the bloody thing. The 35-year-old has rarely put a glove wrong since and is already a Leicester icon.
HIGHLIGHT Five straight clean sheets near the end of 2015-16, when everybody began to believe in the impossible.

91 DION DUBLIN
MANCHESTER UNITED, COVENTRY, ASTON VILLA

LEGACY Quiz question: who scored the winner in Manchester United's first Premier League victory? This guy did.

Just over a week after Dublin's 88th-minute poacher's finish against Southampton, his third United appearance, the towering striker broke his leg at home to Crystal Palace. While Dublin was sidelined, United signed Eric Cantona from Leeds to kick-start a trophy-laden new era at Old Trafford.

"I don't have any regrets, although I'd love to know what could have happened if I'd been able to sustain a longer spell in the United team," Dublin pondered to *FFT* on his *Sliding Doors* moment in 2019.

Still, Dublin did just fine away from Manchester. Flogged to Coventry in September 1994, the forward hit the ground running, netting eight times in his first 10 games. He bagged 13 or more in his first four seasons at Highfield Road, and played an integral role in keeping the Sky Blues up in a frantic end to the 1996-97 season. With six daunting matches to go, Cov were bottom. Then they won at Liverpool with a late Dublin goal, before beating Chelsea with another strike from their talisman. Dublin also earned Cov a point at Arsenal before their final-day showdown against Spurs, where only a win – and other results going their way – would suffice. On a nerve-jangling afternoon, Dublin's early goal sent Gordon Strachan's side on their way to safety, in one of English football's great escape acts.

He stayed to joint-top the Premier League goal charts with 18 in 1997-98, spurning the advances of Blackburn to join Aston Villa for £5.75m after a harsh omission from England's France 98 squad. Dublin couldn't quite match his output down the A45, but was a fan favourite at Villa Park, helped by two braces and a hat-trick in his opening three games for John Gregory's men.

Dublin, though, achieved something deeper still with each passing campaign. The talisman took on cult status in the '90s, with his long-legged stride, rocket shot and infectious energy endearing him to those who watched on. He bounced back to play for Villa just three months after sustaining a broken neck that could have ended his career in 1999, once nutmegged Bolton goalkeeper Keith Branagan with a side-footed volley before standing perfectly still in celebration, and even played at centre-back for Villa – as if that was a perfectly normal thing for a striker to do. Long before social media, he also scored one of the cheekiest goals in history, robbing Shay Given in 1997 by hiding behind the keeper.

If that's not enough, Dublin once lived with actor Jason Statham, went on to invent his own percussion instrument (The Dube) and now successfully presents *Homes Under the Hammer*. Dion, we salute you.
HIGHLIGHT An explosive hat-trick for Coventry against Sheffield Wednesday in December 1995, coming during a purple patch where Dublin began to assert himself as one of the premier marksmen in English football.

90 GILBERTO SILVA

ARSENAL

LEGACY Arsene Wenger built a cathedral of beautiful football at Arsenal, with silky attacking players his architects. Behind them, though, sat Gilberto: the 'invisible wall' who swept up, battled hard and helped to provide an artistic Gunners side with a tough shell. His understated influence underpinned Arsenal: the Invincibles owed their creativity to the ball-winner who let them flourish.

HIGHLIGHT Going unbeaten in 2003-04 was a team effort, but two goals to win the first North London derby at the Emirates Stadium in December 2006 were all Gilberto's.

89 STEVE MCMANAMAN

LIVERPOOL, MANCHESTER CITY

LEGACY Rarely is a side's most talented player also its most hard-working – McManaman was the exception. He almost scorched the Anfield turf with his fierce running, yet so much of the Reds' play went through him. He became El Macca when departing for Real Madrid in 1999, but epitomised everything positive about '90s Liverpool with his flair and determination.

HIGHLIGHT A looping corker against Arsenal in November 1997 – one of his 11 goals that season – summed up the Scouser's cocksure confidence. Great hair, too.

88 FERNANDINHO

MANCHESTER CITY

LEGACY The 37-year-old has sharpened his positional sense, passing and tactical awareness to become indispensable for Manchester City. "Everything we've done wouldn't have been possible without him," Pep Guardiola hummed of the Brazilian utility man ahead of 2017-18 glory.

HIGHLIGHT City pinched the 2018-19 title by just a point thanks to their humdinger of a win over Liverpool in January. Fernandinho, recently back from injury, was outstanding in a 2-1 classic, won by the barest of margins.

87 KEVIN PHILLIPS

SUNDERLAND, SOUTHAMPTON, ASTON VILLA, BIRMINGHAM, CRYSTAL PALACE

LEGACY As a youngster with Southampton, Phillips would clean Alan Shearer's boots. By 2000, the strike pair were on either side of the Sunderland-Newcastle divide and Phillips was pipping his senior to the Premier League Golden Boot.

In fact, Phillips outscored anyone in Europe in his first top-flight season, as the Black Cats finished seventh. He is the only Englishman to win the European Golden Shoe.

As it transpired, Rodney Marsh's assertion that 'Super Kev' wouldn't score more than six goals was about as accurate as an octopus playing darts. "We got smashed 4-0 at Chelsea on the opening weekend – I think I only touched the ball about five times and thought, 'Rodney could be right!'" Phillips chuckled to *FFT* in 2019.

In fact, the striker began with 13 in his first 12 games, including an iconic winner against Newcastle in front of a seething, dropped Shearer at St James' Park. He struck another three doubles before Christmas, most notably at home to Chelsea in a 4-1 redemption victory. Although Sunderland went 11 matches without a win from Boxing Day, Phillips still scored six – including two more against Newcastle. "The Premier League hadn't come up against a pairing like me and Niall Quinn before," said Phillips.

The arch poacher plundered 14 during 2000-01 as the Wearsiders came seventh again, but trouble lay ahead. By April 2002, his goals were keeping Peter Reid's outfit afloat in the top flight on the final day of the season.

In 2002-03, the Black Cats finished bottom with the Premier League's (then) worst points total. Southampton pounced to bring him back to the south coast for £3.25m, where he forged a fine partnership with James Beattie. When Beattie moved to Everton, Phillips struggled without a pacy forward and was again relegated in 2004-05.

The eight-cap England man had spells with Aston Villa and Birmingham, and by late 2013 was still coming off the bench for Crystal Palace at 40, before finally heading back to the Championship.

There, Phillips joined promotion-winning Leicester to play alongside Jamie Vardy, following the previous term's loanee Harry Kane. That trio are the only Englishmen to have won 21st century top-tier Golden Boots – but Phillips did so with the most goals. A remarkable campaign from a remarkable finisher.

HIGHLIGHT A sumptuous drive in that 4-1 win against Chelsea. "It was a 25-yard dipping volley then," smiled Phillips. "It's [become] a 40-yard volley." It was brilliant.

86 STAN COLLYMORE

CRYSTAL PALACE, NOTTINGHAM FOREST, LIVERPOOL, ASTON VILLA, LEICESTER, BRADFORD

LEGACY In April 1996, Collymore was closing in. Closing in on devastating Newcastle's title ambitions in that breathless classic, yes, but also on the brightest of futures. Collymore was 25 years old and Liverpool's starting striker in a formidable 42-goal partnership with Robbie Fowler, having fired 22 the season prior at Nottingham Forest.

And then it all went wrong. Eleven months later, he was on the bench watching the same fixture – another astonishing 4-3 victory. Two months after that, he watched Michael Owen net his first Liverpool goal on his debut against Wimbledon.

By early 2001, Collymore's top-tier career was finished. "I didn't see any beauty in football any more," he later wrote. "I didn't see any friendship or even fraternity. I just saw a wilderness of loneliness and pain. By the end I felt like some sort of f**king circus act."

If Owen's emergence had eventually nudged him out of Liverpool under a cloud by May 1997, what followed was much more serious – a battle with his own head that seemed unwinnable. While Collymore clashed with John Gregory at Aston Villa and later Peter Taylor at Leicester, his mental health struggles also brought with them a lack of understanding around him.

Villa chairman Doug Ellis suggested his striker's 1999 stint in the Priory was "a holiday', according to Collymore, who criticised his team-mates' lack of support.

A switch to Leicester in February 2000 was Collymore's career in a microcosm. Days after signing, he drunkenly decorated a La Manga hotel with a fire extinguisher; new boss Martin O'Neill let him off with a royal wrist slap, then watched his new striker hammer home a brilliant hat-trick against Sunderland on his Filbert Street debut. Four games later, Collymore broke his leg. O'Neill left soon after, to be replaced by another imminent nemesis in Taylor. Within six months Collymore was gone.

And so, after a three-month stint with cash-strapped Bradford, Collymore reached that wilderness of loneliness and pain. It shouldn't have ended like that.

The 1994-95 Stan was a whirlwind of athleticism and lethal class. Forest finished third upon their return to the big time, qualifying for the UEFA Cup thanks to their unplayable frontman. Fans had enjoyed Teddy Sheringham and Nigel Clough before that, but neither thrilled like a peak Collymore.

On the pitch, there wasn't much he *couldn't* do. Off it, sadly, there wasn't much he could do right, struggling on in a world that couldn't understand his issues, often made worse at his own accord.

But remember the footballer, remember

the good. Fire up YouTube, search 'Collymore vs Wimbledon' and marvel at the force of nature that was Stanley Victor Collymore.

HIGHLIGHT Look no further than Newcastle. After teeing up Fowler for the first goal, Collymore hit two of his own, the second, a 92nd-minute jackhammer that sent Kevin Keegan sinking to the advertising boards. Pure theatre.

85 ROMELU LUKAKU

CHELSEA, WEST BROM, EVERTON, MANCHESTER UNITED

LEGACY Future historians may struggle to summarise Lukaku's career. His Old Trafford tenure was largely unhappy, his stints at both Everton and West Brom spectacular. Ultimately, the Belgian's record – 113 goals in 252 appearances – stands up for itself. Lukaku remains the youngest ever foreign player to hit a ton of Premier League goals, aged just 24.

HIGHLIGHT On as a sub in Alex Ferguson's last match as United gaffer, Rom's perfect hat-trick helped West Brom to a 5-5 draw.

84 MARC OVERMARS

ARSENAL

LEGACY The jet-propelled Dutchman took time to catch alight after joining from Ajax in the summer of 1997, but was crucial to Arsenal's subsequent Double-winning campaign. The winger was good for big goals on the biggest occasions, including a brace as Arsene Wenger's outfit wrapped up the title against Everton.

HIGHLIGHT His slotted finish at Old Trafford in March 1998 was essential to the Gunners overturning a nine-point (and three-match) deficit to Manchester United before kick-off.

83 JUNINHO

MIDDLESBROUGH

LEGACY Juninho loved Boro so much he signed for them three times: initially as a fancy new arrival from Brazil in October 1995, then again in 1999 and 2002. His star may have diminished with each return, but the schemer's twinkle-toed displays at the tip of Bryan Robson's midfield in his first spell secure his standing as one of British football's most-loved imports.

HIGHLIGHT In a Boro career of near misses, finishing as runner-up to Gianfranco Zola for the FWA Player of the Year award in 1996-97 was an indication of Juninho's class.

82 TIM CAHILL

EVERTON

LEGACY Cahill is one of the all-time great Premier League bargains. For £1.5m in 2004, Everton bagged a player who would decorate matches with aerial brilliance and corner flag punishment for eight campaigns. The Aussie averaged a goal every four games across 226 league appearances, and is loved at Goodison Park.

HIGHLIGHT No post-war Everton player has scored more Merseyside derby league goals (five). A late Anfield strike in January 2009 snaffled a draw, en route to finishing fifth.

81 DAVID BATTY →

LEEDS, BLACKBURN, NEWCASTLE

LEGACY Batty wasn't like other players. While Gareth Southgate's Euro 96 penalty miss ate away at the future England manager, his Three Lions team-mate had no such demons after missing at a World Cup two years later.

"After the game it was like, 'Unlucky Dave' and he was like, 'What?'" Paul Merson told the *Quickly Kevin* podcast. "David Beckham's in the dressing room crying his eyes out because he's been sent off and let everyone down, and David Batty's sitting there getting changed."

For anyone who watched him in his pomp, it's baffling to imagine such off-field nonchalance. He grafted. As a teenager at Elland Road, he was made to drink sherry and raw egg by Billy Bremner, the legendary midfield general who Leeds fans hoped he would emulate. He was similarly combative: the local boy's idea of injecting fun into the 1992 pre-season Makita Tournament involved hacking Roberto Mancini's riled Sampdoria team to bits, with a mischievous grin.

"It was a friendly, wasn't it?" he shrugged during a rare interview. "So you could do what you wanted."

Batty helped Leeds secure promotion in 1990, before winning the last First Division title. Boss Howard Wilkinson let him move to Blackburn for £2.75m in October 1993, however, with *The Independent* sniffing at a footballer "whose distribution never matched his more destructive skills". Years later, few would have agreed.

It was certainly Rovers' gain. Batty went on to establish a steely midfield partnership with Tim Sherwood as they finished second in 1993-94, but then suffered a broken foot which ruled him out for the majority of their golden campaign a year later. The midfielder refused his winners' medal, having only featured five times.

He asked to leave Ewood Park in 1996 after infamously scrapping with team-mate Graeme Le Saux in the difficult sequel to Rovers' title defence. Newcastle manager Kevin Keegan jumped at the chance to add "the last piece in my jigsaw" to complement Les Ferdinand, Tino Asprilla, Peter Beardsley and David Ginola ahead of him. Again, though, Batty was a nearly man; part of a side that were runners-up twice.

He departed St James' Park weeks after France 98, returning to Leeds as elder statesman of David O'Leary's new era. Injuries limited his impact, but Batty nonetheless helped his local club fly through Europe on the crest of a wave.

The end was sudden. In 2004, when Leeds went down amid financial disaster, the Whites hero retired. He didn't go into coaching. He isn't seen proffering his opinions on TV every week. He barely does interviews. Famously, Batty was the only member of Blackburn's 1995 title winners not to turn up for their reunion 20 years later.

Football was his job. Ultimately, Batty was just another bloke with a life outside work – and loved for it.

HIGHLIGHT Re-signing for his hometown team in 1998, greeted by "Batty's coming home" from the stands.

80 ROBBIE KEANE

COVENTRY, LEEDS, TOTTENHAM, LIVERPOOL, WEST HAM, ASTON VILLA

LEGACY Keane is remembered for his trademark cartwheel following 126 Premier League goals, including six straight seasons of double-digit returns in his first Spurs spell. As Edgar Davids found out, he was also nails. "He went bang – one punch, gone," said ex-Tottenham team-mate Jamie O'Hara of one training ground fracas. "Davids picked himself up and walked off."

HIGHLIGHT Britain's most expensive teen in 1999 tied Derby's Jacob Laursen up in knots during a superb two-goal debut for Coventry.

79 FREDDIE LJUNGBERG

ARSENAL, WEST HAM

LEGACY While Robert Pires was cultured and delicate down the left flank for Arsenal, there was nothing subtle about Ljungberg. The Swede was fearless, feisty and would frequently slip past centre-backs unnoticed to grab big goals. A generation of children dyed their hair pink thanks to Freddie – the Gunners' action man.

HIGHLIGHT Injury to Pires forced Ljungberg to the left in 2001-02's run-in, but he popped up with six goals and helped to create Sylvain Wiltord's strike to win the title at Old Trafford.

78 ROBERTO FIRMINO

LIVERPOOL

LEGACY The Brazilian was once a promising, yet inconsistent attacking midfielder – then perfected the false nine role under manager Jurgen Klopp. Now, his vision and positional nomadism are the template for how traditional forwards – even Harry Kane – can improve their skill set. "I would feel really embarrassed if I had to mention all the qualities of Bobby Firmino," tooted Klopp in 2020.

HIGHLIGHT Three assists for three different players as Liverpool trounced Southampton 4-0 in February 2020 was Firmino at his finest.

77 MICHAEL ESSIEN

CHELSEA

LEGACY Whether Essien was bludgeoning footballs from 30 yards, charging through a sea of midfield legs or crunching into tackles, he did everything with the utmost commitment. The Ghanaian could also read a game like few others, and was a linchpin in eight seasons at Stamford Bridge for Jose Mourinho and Carlo Ancelotti.

HIGHLIGHT Essien's stonker against Arsenal in December 2006 combined brawn with beauty; a glorious outside-of-the-boot strike which almost decapitated Didier Drogba.

76 GARY SPEED

LEEDS, EVERTON, NEWCASTLE, BOLTON

LEGACY Just before Gary Speed finally retired aged 40, having made almost 850 appearances in English football, the midfielder decided he needed another challenge. He was about to join the Sheffield United coaching staff, but that wasn't enough for the all-action Welshman. So, he took up long-distance running, and in April 2010 entered the London Marathon to raise funds for the Sir Bobby Robson and John Hartson Foundations.

I spent a day with Gary at the Blades' training ground in the build-up to the big race, and couldn't understand how someone who claimed he wasn't fit enough to play football should put himself through 26 miles of torture.

"It's a different kind of fitness," he said. "I don't have the power to play at a decent level any more, but if you're plodding in a marathon, then I'll be able to plod all day." Plodding? Well, he plodded his way to smash his pre-race target of beating the four-hour mark. But that was typical Speed, the man blessed with model good looks who could seemingly turn his hand to anything. He mastered the guitar as a young player and became the life and soul at every party.

Those handsome features got me into a spot of bother with the midfielder within days of him joining Sir Bobby's Newcastle from Everton. I'd read that Speed had scooped 'Heartthrob of the Year' in a teenage girls' magazine, and wrote that he'd come to St James' Park looking to add to this latest honour. "Thanks, mate," he said when we met. "Can you imagine the bloody stick I've taken for that?"

It was no more than a gentle ticking off, though. Speed was incapable of worse.

Indeed, you were more likely to be thanked than chided by him – as I found out when he rang me after the *Daily Star* had carried a spread on his marathon preparations. Gary enjoyed the piece so much that he asked if he could include it on his JustGiving page. The honour, of course, was all mine.

As a player, Speed won the First Division title at Leeds, achieved his boyhood ambition by pulling on the blue shirt of Everton and played in the Champions League for Newcastle.

On February 7, 2004, he became the first footballer to achieve 400 Premier League appearances. Ahead of the big game for the Magpies against Leicester, I asked him to name his all-time Premier League XI. His selection contained all the usual suspects – Schmeichel, Adams, Keane, Henry, Giggs and his big pal Shearer – but it also revealed something about the individual.

"No place for Gary Speed in that midfield?" I naively asked. He looked at me with disdain. "Are you joking?"

Speed was modest and a realist. He knew he was good – very good, even – but the Welshman never got too big for his boots. The left-footed midfielder would get into many supporters' best XIs of the Premier League era at Leeds, Everton, Newcastle and Bolton, whom he joined after being sold behind Sir Bobby's back just six months after becoming the 400-club's founding member.

Sam Allardyce's joy was in stark contrast to Robson's despair. "My life is enriched having known Gary," Big Sam later claimed.

Sir Bobby, meanwhile, mourned the huge void that Speed's exit would cause when he left St James' Park in 2004. "We'll miss him on the pitch, we'll miss him in the dressing room, we'll miss him on the training ground, we'll miss him in the restaurant," said the former England boss, in true Churchillian style.

Speed's Toon career hadn't exactly got off to the best start, however. Played wide by Kenny Dalglish early on, he had his critics in the stands but soon became crucial to the Magpies' line-up. Robson considered him among his ever-reliable 'blue-chip brigade', along with Speed's midfield partner Rob Lee, right-back Warren Barton, goalkeeper Shay Given and close friend Alan Shearer. But the pass master was popular with all; young and old, loud and quiet, rebels and diplomats. Arch-firebrand Craig Bellamy, who endured a difficult off-field relationship with Shearer, loved Speed like a big brother.

According to Jonathan Woodgate, who had grown up at Elland Road hearing stories of Speed's exploits, getting into his good books was one of his primary aims upon moving to Newcastle in 2003.

"When I turned up, I realised that not only was I signing for a top manager in Sir Bobby, but I'd be playing alongside two unbelievable pros in Alan and Gary," the ex-defender tells *FFT*. "I wanted to impress them just as much as I did the manager.

"I got to know Speedo well and always stayed in touch with him. You could always speak to him, you could always rely on him. When it came to training well every single day, he set the template. Throughout the game, young players were invariably told, 'If you're looking for a role model, Gary Speed's your man.'"

Over a decade after his tragic death, the man who represented Wales 85 times and went on to manage his country after a short stint at Bramall Lane is still regarded as one of the finest professionals of the modern era. So many former team-mates reminisce about Speed's insatiable work-rate, willingness to do the dirty work, make decoy runs to create space for others, and an instinctive ability of having time on the ball when there was none.

And then, of course, there were the goals – 135 of them across a 23-year career, so many via commanding bullet headers. Speed was equally capable of a crisp left-footed drive or a smart close-range finish after one of those trademark late runs into the box.

The tragedy of Speed's death on that bleak November 2011 morning is still one his mates struggle to come to terms with.

"Could you have done any more, could you help? I don't know," says Given, whose tears as Aston Villa faced Swansea – within hours of Speed's death being announced – remain one of the most evocative images of an awful day. "Gary as a person was among the most bubbly characters you'll ever meet. He was always up for a laugh – even his laugh used to make me laugh.

"You just think he'd be the last person [to take his own life]. I know a lot of people say that when someone does, but genuinely, you would never have seen it coming."

NEWCASTLE BROWN ALE
adidas

75 JURGEN KLINSMANN

TOTTENHAM

LEGACY 'Klinsmann To Be Diving Force' cackled the *Daily Express* after Spurs' £2m capture of the Germany marksman in July 1994. Having arrived at White Hart Lane from Monaco at the age of 30, the experienced frontman's reputation for scoring goals was only overshadowed by his predilection for amateur dramatics.

The 1990 World Cup Final had featured one particularly heinous act of thespianism from him; a textbook stretch-armed leap over a challenge, followed by rolls, cries and the requirement of a full medical team. Replays indicated minimal contact, yet defender Pedro Monzon became the first man to be sent off in a World Cup final as Klinsmann & Co lifted the trophy.

But upon his grand unveiling to a xenophobic press pack, Spurs' new man had the perfect line. "Maybe I can ask you the first question," he smirked with anticipation. "Are there any diving schools in London?" Reflecting on his introduction to *FFT* in 2011, the German said, "Making the joke helped begin to change the perceptions. It came from a German guy I'd met in southern France who'd lived in England for many years. He said, 'When you meet the media, why don't you take a backpack and pull a snorkel and goggles out of it?' In the end, I only said the joke. It just worked."

Soon, focus switched to the German's pedigree. He had been prolific at Stuttgart, Inter and Monaco before moving to north London, and the press soon realised Klinsmann was about more than quick quips.

Naturally, he opened with a goal on his Premier League debut: a trademark thumping header at Hillsborough, followed by his now-legendary diving celebration. In an Ossie Ardiles team built to score, Klinsmann thrived. "It wasn't ridiculous at all playing with five attacking players," he insisted to *FFT*. "I had a lot of fun, and I still think that had we been more consistent defensively, and not made so many individual mistakes at the back, we could have played that system."

The Guardian's Andrew Anthony, who had written an article called 'Why I Hate Jurgen Klinsmann' following the poacher's arrival, wrote another two months later titled 'Why I Love Jurgen Klinsmann'. With that, the marksman got on with what Spurs had paid for: scoring. He bagged 20 in 41 league games across 1994-95, helping Spurs finish seventh.

His sale to Bayern Munich after just one campaign was heartbreaking for Spurs fans – and angered chairman Alan Sugar, who believed the get-out clause in Klinsmann's contract only applied if the club was relegated. The small print didn't denote as much.

Klinsi wasn't gone for long, however, returning on loan from Sampdoria in 1997 to save Spurs from the drop. Nine goals in 15 post-Christmas appearances dragged them to safety, securing his legendary status forever.

HIGHLIGHT Klinsmann's four-goal haul at Wimbledon in May 1998 sealed troubled Tottenham's top-flight status with a match to spare.

74 PATRICE EVRA

MANCHESTER UNITED, WEST HAM

LEGACY Alex Ferguson likened finding a decent full-back to "searching for a rare bird" in his 2013 autobiography. In Evra, he found what he was looking for. "He was quick, had superb technique and a strong personality," wrote Fergie. United paid Monaco just £5.5m for the Frenchman in 2006, receiving more than eight years of fantastic service in return.

HIGHLIGHT It takes strength to recover from being subbed at half-time on your debut. He hung on, delivering a terrific goal-and-assist display against Everton later that year.

73 SAMI HYYPIA

LIVERPOOL

LEGACY The £2.6m arrival from Dutch outfit Willem II in 1999 was no headline-maker. Yet the centre-back soon transformed Gerard Houllier's Merseysiders into a different beast; from leaking 49 goals in 1998-99, the Reds conceded only 30 in two of the next three league campaigns. "He was so consistent, it was a shock if he had a bad game," Jamie Carragher told *FFT*.

HIGHLIGHT The Kop's mosaic tribute for the Finn's final Liverpool match in May 2009 was a fitting way to honour him.

72 DAVID DE GEA

MANCHESTER UNITED

LEGACY Schalke giant Manuel Neuer had been sought by Alex Ferguson in 2011, but United's goalkeeping coach Eric Steele believed the younger De Gea was a sounder option. "In three years, he'll be better," stated Steele. After a wobbly start, De Gea grew into a world-class stopper who bailed an ailing Red Devils side out for years, and was their player of the season in four of the five campaigns from 2013-14.

HIGHLIGHT An unbeatable, 14-save display against Arsenal in 2017 helped United pinch a 3-1 win at the Emirates Stadium.

71 JIMMY FLOYD HASSELBAINK

LEEDS, CHELSEA, MIDDLESBROUGH, CHARLTON

LEGACY After netting 24 goals for Boavista in 1996-97, Dutch ball-batterer Hasselbaink picked Leeds ahead of Werder Bremen – then plundered 34 goals over two Premier League seasons. After leaving for a prolific year at Atletico Madrid, Chelsea paid £15m for him in 2000, and were rewarded by back-to-back scoring seasons of 23.

HIGHLIGHT A thunderbolt at Old Trafford in 2000 was one of numerous Jimmy specials, opening the scoring in a see-saw 3-3 draw.

70 EMMANUEL PETIT
ARSENAL, CHELSEA

LEGACY Where Patrick Vieira was fire and might, Petit may be reflected on as the cooler antithesis. In reality, the sultry Frenchman embodied Arsenal's late-90s passion, and played with similar bite to his midfield partner. 'Manny Small' helped to deliver Wenger's first Double, and later moved to Stamford Bridge via one unhappy season at Barcelona.
HIGHLIGHT As Arsenal gunned towards the finish line in 1998, Petit's terrific goal decided a tight April encounter against Derby which set up their imminent trophy lift at Highbury.

69 LUKA MODRIC
TOTTENHAM

LEGACY Harry Redknapp telling his players to "just give the ball to Luka" might have appeared a rudimentary approach – but watching the Croatian, it didn't take a genius to understand why. Although he initially struggled, Modric's mastery of the ball soon came to the fore over four brilliant seasons at White Hart Lane.
HIGHLIGHT In an outstanding 2010-11, he was otherworldly in a goalless draw against Manchester United; later, Fergie would name him his player of the season.

68 JERMAIN DEFOE
WEST HAM, TOTTENHAM, PORTSMOUTH, SUNDERLAND, BOURNEMOUTH

LEGACY Only seven men have scored more Premier League goals than Defoe, who struck 162 times for five teams. The Londoner carved out a career of expertly hanging on defenders' shoulders, posting 10 double-digit top-flight seasons in a streak of healthy goal-getting. Anyone who can net 15 goals in back-to-back campaigns for Sunderland deserves a nod.
HIGHLIGHT Five second-half goals in a 9-1 Tottenham drubbing of Wigan had Redknapp hailing Defoe as the best finisher in England.

67 CARLOS TEVEZ
WEST HAM, MANCHESTER UNITED, MANCHESTER CITY

LEGACY At first, the circus of Tevez's disputed move to West Ham seemed silly – his first 16 league games passed without a goal, as the Hammers looked doomed. Then it all changed – seven strikes in the run-in saved the Londoners, before the Argentine proved his class in title triumphs at both Manchester clubs. Life was rarely quiet.
HIGHLIGHT With West Ham requiring a win on the final day of 2006-07 at Old Trafford, Super Tev stepped up, netting the only goal.

66 FERNANDO TORRES →
LIVERPOOL, CHELSEA

LEGACY In hindsight, it should have been very easy to foresee that Torres would outsmart the Premier League's bruising defenders – after all, he had once been Diego Simeone's captain at just 19 when the pair played together at Atletico Madrid. 'El Nino' was a precocious talent with searing pace, but he also commanded the respect of men from a tender age.

It was compatriot Rafael Benitez who managed to convince La Liga's hottest prospect to swap sunny Spain for the watercolour sprawl of English football. Liverpool pipped Chelsea to his services in 2007, paying around £20m and letting Luis Garcia leave in the opposite direction.

Pressure for a speedy start was on, but the Spaniard was quick to deliver. He set a new record as the most prolific foreigner in a debut season, usurping Ruud van Nistelrooy's 23-goal collection of six campaigns earlier with a 24th on the final day of 2007-08. He was an instant Kop hero and the subject of a classic Nike advert, which reflected his cult standing.

Torres looked like the complete striker: defenders knew about his Bugatti-esque acceleration and intelligence, but his power staggered them. For such a slender forward, he was hard to bustle off the ball – you would only get within a yard of him when he burned beyond or released a shot.

Steven Gerrard claimed that the talisman turned "all of my bad passes into good ones".

Chelsea again hovered as Torres headed for Euro 2008, but the player himself stated his desire to play on at Anfield "for many years". "It's been quite easy for me [so far]," he added, correctly.

On the first weekend of his second season, he showed why by curling home a beauty at home to Sunderland. His 2008-09 was littered with niggly injuries, but he struck 14 league goals in 24 appearances anyway. Knee problems dogged a tough third campaign too, but Torres managed more goals – 18 – in even fewer outings (22).

Roman Abramovich continued to lurk. Having tried to sign him in 2003, 2005 and 2006, Chelsea's owner finally landed his man for £50m. Reds were heartbroken – but behind the scenes, Torres' former colleagues knew the deal was excellent. "We didn't want to stop him signing," Jamie Carragher later admitted. "I was shocked by the money they paid."

The proof was in his performances. Torres notched a late breakaway goal in Barcelona as Chelsea reached the 2012 Champions League Final, but such moments were the exception rather than rule of his career at Stamford Bridge. The blond-haired boy was now dark on top, and netted just eight league goals in his best season for the Blues. At times, it was difficult to watch.

Torres' Premier League story was not one of longevity, then, but had a much shorter fuse. The fireworks, while brief, were also quite brilliant.
HIGHLIGHT Liverpool hammered Manchester United 4-1 at Old Trafford in March 2009, with Torres using Nemanja Vidic and Rio Ferdinand as his playthings. The Spaniard's goal that afternoon is always his go-to highlight.

65 MATT LE TISSIER

SOUTHAMPTON

LEGACY St Mary's Stadium might never have been built had Southampton not remained in the top flight for 27 years – many of them due to Le Tissier and his feats of crucial escapology. It was no coincidence that a man with a fondness for tense run-ins weighed in with eight goals on the final days of the season for the south coast outfit.

He was certainly the best penalty taker in the history of the Premier League – Mark Crossley's famous save in March 1993 gave Le Tissier a meagre 98 per cent success rate across his career – and arguably the foremost bottom-half player in the rebranded division. Criminally, the Guernsey demigod never finished above 10th in the renamed league.

But perhaps no other player had ever assembled such a collection of goals; a compendium of free-kicks, volleys and inch-perfect long-range efforts that were necessary to prevent him from doing any more running. "Outrageous, sickening goals," eulogised Barcelona idol Xavi, who developed an obsession with Le Tissier.

The Saints hero's favourite was his 40-yard strike against Blackburn, in part because the beaten goalkeeper was his friend, Tim Flowers. But consider his 1993 double against Newcastle: the first started with a backheel flick, before he juggled the ball past two defenders and rolled home; for the second, he nudged the ball up with his thigh for a dipping volley from 25 yards. It was extra satisfying for Le Tiss, who had been dropped for the previous five games by long-ball merchant Ian Branfoot.

That most emphatic of comebacks started a run of form that remains virtually unrivalled. Saints scored 49 goals in 1993-94; Le Tissier netted 25 and assisted another 10, meaning he was directly involved in 71 per cent of their total.

The following year, he notched 19 and assisted 15. No one has come closer to being a one-man team. Few others have combined loyalty with such brilliance.

HIGHLIGHT That final game at The Dell, Southampton's home for 103 years. Its greatest player came on with 16 minutes left against Arsenal; even by his standards, the 32-year-old Le Tissier looked out of shape. But when the ball fell his way, he swivelled to dispatch a magnificent left-footed half-volley. It proved his last goal, as well as the ground's.

64 DIMITAR BERBATOV

TOTTENHAM, MANCHESTER UNITED, FULHAM

LEGACY Berbatov shared the Premier League Golden Boot in 2010-11, but in one of his boss' most brutal decisions, wasn't even named among the substitutes for the Champions League final that followed. But such is the lot of the misunderstood genius: according to Alex Ferguson, running statistics actually showed that Berbatov covered more ground than Wayne Rooney.

However, on a field of athletes he invariably looked the artist: operating in his world, at his speed, a man apart from everyone else. There were occasions when the Bulgarian mooched around, his sleeves pulled over his hands like a student who had forgotten his coat – but Berbatov, who famously learned his English from watching *The Godfather*, acquired a cult following of his own. No one else plucked a sweeping pass out of the air as effortlessly. Maybe it was the product of a childhood smashing basketballs and pigs' bladders around, but only Dennis Bergkamp in Premier League history blended technical perfection with elegance in a similar way.

Perhaps Berbatov's body language made him seem still more languid. The frontman had a fondness for nutmegs and volleys – often, it felt as though the most energetic thing he did was scissor-kicks.

His two Premier League crowns came with Manchester United, but his influence was possibly greater at Tottenham: the striker's instinctive understanding with Robbie Keane yielded 91 goals in all competitions across two seasons before Ferguson came calling. They were an attacking duo of such lethal chemistry that it made them the Harry Kane and Son Heung-min of their day.

This iconoclast might have looked like a bit of a loner, but it also meant Berbatov fitted firmly into Spurs' tradition of stylish crowd darlings. He would have had it no other way.

HIGHLIGHT His September 2010 hat-trick for United against Liverpool featured a fine overhead kick. It also proved the last league treble against the Merseysiders for a decade, until Ollie Watkins' shock glut for Aston Villa in October 2020.

63 PAOLO DI CANIO

SHEFFIELD WEDNESDAY, WEST HAM, CHARLTON

LEGACY There's a reason why every subsequent West Ham flair player has been compared to Di Canio: he still represents the gold standard. The Italian is arguably Hammers fans' favourite player of the Premier League era – surely the finest dribbler and volleyer in their history – and a maverick who felt different in everything he did.

Di Canio offered excitement and identity. Combustible, controversial and charismatic, he overshadowed the exciting generation of homegrown talents who went on to scale greater heights – although none performed with such elan or such unpredictability. He was the master of the feint, often beating the defender or goalkeeper an extra time before shooting. Even Di Canio's penalties – one famously wrestled off a furious Frank Lampard – could be Panenkas.

The icon was a mass of contradictions: the player banned for 11 games after shoving referee Paul Alcock, but also the winner of FIFA's Fair Play award, for catching a cross rather than scoring because Everton keeper Paul Gerrard was injured. His West Ham career ended in the ignominy of relegation; his spell at Sheffield Wednesday in disgrace for pushing Alcock.

But in between, Di Canio was simply one of the best footballers in the division. His 16 Premier League goals in 1999-2000 remain the highest haul from a West Ham player, and were complemented by 13 assists. Alex Ferguson wanted to sign the Italian in 2001 and, given his temper, his swagger and his catalytic qualities, he bore certain similarities to Eric Cantona.

Instead, he was Upton Park's Cantona.

HIGHLIGHT Egil Olsen's notoriously direct Wimbledon were rarely associated with things of beauty... that is, until Trevor Sinclair launched a 50-yard diagonal pass against them. Rather than controlling, Di Canio met it on the volley with a scissor-kick that flew past Neil Sullivan. In its technique, audacity and execution, it's among the top Premier League efforts of all time. His 2002 volley at Chelsea was almost as good, though.

62 JAY-JAY OKOCHA

BOLTON

LEGACY Bolton's greatest player since Nat Lofthouse: a status their subsequent decline into League Two means the Nigerian is likely to keep for years to come.

It never felt normal that Okocha played for Bolton, but today it seems even more surreal. Sam Allardyce may now be a byword for dullness and direct football, but 19 years ago he was a pioneering force, assembling the Reebok Galacticos by melding Youri Djorkaeff with Okocha; those 2002 signings were then followed by Ivan Campo and Fernando Hierro. They reinvented a yo-yo club as annual top-eight finishers, combining Allardyce's pragmatism with style and a swagger.

"We agreed a deal at Charles de Gaulle airport, and he promised to follow the next day to complete paperwork," Allardyce later wrote. "Would he turn up? He drove all the way from Paris Saint-Germain to Bolton, parked, got out of his car, marched into the Reebok and signed. Quality."

Okocha was the Ronaldinho of the Reebok. More than anyone else, he made Bolton fashionable with a dazzling array of flicks and tricks, rabonas and stepovers. He could fool foes using his fancy footwork, allied with seemingly elastic legs that appeared to bend during some skills. Few have found more imaginative ways to lift a ball; indeed, one mind-boggling piece of magic involved a rainbow flick over a baffled Ray Parlour.

Okocha feels the least likely of Allardyce captains, but fought back after a false start with Wanderers – he was hauled off at half-time on his debut, as Henrik Pedersen came on against Fulham – to assume the armband after a year. By then, he had been the driving force in winning a relegation battle – the Nigerian scored in four of Bolton's last five victories, netting deciders in three of them. In 2003-04, he took Bolton to only their second cup final since the 1950s; his performance in the first leg of the semis against Aston Villa, including an extraordinary free-kick, was probably his best for the Trotters.

Okocha packed a vicious long shot and even a long throw, which almost definitely endeared him to Allardyce. He was, as the club merchandise used to say, so good they named him twice.

HIGHLIGHT Pick from the solo run and missile to defeat West Ham and help keep Bolton up in 2003... or the dance with Big Sam when survival was secured.

61 RIYAD MAHREZ

LEICESTER, MANCHESTER CITY

LEGACY "I didn't know Leicester," Mahrez told *FFT* two years after his defining transfer to the then-Championship club. "In France, I thought they were a rugby club." It's safe to assume the feelings were mutual.

Signed on the recommendation of Leicester's expert talent spotters, the winger's bargain arrival from Ligue 2 side Le Havre was greeted with little more than Partridge GIF shrugs by supporters. A street footballer who cut his teeth at fourth-tier outfit Quimper, Mahrez hadn't even been the Le Havre player that Leicester's recruitment chief Steve Walsh was hot for – that honour belonged to Ryan Mendes, who later floundered at Nottingham Forest.

But the 22-year-old Mahrez's velvet touch and dribbling impressed Leicester, who swooped midway through their 2013-14 promotion campaign. In the Premier League return that followed, Nigel Pearson's Foxes survived with a late-season flourish, but Mahrez struggled to assert himself until a swashbuckling run-in.

There was no indication of what happened next. With Claudio Ranieri an underwhelming replacement after Pearson's acrimonious exit, relegation was widely tipped. Yet Mahrez notched four goals across the opening three weekends, as Leicester took seven points from a possible nine. Bandy-legged and ludicrously languid, the Algerian was quick-stepping through rearguards with jaw-dropping regularity, with the killer instinct to match.

It quickly became clear that this was no purple patch: it was a major breakthrough. In tandem with Jamie Vardy, Mahrez sucker-punched unsuspecting rivals at lightning speed as soon as possession was turned over. Throughout a breathtaking season, Mahrez hit 17 goals and assisted 11 as Leicester powered towards Premier League glory. His 14th goal of the campaign, the second in a 3-1 win at Manchester City in early February, was the moment Foxes fans believed in a miracle.

A relentless side romped to the title. "When you start winning games, you gain even more confidence," Mahrez summed up matter-of-factly to *FFT*.

Vardy may have scored more goals and N'Golo Kante became a global sensation, but Mahrez was crowned PFA Players' Player of the Year after providing the artistry that kept teams on the back foot all season. Defences knew exactly what was coming – the nightmarish, trademark chop inside – but could do nothing about it.

The winger was finally flogged to Manchester City two summers later for £60m. While not always a guaranteed starter for Pep Guardiola's side since, Mahrez deserves his place at the elite level. He has since added three more Premier League winners' medals with City to the one he won at Leicester. At his best, there are few you would rather watch.

HIGHLIGHT Scoring Leicester's second in that masterful win at the Etihad Stadium in February 2016, hopping over Nicolas Otamendi, then wrong-footing Martin Demichelis to fire past Joe Hart. Dilly ding, dilly dong: it was really on.

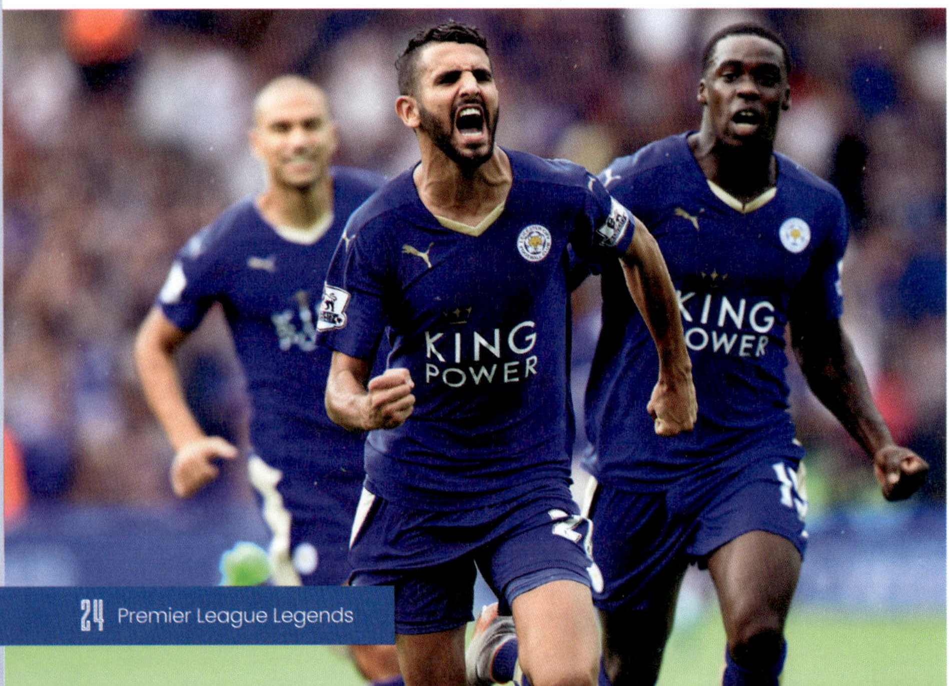

60 MICHAEL CARRICK

WEST HAM, TOTTENHAM, MANCHESTER UNITED

LEGACY Manchester United almost didn't sign Carrick in 2006, when chief executive David Gill phoned a golfing Alex Ferguson to say Spurs had upped the price – "typical Daniel Levy," hissed the Scot. Some baulked at the £18m price tag, but Carrick's class across 450-plus appearances brought five Premier League titles and proved he was worth every penny.

HIGHLIGHT Being crowned United's Player of the Year in 2013, as the Red Devils won a final Premier League title under Fergie.

59 GARY NEVILLE

MANCHESTER UNITED

LEGACY Younger generations recognise the straight-talking pundit, but those who watched G-Nev play will recall his days as a boisterous right-back over almost 20 years at United. His intelligence, tough tackling and top-notch crossing made him an Old Trafford mainstay, even as his manager rebuilt several title-winning sides.

HIGHLIGHT Zealous celebrations after a late Rio Ferdinand winner against Liverpool at Old Trafford in January 2006 secured legendary status among Red Devils. And an FA fine. Boo.

58 LES FERDINAND

QPR, NEWCASTLE, TOTTENHAM, WEST HAM, LEICESTER, BOLTON

LEGACY For the first six years of the Premier League, only Alan Shearer hit more goals. 'Sir Les' shone in a functional QPR team, then plundered 41 league strikes over back-to-back seasons for Newcastle's 'Entertainers'. A move to Spurs didn't take off, but at Leicester Ferdinand's dozen goals showed his class.

HIGHLIGHT Ferdinand headed the Magpies' third goal in the 5-0 drubbing of Manchester United from Shearer's centre – a partnership which sadly lasted just a single campaign.

57 DAVID SEAMAN
ARSENAL, MANCHESTER CITY

LEGACY Somehow, Seaman made his £1.3m British record move (for a goalkeeper) from QPR to Arsenal in 1990 look like a steal. He delivered 141 clean sheets in 344 Premier League matches, en route to two titles (after another in 1990-91) and more than a decade of reliable service.
HIGHLIGHT Posting 19 shutouts and leaking only 15 goals during a silverware-less season is hardly fair, but that was Seaman's superb 1998-99. Arsenal finished one point behind Treble-winning Manchester United.

56 NICOLAS ANELKA →
ARSENAL, LIVERPOOL, MANCHESTER CITY, BOLTON, CHELSEA, WEST BROM

LEGACY Anelka was 17 years old when he swapped PSG for Arsenal in a £500,000 deal in February 1997, becoming Arsene Wenger's first official signing at Highbury.

Without an early fatherly Wenger intervention, though, things could have ended quite abruptly. When an afflicted Anelka didn't show up for the Gunners' last game of the 1996-97 season at Derby, Wenger found him packing his bags. "Make an effort," the Arsenal supremo told him, "and it will pay off." Anelka was convinced to travel.

When Paul Merson went off injured after only nine minutes, on went the youngster to set up two Ian Wright goals in a 3-1 victory.

In November 1997, the Frenchman netted the opening goal in a 3-2 win over title rivals Manchester United on his second start of the campaign. The Gunners' famous Double followed – as did the PFA Young Player of the Year award a season later, having top-scored for Arsenal with 17 goals.

But discontent was never far away. Years later, Anelka revealed he had been plotting his exit – to Real Madrid, for a huge £22m in 1999 – ever since discovering a poll where Arsenal supporters doubted his ability to succeed Wright. "Seeing the result hit me hard," he sniffed. "I thought, 'So that's how it is. This is how you thank me. I'm going to play, score my goals, and just when you're all cheering for Anelka, that's when I'm going to leave'."

Short-lived spells with Madrid and PSG led to an English return with Gerard Houllier's Liverpool. Anelka wanted to remain at Anfield, but Houllier wasn't so keen. Instead, Kevin Keegan's middling Manchester City made him their record signing for £13m in 2002 – he notched 30 league goals across his first two seasons.

Champions League football with Fenerbahce followed in 2005, but England continued to tempt Anelka back.
A successful 18 months at Bolton yielded 21 goals in 53 matches and resulted in a January 2008 move to Chelsea.

Since joining Arsenal, the forward hadn't stuck around anywhere for more than two and a half seasons, but he found a home in SW6. He bagged 19 league goals in 2008-09 to snatch the Golden Boot ahead of Cristiano Ronaldo, and won a second Premier League and FA Cup Double in 2010 – 12 years after his first.

There was a swansong for Anelka at West Brom in 2013-14 but, like many of his footballing experiences, it was tinged with regret. He scored two league goals for the Baggies, infamously celebrating the latter at West Ham with his *quenelle* gesture popularised by comedian pal Dieudonne. He denied its links to racism and anti-Semitism, instead insisting the act was directed at boss Steve Clarke.

Sadly, that summed it all up – it was always him against the world. Sometimes, the world bit back harder.
HIGHLIGHT Anelka's brilliant, rifled finish against United at Highbury in November 1997 was crucial to Arsenal's Double and marked the real arrival of a thrilling prospect.

55 GARETH BALE
TOTTENHAM

LEGACY Bale went 24 Premier League matches without a win for Tottenham, stretching from his bow in August 2007 through to September 2009. Four years after that first win, he was the planet's most expensive player. The Welshman's evolution from skinny left-back to world-class attacker culminated in an explosive 2012-13 – one of the greatest individual campaigns in English football – in which he scored 21 league goals.
HIGHLIGHT A 90th-minute rocket to down West Ham at Upton Park in February 2013 encapsulated Bale at his best. Devastating.

54 DWIGHT YORKE

ASTON VILLA, MANCHESTER UNITED, BLACKBURN, BIRMINGHAM, SUNDERLAND

LEGACY Yorke had already hit 60 Premier League goals by the time he arrived at Old Trafford in the summer of 1998 – but better was to come. Alongside Andy Cole, the £12.6m man from Aston Villa registered 18 league strikes during United's Treble-winning campaign, pocketing himself the Golden Boot for good measure.
HIGHLIGHT A hat-trick and assist in a 6-1 stuffing of title rivals Arsenal at Old Trafford in February 2001 showcased Yorke's class.

53 RAHEEM STERLING

LIVERPOOL, MANCHESTER CITY, CHELSEA

LEGACY Sterling was almost a title winner at 19; key in the fearsome Liverpool frontline of 2013-14. Many mocked City for shelling out £52m to sign him in 2015 nonetheless, but they were wrong to: Sterling has since honed his forward play to become a phenomenon for Pep Guardiola, helping City win consecutive Premier League crowns on two occasions before making the switch to Chelsea in 2022. An inspiration.
HIGHLIGHT Being named PFA Young Player of the Year and FWA Footballer of the Year as the Sky Blues pipped old club Liverpool to the title by a point in 2018-19.

52 RICARDO CARVALHO

CHELSEA

LEGACY "Carvalho was horrible to play against," Bobby Zamora told *FFT* in 2020. "He'd always know where the referee was, and he'd be getting in these little fouls when nobody was looking." The Portuguese defender followed manager Jose Mourinho in swapping Porto for Chelsea in 2004, forming a watertight partnership with John Terry on the way to three league titles.
HIGHLIGHT With Carvalho in tow, Chelsea conceded just 15 goals as they sealed their maiden Premier League triumph in 2004-05.

51 DAVID GINOLA

NEWCASTLE, TOTTENHAM, ASTON VILLA, EVERTON

LEGACY Few could dazzle like David Ginola. With his good looks, musketeer locks and swashbuckling dribbling, the French left-winger stood out so much that he sometimes resembled the lone pro on the field, carving his way through a rearguard of over-matched amateurs.

Ginola came to the Premier League in 1995 from winning cups and a league title with PSG to join a recently promoted, ambitious Newcastle side led by Liverpool legend Kevin Keegan. 'Le Magnifique' flourished under Keegan's "instinctive football" at Newcastle, liberated from defensive duties and allowed to give his best in attack in his flamboyant style. The 1995–96 season was a heartbreaking one in the end for Ginola and Newcastle. At one point top of the league by 12 points, 'The Entertainers' were filled with the raw talent of Ginola, Les Ferdinand and Peter Beardsley but were pipped to the title by Sir Alex Ferguson's relentless Manchester United side led by Eric Cantona. When Alan Shearer joined the next season for a world record fee, Newcastle seemed primed for the top.

But there was a shock exit in 1996–97 when Kevin Keegan was replaced by the much colder, sterner Kenny Dalglish. For Ginola, this change in management style was not to his benefit, and he was frozen out. Just weeks before his departure, Keegan also infamously blocked Ginola's dream move to Barcelona, stranding him at the club. Terrible timing.

Ginola's inevitable departure from Newcastle was sealed on a meeting on a boat in the Mediterranean with then-Spurs chairman Alan Sugar. The switch was confirmed with a £2.5m bid in 1997, and Ginola joined a struggling Spurs side close to relegation. Ginola embraced the challenge, saying "I liked that pressure – it gave me even more power and I felt that from the beginning. I thought 'Let's make the club better'".

This approach worked, and the following season of 1998–99 was Ginola's best yet. Disciplinarian George Graham arrived that summer, and Ginola used this change to prove that he was a team player as well as a flamboyant fashion icon. He ended the season winning the 1998–99 PFA Player of the Year award at 32 years old, proving his dedication: "You can't be player of the year at 32 if you're not 100 per cent committed to your job".

Just a year later, however, Ginola was out at Tottenham. Another offseason meeting forged a move to Aston Villa, the start of a forgettable 18 months highlighted by a blockbuster strike against Manchester City. Ginola then passionately stripped off his kit and flexed at manager John Gregory, who had criticised the then-older Ginola's physique. Safe to say Gregory was proved wrong.

Ginola retired at 35 after brief appearances at Everton. Ever the entertainer, 'Le Magnifique' is adored by droves of Newcastle and Spurs fans for his thrilling displays and film-star looks. Some say he was capable of even more: he never got his dream Barcelona move, nor played in a major tournament for France. Nonetheless, a true Premier League great.
HIGHLIGHT The finest moment of his PFA Player of the Year 1998/99 season was his magnificent solo goal at Barnsley in the FA Cup quarter-final. He picked the ball up on the left, rhythmically slalomed left and right between defenders and nonchalantly stroked the ball home.

50 MICHAEL OWEN

LIVERPOOL, NEWCASTLE, MANCHESTER UNITED, STOKE

LEGACY At one point, there wasn't a child in Britain who didn't pretend to be Owen in the playground. His rise felt scripted by Hollywood screenwriters; the Lilleshall graduate scored a goal on his Liverpool debut aged 17, netted a glorious World Cup goal at 18 and even had his own TV show. For years, everything he touched turned gold.

Fortunately, he was just in time for Gerard Houllier. Owen had scored 18 goals to share the Golden Boot in 1997-98, and offered the incoming Frenchman a thrilling partner for erstwhile boy wonder Robbie Fowler.

Under Houllier, Owen plundered another 18 goals in 1998-99 – but the high was short-lived. Having struggled with a troublesome hamstring problem all season, a mid-April clash against Leeds finally took its toll. The striker was out for nearly five months and, although he returned in fine fettle, his bullet-speed game was forever hampered by the ominous threat of a repeat.

History tells us that Owen never managed 20 goals in a Premier League campaign, yet his record at Liverpool stood at an excellent 118 goals in 216 league games by the time he departed for Real Madrid in 2004. In reality, injuries forced him to miss a fifth of every league season at Anfield on average.

The Reds finished in the top two spots only once during Owen's career on Merseyside, but they did win a brilliant treble of trophies with their ace marksman in 2000-01 – not least thanks to his deadly intervention which earned them the FA Cup against Arsenal. It also bagged Owen the Ballon d'Or. "I didn't have a clue how big that was," he later told *FFT*. "Gerard Houllier said, 'You've won the Ballon d'Or' and I thought, 'That's good'. I was delighted, but I can guarantee I went to bed having totally forgotten about it. It was, 'Right, that's in the arse pocket, what's the next thing I can win?'"

When Houllier stepped aside in 2004, Owen swapped Anfield for Madrid – but something wasn't right.

"You know when you sign something and think there's no going back?" he reflected. "When you think, 'Oh my God, what have I done?' I remember crying my eyes out as I went off to the airport."

His year-long stint in La Liga set off the downfall. By the time he returned to England, Liverpool had moved on – his only option was a club-record £16.8m switch to Newcastle in 2005. It was always an unhappy marriage of convenience from the outside, made worse by metatarsal and cruciate ligament injuries which meant he barely played for two years.

A free transfer to Manchester United all but killed his Liverpool legacy, although Owen wasn't quite done: his 96th-minute winner against rivals City in September 2009 sealed a famous 4-3 derby win. Alas, those highs had all but died out long before.

HIGHLIGHT An 18-year-old Owen, floating after France 98 and at the peak of his powers, slotted four goals past Nottingham Forest four months later.

49 CLAUDE MAKELELE

CHELSEA

LEGACY A man so good that he has a position named after him, Makelele was perhaps Chelsea's most important signing of the early Abramovich era. A defensive midfielder who kept the Galacticos grounded, he played the same role at Stamford Bridge, providing the engine for two Premier League crowns.

HIGHLIGHT Bundling in the rebound of his own missed penalty against Charlton on the final day of 2004-05's title-winning season: his Blues team-mates loved him that much, they gave him the spot-kick.

48 JAMIE VARDY

LEICESTER

LEGACY He is Leicester's best ever player. His eye-bulging effort and pantomime hustling lend themselves to cult status, but the former factory worker has backed that up season upon season with a stream of talismanic strikes. Vardy is now chomping into the Premier League's top 15 scorers of all time, having not played a game in it until the age of 27.

HIGHLIGHT Breaking Ruud van Nistelrooy's record by netting in 11 consecutive Premier League games en route to 2015-16 title glory.

47 TEDDY SHERINGHAM

NOTT'M FOREST, TOTTENHAM, MAN UNITED, PORTSMOUTH, WEST HAM

LEGACY Sheringham was 31 when he joined Manchester United in 1997, handed the unenviable task of replacing Eric Cantona. The frontman recovered from a slow start to thrive among fierce Old Trafford competition. Teddy scored in Forest's first Premier League game in 1992, was still going at West Ham by 2006, aged 40, and was loved at Tottenham in between.

HIGHLIGHT A superb hat-trick at home to Southampton in October 2000 preceded PFA and FWA Footballer of the Year gongs.

46 DENIS IRWIN

MANCHESTER UNITED

LEGACY Seven-time Premier League champion Denis Irwin tells FourFourTwo about life as Fergie's favourite, toppling Liverpool, and smashing Eric Cantona at chess.

Alex Ferguson said you were the only player guaranteed to make his best Manchester United XI. Why were you so loved by him?

I went in and just got about my job. I wasn't a star player, but Fergie still appreciated me. I didn't cause him too much stress. My peers appreciated what I did, too. Maybe to the fan in the street I didn't make headlines because I wasn't a star player, but I didn't want the limelight. I worked my socks off, trained hard and tried to learn from mistakes. Gary Neville was the same as me. Full-backs were pawns on a chessboard when I played. They're more important now in the game. We had Giggsy or Becks in front of our full-backs to cross the ball. Twenty years ago, if one full-back went forward, the other stayed back. Now, both go forward in the top teams.

How did you see the team develop from one that hadn't won the title in years, to one that ruled? How did you keep up?

Personally, I was getting better. Being let go by Leeds at 20 [in 1986] was a major turning point. It motivated me, and I had a couple of great years at Oldham where my confidence lifted back up. I felt ready for a big club when I joined United, who'd just won the FA Cup but finished 13th [in 1989-90]. We won the Cup Winners' Cup the following year, when Peter Schmeichel and Paul Parker arrived – then the League Cup in 1992, after which Eric [Cantona] signed. We had young lads like Ryan Giggs and Lee Sharpe, who were flying. We finally won the league in 1993, the year we bought Roy [Keane]. We were building confidence all the time, bringing good players in. Winning that first title was a big deal, because it gave us the know-how of how to do it. It was a tree with branches getting bigger and stronger.

You were famously the subject of Leeds' attention in the episode that took Cantona to Old Trafford. Would you have gone to Elland Road if Fergie had said yes to them?

That's the first time I've ever been asked that. Would I have wanted to leave? No. But when a manager doesn't want you any more, you have a decision to make. Eric gave the team something different. We already had loads of runners in the squad, like Giggsy, Sharpey, Incey, Brian McClair and Andrei Kanchelskis, while Sparky [Mark Hughes] could hold the ball up extremely well. But we didn't really have someone to play between the lines – we'd not seen that before. Cantona would do that; he played in the little holes. He was big, strong, and suited the Premier League. He had pace as well, which people don't always associate with him, and he could score goals. We had four and a half years with Eric. I wish it was more, as he was a special player. I've not seen a player like that before and neither had opponents. He was a catalyst for us and for United to become the club they are now.

How satisfying was scoring that excellent free-kick against Liverpool in the famous 3-3 draw of January 1994?

Very. Liverpool had been dominant during the '70s and '80s. They'd had their time, and Arsenal had also won the league a couple of times. But we still needed to win the league, and were well placed when we finally did: the ground was expanded, the merchandise sold. When I joined the club, the physio handed us hats from one of his mate's firms – Morson – for the celebration photos whenever we won trophies. Imagine that now!

Which was the strongest title-winning United team you were part of, and why?

The 1994 team was physical, powerful and difficult to beat. The league was much more physical, and football changed between '94 and '99. The '94 side weren't as easy on the eye as the '99 team, and there weren't as many options, but we had guts and won the Double. I loved playing with that team, and the XI was pretty set. Nothing can top '99 – we had drive in abundance, and goalscorers all over the pitch. I'm one of the few that played in both teams, but that '94 side was such a joy to play in.

You joined Wolves in the second tier, but had one last crack at the Premier League with them in 2003-04. Did that final hurrah in the top flight come as a surprise?

I was 36 when I left United in 2002, and felt like I could get another year out of my body. I'd supported Wolves when I was growing up – they weren't a bad team in the mid-70s. A lot of my mates were Liverpool fans, so I'm glad I didn't go down that route! I played 52 games during my first season at Wolves, and thoroughly enjoyed it – we got to the play-off final and beat Sheffield United 3-0 to go up. I contemplated calling it a day, as I was 37, but they convinced me to play for another season. The second year was a difficult one. We didn't spend a lot of money and our two best players, Joleon Lescott and Matt Murray, were injured, but it was good to be in the Premier League again. I was disappointed to be relegated for the first time in my career.

We've learned that you were a national chess champion in your youth – what's the story there?!

I wasn't a national chess champion. I played for my school and we finished second in the national championship. I was a decent chess player, don't worry about that. I used to play Eric, but games wouldn't last long. I've been watching *The Queen's Gambit* on Netflix...

45 YAYA TOURE

MANCHESTER CITY

LEGACY People often talk of the trophy that kick-starts a revolution; that piece of silverware which convinces a team that they are capable of something more. Something a bit special. The origin of Manchester City's current era of excellence – a decade in which a conveyor belt's worth of world-class talent have greedily collected more than 10 major trophies – can be traced back to an exact day: May 14, 2011. With 73 minutes gone of an FA Cup final seemingly destined for a dull denouement, Yaya Toure slammed home a close-range winner against Tony Pulis' stubborn Stoke.

This was the moment that City fans had been waiting for; three years and approximately £350m into the Abu Dhabi project, a first major title since they lifted the League Cup in 1976. Yet it was far from the Ivorian's maiden success. After three years at Barcelona which overlapped with Pep Guardiola's rise to the first team, Toure joined City for £24m in the summer of 2010, alongside David Silva.

Toure was a pivotal member of Pep's Treble winners of 2008-09, before celebrating another La Liga success in his final season. He hadn't wanted to leave, but felt betrayed by Guardiola, problems that would resurface later in his career. "Whenever I asked him something, he always gave strange answers," Toure commented after his departure. "He pretty much ignored me until City's offer came in. If he had talked to me, I would have stayed in Barcelona."

If it sounded like Toure didn't want to be in England, his subsequent performances didn't show it. Under the more appreciative boss Roberto Mancini, Toure gave his all in City's bold new world. The 6ft 2in powerhouse, who had resented playing at centre-back in Barcelona, was moved into his natural midfield domain – frequently, as the most advanced man. Alongside Silva's subtle artistry, Toure's impressive passing range, tackling and box-to-box bursts helped to take Mancini's talented team to another level.

In his second campaign, the Ivorian was at the heart of City's Premier League title – his sixth assist of the season teed up Pablo Zabaleta's opener during the nail-biting 3-2 final-day win over QPR.

The first success always elicits the best memories, but Toure's displays in City's second title win two years later were outstanding. He plundered 20 league goals in a rampaging free role, as Manuel Pellegrini's Sky Blues pipped Liverpool by just two points. Free-kicks, howitzers, individual runs, penalties, tap-ins, headers: there was no type of goal that City's most influential player couldn't score.

Toure's final years at the Etihad Stadium were marred by curious grievances with cake and a second string of spats with Pep, but those early years are the ones City fans cherish. Toure struck fear into the opposition whenever he revved up to imminently destroy them.

HIGHLIGHT A March 2014 hat-trick against Fulham, with a trademark screamer, helped City to a rampant 5-0 win. A captain's display en route to a second league triumph.

44 ROBBIE FOWLER

LIVERPOOL, LEEDS, MANCHESTER CITY, BLACKBURN

LEGACY Four minutes and 33 seconds was all it took for Liverpool to go 3-0 up against Arsenal in August 1994 thanks to Fowler's record-breaking Premier League treble, which stood for more than two decades. Dubbed 'God' by the Kop for his supreme natural finishing, Fowler's later spells with Leeds, Manchester City and Blackburn were blighted by injury.

HIGHLIGHT Successive PFA Young Player of the Year awards in 1994-95 and 1995-96, after stellar campaigns of 25 and 28 goals.

43 ROBERT PIRES

ARSENAL, ASTON VILLA

LEGACY "Wow, this football is not for me," Arsenal's new £6m signing muttered before coming off the bench for his August 2000 Premier League debut. He couldn't believe the physicality. Pires grew to love English football, shining during the Gunners' greatest spell with 14 goals in three seasons running from 2002-03.

HIGHLIGHT With Arsenal chasing down Manchester United for the 2002 title, Pires' gorgeous lob over ex-Red Peter Schmeichel at Villa Park sealed all three points in style.

42 XABI ALONSO

LIVERPOOL

LEGACY When Liverpool went toe-to-toe with Manchester United for the 2008-09 title, they did it with their greatest midfield of the Premier League era. Captain Steven Gerrard rampaged, Javier Mascherano hared and, next to them, Alonso glided. The Spaniard was an instant hit from Real Sociedad in 2004, stunning team-mates with his pristine passing. Gerrard later called him "my most enjoyable partner".

HIGHLIGHT Netting twice from inside his own half. The second, in September 2006 against Newcastle, put Steve Harper on his backside.

41 TONY ADAMS
ARSENAL

LEGACY The only player to captain a title-winning team across three different decades. For all Arsene Wenger's sexy football, it's the rugged Adams who supporters hold among their dearest. His leadership offered Wenger the canvas on which to create art – not least after returning from rehab to win the league in 1997-98.

HIGHLIGHT Latching onto Steve Bould's looping ball to batter home Arsenal's fourth goal against Everton in May 1998. A third title was his – would you believe it, indeed.

40 IAN WRIGHT ➔
ARSENAL,
WEST HAM,

LEGACY Wright worked as both a plasterer and bricklayer until he was almost 22. Football? He played in a Sunday League side each week. He shouldn't have had a chance of playing in the Premier League – not least because it was founded when he was 29.

But Wright never took no for an answer. Rejected after trials at professional clubs, he settled for a £30-a-week gig at Greenwich Borough and was swiftly noticed by a Crystal Palace scout. Six years later, at the age of 27, he left the Eagles as their record post-war scorer.

Wright was the very definition of a late bloomer, but the chance to spend his prime at Arsenal simply couldn't be missed. He grew up in a Gooner-supporting estate, thanks to local boy David 'Rocky' Rocastle joining the club as a boy. Wright was glued to his TV when Arsenal became champions at Anfield in 1988-89. When Rocky told Wrighty, "It's all about the fans" at Highbury, the goal-getter didn't think twice about signing.

Keen to make up for lost time, Wright hit 24 goals in 30 games during his debut First Division season as a Gunner. Arsenal came 10th in the first Premier League campaign but won both the FA Cup and League Cup, with their No.8 tallying 30 in all competitions. Wright bagged at least 15 league goals in the first six of his seven Highbury seasons, and at least 23 in half of those, thriving alongside Alan Smith or Kevin Campbell in attack for George Graham's last few league campaigns.

In 1995, Arsenal signed Dennis Bergkamp from Inter. It was assumed a 31-year-old Wright would wind down, but the striker hadn't lost the 18-yard box hustling, quicksilver pace or desire to dance in front of the North Bank.

Bergkamp was a more introverted character, but they made a perfect couple; the Non-Flying Dutchman knew instinctively where Wright would be and could practically thread him through-balls with his eyes closed.

An injured Wright missed several chunks of Arsenal's Double-winning 1997-98 campaign, but still hit 10 goals to maintain a run of posting double digits in each Premier League season. Nicolas Anelka was now on the scene, and Arsenal were devastatingly quick, physical and fit. At nearly 35, Wright kept up with his team-mates. He left north London at the end of the season on a high, with 185 goals to his name.

A short stint at West Ham followed before Nottingham Forest, Celtic, Burnley and a TV career.

Wright was a lesson that good things come to those who work hard, and remains a huge fan favourite more than two decades after exiting Arsenal. He was nearly 30 when the Premier League came calling – but wasted no time lighting it up.

HIGHLIGHT With Arsenal's all-time scoring record on the line, Wright notched against Bolton in September 1997, then gleefully revealed his famous T-shirt bragging, "179. Just Done It." He had only equalled Cliff Bastin's 60-year record, so netted two more before full-time to make sure.

39 SADIO MANÉ
SOUTHAMPTON, LIVERPOOL

LEGACY Mané has evolved from a talented, but erratic winger at Southampton into a world-class forward at Anfield, turning raw talent into consistent numbers. With a relentless work rate to chase balls in the channels, thumping striking ability on both feet and impressive heading ability for his size, he partnered Mo Salah as wing-striker extroardinaires.

HIGHLIGHT A goal and two assists in a 2019 5-2 derby thrashing of Everton set a new Red record of 32 top-tier league games unbeaten – but nothing beats his ludicrous Saints treble against Aston Villa in May 2015: struck in just two minutes and 56 seconds.

38 JAAP STAM

MANCHESTER UNITED

LEGACY Stam made just 79 Premier League appearances, yet those three title-winning seasons from 1998-99 have loomed large ever since. He set the gold standard of modern defending, making strikers look weak and slow in his considerable shadow. His 2001 sale to Lazio remains Alex Ferguson's biggest regret.

HIGHLIGHT United went unbeaten for the last 20 games of their Treble season. Stam played in 14 of them, leaking only nine goals – with seven clean sheets – to pip Arsenal.

37 N'GOLO KANTE

LEICESTER, CHELSEA

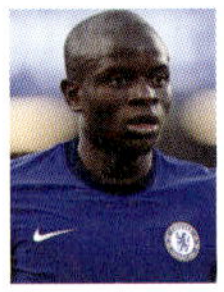

LEGACY How many players arrive in England as genuine unknowns? Kante did in 2015 – then enjoyed one of football's most magnificent breakout seasons in the unlikeliest of Premier League titles. The 5ft 6in dynamo was in France's third tier as recently as 2013, but captured hearts – and opposition players – to secure successive titles with the Foxes and Chelsea.

HIGHLIGHT Ten-man Leicester lost against rivals Arsenal in February 2016, but Kante's one-man show of industry almost earned the champions-in-waiting an unlikely draw.

36 CESC FABREGAS

ARSENAL, CHELSEA

LEGACY Fabregas trained with the Invincibles at 15 and grew to become a new revolution's poster boy, persuading Arsene Wenger to bend his philosophy. The Spaniard was defter than past midfield generals, his gift an ability to kill teams with devastating simplicity. He made 18 assists in 2014-15, the first of two title wins at Chelsea.

HIGHLIGHT Four assists – to different players – plus a goal against Blackburn in October 2009. Only Ryan Giggs can beat his Premier League assist haul of 111.

35 LUIS SUAREZ

LIVERPOOL

LEGACY There may never have been a greater individual performance over a Premier League season than Suarez's in 2013-14; rarely has one player ever shaped a year to their will like Liverpool's electric forward throughout that near-miss of a title campaign. However, as was so often the case with the Uruguayan, it began with controversy.

Suarez scored 31 goals and 12 more assists in a devastating season – but he wasn't even available for the first five fixtures. It could have been worse: after the 10-match ban he received for biting Chelsea defender Branislav Ivanovic in April 2013, the Reds man wanted out completely. No offer from preferred suitors Barcelona was forthcoming, and Suarez was annoyed Liverpool didn't accept a £40m+£1 offer from Premier League rivals Arsenal, who believed they were triggering his release clause. "What do you think they're smoking over there at the Emirates?" tweeted Reds owner John Henry.

Liverpool held firm. Suarez was promised a 2014 move and boss Brendan Rodgers advised his star attacker to use the remaining five games of his sentence to get his head together. In late September, the No.7 entered stage left.

The Reds sat second in the table following a grim home defeat to Southampton, but Suarez flew out of the blocks, firing a brace in a 3-1 victory at Sunderland, then opening the scoring a week later in a home win over Crystal Palace.

Liverpool's smarting forward produced 19 goals in his first 12 games back – including five braces, one hat-trick and even a four-goal haul. Suarez led from the front in a feared frontline alongside Daniel Sturridge and Raheem Sterling, harrying and hustling defenders as if his place on Earth depended on it. Such inspirational determination transformed a young squad into title contenders.

Successive defeats against Manchester City and Chelsea in December could have crushed the Reds, but Suarez & Co powered on. From New Year's Day they won 14 of their next 16 games, their Uruguayan talisman scoring another 11. A maiden Premier League title was so close.

But it wasn't to be. After slipping at home to Chelsea, the Red dream ended with Suarez's tears at Selhurst Park and the notion of what might have been. "Suarez was banned for those five matches and we dropped five points," ex-Liverpool defender Jamie Carragher told Sky Sports in 2019. "If he'd played in those games it would have been different."

It's tough to disagree. In 2013-14 Suarez was a one-man wrecking ball; a lethal hitman, yes, but also the ideal team-mate who facilitated the fine individual campaigns of Sturridge and a teenage Sterling. That summer, Barcelona finally made their move. Even at £65m – somewhat more than £40m+£1 – he looked like a bargain. Suarez departed Anfield with a clean sweep of England's individual awards, but no winner's medal.

LUIS WAS A ONE-MAN WRECKING BALL – A LETHAL HITMAN AND AN IDEAL TEAM-MATE

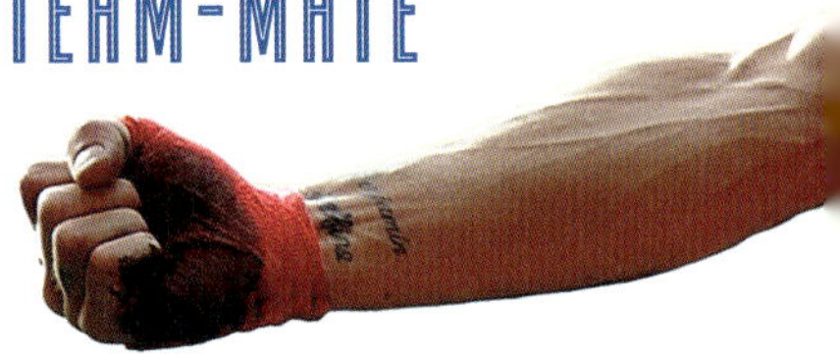

HIGHLIGHT Four goals of outstanding class obliterated Norwich as Liverpool won 5-1 in December 2013 – having struck a hat-trick past the same opposition a year earlier.

34 EDEN HAZARD
CHELSEA

LEGACY Juan Mata described the Belgian as the Premier League's greatest ever player. That may be a stretch, but there was little doubting the schemer's talents or the ease with which he could destroy defences single-handedly. Hazard, who hit 85 goals in seven seasons, was the standout player of two Chelsea title triumphs in 2015 and 2017.

HIGHLIGHT A solo stunner against Arsenal in February 2017 was peak Hazard: glorious dribbling from inside his own half, opposition faintly embarrassed and a finish to match.

33 ROBIN VAN PERSIE
ARSENAL, MANCHESTER UNITED

LEGACY Van Persie vexed the Gunners by swapping north London for Manchester after eight years and 132 goals at Arsenal but, desperate to bag a Premier League medal after a sensational 30-goal season in 2011-12, he was proved right. Another 26 strikes helped Manchester United to their 13th Premier League crown under Alex Ferguson, in the Scot's final year.

HIGHLIGHT His perfect volley from a raking Wayne Rooney pass – part of a title-sealing hat-trick against Aston Villa in April 2013.

32 SOL CAMPBELL
TOTTENHAM, ARSENAL, PORTSMOUTH, NEWCASTLE

LEGACY Campbell's crossing of the north London divide is still the most contentious Bosman deal in English football history, but in his pomp, he was the country's best centre-back: a towering, brave, fast and intelligent defender who could rule either penalty area. Spurs fans don't like to hear it, but the move was smart – Campbell won two league titles at Highbury.

HIGHLIGHT A pillar of reliability as Arsenal leaked just 26 goals across their Invincibles campaign of 2003-04.

31 RUUD VAN NISTELROOY
MANCHESTER UNITED

LEGACY Death, taxes and Van Nistelrooy tap-ins. After the Dutchman (eventually) signed from PSV for £19m in 2001, the prime poacher plundered 95 goals in 150 Premier League appearances across five campaigns with the Red Devils – pocketing a Premier League title and Golden Boot combo in 2002-03.

HIGHLIGHT OK, so they weren't *all* tap-ins. An uncharacteristically mazy run from inside his own half preceded a cool finish against Fulham in March 2003, part of a fine hat-trick.

30 GIANFRANCO ZOLA

CHELSEA

LEGACY Gianfranco Zola arrived at a Chelsea side not used to success: between 1971 and his arrival in 1996, the club won no major titles and finished outside English football's top 10 on 21 occasions. In the 25 years after the diminutive Sardinian's arrival, Chelsea never finished outside the top 10 and celebrated 20 major trophies. Few players have altered the course of history in such pivotal fashion.

Zola started his career learning from a half-decent mentor: Diego Maradona. At 5 ft 6 in tall, Zola had to rely on his technique and genius footballing brain, two things Maradona was perfectly placed to teach him about during his stint at Napoli. Playing only an outside role in Napoli's 1989–90 Scudetto, Zola announced himself after Maradona left the club in 1992. Taking his mentor's famous No.10 shirt, Zola scored 12 goals and provided 12 assists (the joint-highest tally in the league) in the 1992–93 season.

The following season, Napoli found themselves in financial trouble, so Parma swooped in and took the promising Zola for a £6m fee. Zola kept improving, with 18 goals in his first campaign and a career-high 28 in his next season at the Stadio Enrio Tardini. But, following the arrival of Hristo Stoichkov and manager Carlo Ancelotti, Zola was put on the left of a rigid 4–4–2 – not his preferred position. Other clubs and other lands came calling. Amid scepticism, Zola jolted to Stamford Bridge to join Gianluca Vialli's fashionable European Blues.

Already 30, Zola was desperate to make an impact. He made his debut at Blackburn in November and was Premier League Player of the Month by the end of December, netting 5 times in 6 games. He dragged Chelsea through the FA Cup, scoring a long-range stunner to lead a comeback from 2-0 down against Liverpool in the fourth round and then providing a brilliant piece of skill to outfox the Wimbledon backline as he scored in the semi-finals at Highbury. He finished this run with a classic Zola flick for Eddie Newton as the Blues beat Middlesbrough 2-0 in the final. Chelsea's 26-year major trophy drought was over.

Not only did Zola bring Chelsea silverware, but he led them to a sixth placed finish, their first top 10 finish since 1990. He was named Football Writers' Association Player of the Year, the only player to win the award despite arriving in England partway through a season. And, season after season, the magic continued. In 1998–99, Zola helped Chelsea come third and seal Champions League qualification for the first time, and in 1998 led them to UEFA Cup Winners' Cup glory. With his second touch of the game after coming on as a substitute, Zola thumped a half-volley right in the top corner to clinch the trophy.

These on-pitch heroics have led some Chelsea fans to name Zola their greatest-ever player. But it was the off-pitch impact to transform the club into perennial winners where Zola had arguably his greatest effect. From ex-Blues defender Michael Duberry: "It was the influence he had on other Chelsea players like Frank Lampard, too. The attention to detail, to practise and work hard – it rubbed off on anyone who joined the club. People talk about Jose Mourinho putting that mindset into Chelsea, but Zola had already been doing it. He had such an impact there. He transformed the club." Legacies don't come much better than that.

HIGHLIGHT Fighting for his place in the 2001–02 FA Cup, the ageing Zola showed he still had it as he met a low corner with a stunning backheel volley to score against Norwich at the Bridge. Genius, artistic. Only Zola.

29 EDWIN VAN DER SAR

FULHAM, MANCHESTER UNITED

LEGACY The Dutchman had been a European champion at Ajax and regular at Juventus before joining newly promoted Fulham in a shock 2001 move. Four seasons later, Manchester United came calling, Alex Ferguson ending a six-year wait for the reliable stopper he had been hunting since Peter Schmeichel's exit. The prototype for the sweeper keeper.

HIGHLIGHT A record 14 consecutive clean sheets between November and February led the Red Devils to Premier League title glory in 2008-09. Impregnable.

28 DAVID SILVA

MANCHESTER CITY

LEGACY Slight, short, foreign: would Silva be able to cope in English football? So pondered the pundits when City coughed up £24m for the Valencia man in 2010. 'Merlin' soon dropped jaws with his effortless displays for a side on the ascent, and proved the fulcrum of four league titles under three managers. They all adored him.

HIGHLIGHT A masterful performance as City gubbed Manchester United 6-1 at Old Trafford in October 2011. "The best individual display I've ever seen," Micah Richards later told *FFT*.

27 ANDY COLE

NEWCASTLE, MANCHESTER UNITED, BLACKBURN, FULHAM, MANCHESTER CITY, PORTSMOUTH, SUNDERLAND

LEGACY Cole's shock £7m switch to Old Trafford in January 1995 had Newcastle fans seething with manager Kevin Keegan. The striker had scored for fun at St James' Park, including a stellar 34-goal 1993-94. Predictably, Cole hit 93 more league strikes for the Red Devils, bagging five titles over seven full campaigns.

HIGHLIGHT Cantona's 1997 exit helped Cole, but Eric's spirit lived on. Cole's lesser-heralded chip against Everton that Boxing Day was ace.

26 DAVID BECKHAM

MANCHESTER UNITED

LEGACY A star was born on August 17, 1996. David Robert Joseph Beckham may have been a regular starter at Manchester United for the best part of a full season before the opening game of 1996-97, but it was that summer's day when he truly announced himself to the world.

With United two goals up and only minutes remaining at Wimbledon, a floppy-haired Beckham went for the audacious. But when he sent the ball sailing towards Neil Sullivan's net, he knew what he was capable of: it landed beneath a sun-kissed crossbar without a bounce. Beckham-mania had officially begun. And he wasn't even wearing his own boots, donning the borrowed Adidas Predators of Rangers prodigy Charlie Miller.

The Class of '92 hero had made his Premier League debut against Leeds in April 1995. He was a winger without obvious pace or dribbling ability, but carried a wand of a right foot that he worked hard on to improve with every passing campaign. Has any player before or since boasted such natural ability to bend, spin and weigh passes with the effortlessness of United's former No.7?

No player has ever been so devastating from set-pieces, either: 18 of Beckham's 62 Premier League strikes came courtesy of direct free-kicks – six more than anyone else. His corners, too, were beamed in with swerve and pace that wreaked havoc; Beckham is one of only two players in Premier League history to provide 10+ assists in four consecutive seasons (from 1997-98 to 2000-01).

Eight goals and seven assists over the 1996-97 season earned a 21-year-old Becks the PFA Young Player of the Year gong but, like so many United players, he enjoyed his greatest season in their Treble-winning campaign of 1998-99. He had returned from France 98 a pariah, facing burning effigies and terrace abuse wherever he travelled, but the Englishman embraced the support of Old Trafford to shine. By the end of 1999, he had finished runner-up to Rivaldo in the Ballon d'Or voting. "It was the season when I lived a nightmare and dream at the same time," he said "In the end, the dream won."

Beckham would win three more Premier League crowns after that, before off-field issues (and a swift boot to the face) with his boss led to him being increasingly marginalised throughout the 2002-03 campaign. Fed up with the midfielder's celebrity status, Ferguson decided to sell him to Real Madrid for £25m. "The minute a Manchester United player thought he was bigger than the manager, he had to go," the Scot explained in his autobiography. Later reflecting on the departure to *FFT*, Beckham admitted,

"I was angry – when the club said that they wanted me to leave, I was gutted."

Fergie's mantra served him well over 27 years in charge, with perhaps only one exception.

HIGHLIGHT *That* halfway line goal at Selhurst Park which shot Beckham into the Spice Girl-marrying stratosphere. Sullivan may still have nightmares.

25 HARRY KANE

TOTTENHAM, NORWICH

LEGACY Harry Kane found himself among the substitutes for his first taste of a North London derby in March 2014. He stayed there too, as an early Tomas Rosicky effort secured a 1-0 Arsenal win. Manager Tim Sherwood rarely turned to the 20-year-old to make the difference – Kane was used to it.

By then, he had spent four loan spells away from White Hart Lane with varying success; four years of temporary accommodation and waiting for a shot. Some had written his Spurs career off already. So, when Kane finally got a first Tottenham league start against Sunderland a month later, he was determined to do anything he could to make himself undroppable from there on.

Just before the hour mark, with both Gylfi Sigurdsson and Andros Townsend getting ready on the touchline, it happened – Kane stuck a toe out at Christian Eriksen's cross and got just enough on the ball to turn it home. He would have had a second goal, had Emmanuel Adebayor not tapped in a netbound shot later on.

Kane scored in Spurs' next two matches, but Sherwood didn't survive the summer. Appearances under Mauricio Pochettino were initially restricted to cups and the Europa League, where he was deadly, and it wouldn't be until mid-December when the shackles were released for good. Kane found his scoring touch around Christmas, bagging a New Year's Day brace in a 5-3 win over Chelsea as the Blues conceded four goals in a league game for the first time under Jose Mourinho. From December 14 to March 21, Kane plundered 17 goals in 15 matches – including a double to turn around January's North London derby, the first of a record-breaking 11 in the fixture.

He ended his maiden full season with 21 league goals, but needed more to shrug off mischievous suggestions of being a one-season wonder. History now makes them look suitably ludicrous, of course: in the intervening years, Kane has never netted fewer than 17 goals in a Premier League season, and struck at least 25 in each campaign from 2015-16 to 2017-18.

Top scoring exploits haven't yet brought a league title, but in 2023 he is also England captain, a World Cup Golden Boot winner, Euro 2020 finalist and chomping at the heels of Wayne Rooney for second in Premier League scoring history. Alan Shearer's record haul of 260 is a lofty, but certainly not insurmountable target. He tried to force a move to Manchester City in 2021, but now, seemingly destined to stay at Spurs, can he turn his goals into trophies?

Kane became one of Europe's unlikely playmakers under Mourinho. In his deeper role, he struck up a defining partnership with Son Heung-min while maintaining his own lethal scoring record, making a great all-rounder even more complete. In 2023 under new boss Antonio Conte, Kane bested Tottenham legend Jimmy Greaves for top all-time Tottenham goalscorer with 267 – a record held since 1970. Shearer here he comes.

HIGHLIGHT That brilliant brace against Arsenal in 2015, as Spurs fans returned Gooners' taunts that he was "one of their own". Hubris, meet Nemesis.

24 DIDIER DROGBA

CHELSEA

LEGACY The Ivorian embodies Abramovich-era Chelsea. Both physically elite and mentally resilient, he was an ace card in the Blues' biggest games, but a flat-track bully as well. Drogba became the prototypical Mourinho forward who inspired a tactical change to lone frontmen in English football – every Chelsea striker since has had to measure up to his lofty standards.

HIGHLIGHT Drogba struck 29 goals in a title and Golden Boot-winning 2009-10, his brace at Arsenal in November featuring a stonking free-kick to wrap up a 3-0 victory.

23 VIRGIL VAN DIJK

SOUTHAMPTON, LIVERPOOL

LEGACY To quantify Van Dijk's influence at Liverpool is nigh on impossible. It's not just the Dutchman's terrifying 6ft 4in frame and effortless approach to defending which stand out, his leadership spreads calm where others breed chaos. "He has no weakness," opined Sami Hyypia, who knows a thing or two on the subject.

HIGHLIGHT A towering header at home to Manchester United in a January 2020 win. Face to face with Harry Maguire, Van Dijk proved why he's a different class altogether.

22 KEVIN DE BRUYNE

CHELSEA, MANCHESTER CITY

LEGACY City now orbit around De Bruyne. The Belgian is more than Pep Guardiola's creative hub, he has a midfield role all of his own; their multi-talented action hero with an unrivalled passing range. The maestro has won five league titles and the Champions League with City and has equalled Thierry Henry's long-standing single-season assist record of 20.

HIGHLIGHT It's almost unfair to choose one. De Bruyne's highlight reel of assists deserve an adult rating, but his inch-perfect pass to tee up Leroy Sané in a 7-2 thumping of Stoke in October 2017 was next level.

21 NEMANJA VIDIC
MANCHESTER UNITED

LEGACY Rio Ferdinand's 2002 arrival at Old Trafford was huge, but the picture was incomplete until £7m bargain Vidic rocked up at the start of 2006. United uncovered another leader with no significant weaknesses in the terrace favourite – the Serb is still the only defender to be named Premier League Player of the Season twice.
HIGHLIGHT Vidic endured a difficult first six months after moving from Spartak Moscow, but was captain by 2010. It was a measure of the "uncompromising sod" – Fergie's words.

20 VINCENT KOMPANY
MANCHESTER CITY

LEGACY Captain Kompany was the constant throughout City's astonishing ascent. From his raw arrival at a club still finding its way in 2008, to becoming its beating heart across four title triumphs, the Belgian led by example in steering the team to hitherto unscalable heights.
HIGHLIGHT He was a man for the biggest occasions. First, a bullet derby header swung the 2011-12 title race to City. Seven years on, his swerving 30-yard thunderbolt at home to Leicester meant another winner's medal. An iconic Premier League moment.

19 PETR CECH
CHELSEA, ARSENAL

LEGACY Glovemen in England have long had a reputation for being fiery or eccentric. Not the ice-cool Cech, though. He let in a poxy 15 goals in his maiden campaign at Chelsea, which set the tone for an outstanding top-flight career in which he won four titles and four Golden Gloves.
HIGHLIGHT In 2015, just over a decade after arriving in England, Cech kept a record 170th Premier League clean sheet as Arsenal beat Bournemouth. His final tally of 202 is unlikely to be topped any time soon.

18 MOHAMED SALAH
CHELSEA, LIVERPOOL

LEGACY Salah arrived in the wrong place at the wrong time at Chelsea in 2014. Undeterred, he joined Liverpool three years later, following success with both Fiorentina and Roma, and couldn't have picked his moment any better. The 'Egyptian King' was the catalyst in turning a promising outfit into conquerors. A pair of Golden Boots have come amid domestic, European and world titles in his time at Anfield.
HIGHLIGHT Records tumbled in his debut Reds campaign, including an all-time Premier League high 32 goals for a 38-game season.

17 DENNIS BERGKAMP
ARSENAL

LEGACY It's apt that his statue at Arsenal depicts him pulling a ball out of the sky. The Dutch maestro celebrated three titles and 87 league goals in north London, but it's his elegance which endures. Lethal and incisive, Bergkamp's gift to English football was his artistry. Few are universally loved beyond the clubs they made their name with. The 'Ice Man' is, though.
HIGHLIGHT Any excuse to watch that 1997 Leicester hat-trick – his third, physics-defying goal the pick of a stunning triple.

16 SERGIO AGUERO

MANCHESTER CITY

LEGACY Is it even possible to think of Sergio Aguero's name in the same way ever again? The most climatic moment of Premier League history in May 2012 is unlikely to be matched for its importance or drama.

When we pore over the Argentine's career in years to come, analysts will struggle to look beyond that magical moment against QPR in his maiden Etihad Stadium campaign. Without having watched Aguero ruthlessly put teams to the sword over almost a decade as a Premier League player, it's hard to do his time at Manchester City full justice. What is it to witness a talisman narrowing towards goal, a certain inevitability that the net will bulge seconds later? For years, City fans have been able to rest in that kind of strange, qualitative comfort.

It's easy to forget that Aguero's Etihad career was cast into doubt when Pep Guardiola arrived in 2016. Could he get away with 'just' scoring goals? Actually, he couldn't – so instead, adapted to become an even better player. The Argentine dropped deeper to link play around the box as City shone, but still delivered 20-plus goal seasons in each of the Catalan's first three years in charge.

Ultimately, Aguero's career boils down to big numbers: he scored 184 Premier League goals before leaving City in 2021, at a rate of one roughly every 108 minutes. His dozen hat-tricks are an all-time high. Six times, he has scored 20 league goals in a campaign.

Nobody will talk about anything else because they don't need to: Aguero was simply a master in the art of scoring. For a long time, nobody did it better.

Still, a testimony from a trusted former colleague and compatriot can't hurt...

HIGHLIGHT A record-equalling five-goal thumping of Newcastle in 2015.

15 PETER SCHMEICHEL

MANCHESTER UNITED, ASTON VILLA, MANCHESTER CITY

LEGACY "Bargain of the century," was Alex Ferguson's assessment of the great Dane, plucked from Brondby for £505,000 in July 1991. Schmeichel was United's finest goalkeeper, his leadership, bravery and reflexes essential in five title wins, before bowing out on a high after the 1999 Treble.

HIGHLIGHT A sensational display against rivals Newcastle in March 1996 – pulling off save after save in a 1-0 win – proved pivotal in the title race. Stunning.

14 ASHLEY COLE

ARSENAL, CHELSEA

LEGACY Having Ashley Cole in your team was like having two players in one on the left. The defender melded intelligence with athleticism to become an Invincible at 23, then swapped north London for west to win every other trophy going at Stamford Bridge. Probably the most complete full-back in football history.

HIGHLIGHT Cole bested Cristiano Ronaldo in a draw against Manchester United in 2006. "He kind of put his hand up and said, 'I want to go off' – I think that was a good time to say I had him in my pocket," winked Cole.

13 RIO FERDINAND

WEST HAM, LEEDS, MANCHESTER UNITED, QPR

LEGACY As a lad, the Peckham native famously turned down a five-year scholarship at the Central School of Ballet to focus more on football. His career was no less *en pointe*. Tall, strong, graceful and effortlessly calm in possession, there was something gloriously cultured to Ferdinand, twice the world's most expensive defender.

HIGHLIGHT Rio was key to a United defence which conceded just 22 goals as they won the 2007-08 Premier League, his third of six.

12 JOHN TERRY

CHELSEA

LEGACY 'Captain, Leader, Legend' adorns the famous banner at Stamford Bridge. Tautology aside, it's a neat summary of Terry's career at Chelsea. Two years after making his league debut on Boxing Day 1998, the lion-hearted stopper had assumed the first-team spot that he wouldn't relinquish for another decade and a half.

Playing alongside Marcel Desailly helped iron out early immaturity and it wasn't long before the Barking boy was replacing his World Cup-winning colleague as captain. Terry was still only 23 when Jose Mourinho arrived from Porto in 2004, but served as the Portuguese's perfect general to lead a new era – even if he didn't strike everyone as skipper material at first.

"In my very first training session, I saw this guy from the academy with us – he had this baby face," explained Didier Drogba. "Then they told me, 'This is the captain...'"

But Terry was named PFA Players' Player of the Year as Chelsea broke the Premier League record for fewest goals conceded in Mourinho's first campaign, then honed their menacing brand of bastardry to enjoy the three greatest defensive campaigns of their history.

Terry was at the heart of it all, with his fearless style and vocal leadership steering five Chelsea teams to Premier League crowns. He finished just eight league games short of 500 for the Blues – only 15 men have featured in more since the division's 1992 launch. Nor was it just Mourinho who loved him.

"John Terry is the captain of all team captains – he was born with the armband on his arm," said Carlo Ancelotti, another former manager. "Even without the band, it's as if he wears it anyway, and that's how it ought to be. He's different from all the others.

11 ROY KEANE

NOTTINGHAM FOREST, MANCHESTER UNITED

LEGACY Many young fans nowadays will know Roy Keane as a brutally honest, uncompromisingly contrarian TV pundit. And he certainly is. But 'The Irishman', as he was dubbed by the legendary Brian Clough at Nottingham Forest, was first a combative, edgy and inspirational presence in English football.

Keane started his career in England being thrust onto the pitch by Clough at Anfield against Liverpool in 1990. He had transferred from Cobh Ramblers in Ireland only the day before, and got in a car to Anfield expecting to be a ball boy. Instead, Clough handed him with a pint of milk and said "Here, Irishman, get this down you". Keane hated milk. He downed the lot, and proceeded to start at only 18 without any squad member knowing his name.

This strange start to his Forest life showed Roy's unshakeable nature and unbelievable confidence. He proceeded to turn out 154 times for Forest, scoring a surprisingly high 33 goals in three seasons at the City Ground. "Brian loved good players – managers tend to!" former Forest captain Stuart Pearce explained to FFT. "By the time he left for Man United, he was our standout player, without a doubt. He played in midfield, he played in defence –wherever he played he was outstanding."

After a summer transfer battle with Blackburn and Kenny Dalglish in 1993, Sir Alex Ferguson and Manchester United snapped up Keane for a British record £3.75m. He made an immediate impact as United won the league and FA Cup Double for the first time in 1993–94, playing 54 games. This consistency and brilliance led to Keane winning seven Premier League titles, four FA Cups, the Champions League and Intercontinental Cup during his 12 years at the club, eight of which he was the captain.

Arguably the key to this personal and club success was Keane's fiery nature and relentless drive to win. "Maybe sometimes I'm harsh, and I've left the training field feeling like I've been a bit out of order, particularly with the younger players. But if I wasn't trying to make a point, I'd feel like I was cheating them. If something needs to be said, then I'll say it," Keane confessed to FFT. His friend and United teammate Paddy Irwin had a more positive idea of Keane, saying: "He was a huge driving force in training and in being Manchester United".

This attitude was the cause of much tension in Keane's career, even with the old master Ferguson. "His Irish fire was fundamental to his value as a footballer, but his tendency to go beyond the bounds of acceptability would have to be curbed," said Ferguson of the 1995 Keane. This tension led to an acrimonious fallout between boss and captain in 2005, but not before a period of unparalleled success. Keane was an unmatched leader and driver of success for Manchester United, earning him legendary status and this spot on our top 100 list.

HIGHLIGHT "I don't think I could have a higher opinion of any footballer than I had of the Irishman, but he rose even further in my estimation at the Stadio delle Alpi," gushed Ferguson after Keane's greatest United performance as he helped them come from 2-0 down to beat Juventus 3-2 in the Champions League semi-finals. Keane would miss the 1999 final through suspension, but his role in that treble would never be forgotten.

10 PAUL SCHOLES

MANCHESTER UNITED

LEGACY Scholes was not only the best player – he was the best English player of a generation. A raw, once-in-a-lifetime talent.

Thierry Henry names him as the one player he wishes he could have played alongside – as did Pep Guardiola. Barcelona legend Xavi claims Scholes would have been rated even higher had he been Spanish. Andrea Pirlo calls the Class of '92 graduate the "truly great English midfielder of his generation". Zinedine Zidane, one of the game's legends, cites not playing with Scholes as the biggest regret of his playing career. You get the idea: Scholes was a true players' player.

Liverpool and Chelsea supporters will say he was shoved over on the left for England because Gerrard and Lampard were better. Sven-Goran Eriksson will say it was because he was the only one of the three who could adapt to the positional change.

His England team-mates plundered more goals, yes, but remove Gerrard's 32 Premier League penalties and his tally (88) drops well below Scholes' 106. Remove Lampard's 43 spot-kicks and his goal average moves in line with the United man's.

Arsenal supporters will bring Patrick Vieira into the debate. The Frenchman was indeed phenomenal for the Gunners, but even he concedes that Scholes was the player "who could do everything".

The only answer is Scholes... and I haven't even mentioned his trophies.

09 PATRICK VIEIRA

ARSENAL, MANCHESTER CITY

LEGACY Although Thierry Henry's name rebounded from the North Bank so often, it was Vieira who drew the real choral affection of Arsenal's crowd. The towering skipper's song, to the tune of Italian Eurovision ditty Nel Blu, Dipinto Di Blu (Volare), was top of the Highbury hit parade.

Supporters recognised Vieira as the symbol of one of the Gunners' greatest ever teams. The midfield icon once described himself as having "French feet and an African heart" – exactly what he gave Arsene Wenger's side.

Vieira was a warrior who had the feet of a ballerina. His countless disputes with Roy Keane and "occasional" fits of temper had him portrayed as a hard man; the enforcer around whom Arsenal's team of sprinters and talented dancers orbited. However, to remember him that way is to unfairly reduce his repertoire of skills.

Vieira had a silken touch, his feet as soft as pillows as he cradled the ball on the end of his boot shortly after chapeau-ing another hapless opponent. He could slalom past you or just bulldoze beyond you: ultimately, the painful choice was yours.

There's a good reason why new midfield starlets are still labelled 'the new Vieira' after all these years. The truth is, there hasn't been a player with his blend of qualities since – at Arsenal, nor any other team. Vieira was, and continues to be, unique.

08 FRANK LAMPARD

WEST HAM, CHELSEA, MANCHESTER CITY

LEGACY Roman Abramovich's arrival at Chelsea in 2003 changed English football. The inflated wages and transfer fees have reshaped the landscape of the Premier League ever since.

For all the Russian billionaire shook things up, Lampard did the same for his position in midfield. We can get lost in the conversation about Vieira, Scholes and Gerrard's individual brilliance, but what did they truly accomplish outside of winning silverware?

Lampard's legacy, after those trophies won and 177 Premier League goals, was to alter what we've come to expect from a raiding central midfielder. These players are treated like strikers now. It's not enough to do 'the things we don't see'. Fans, pundits and – most importantly – managers, expect their No.8 to fire home in the high teens each season. End product isn't desired – it's demanded.

While Vieira was inspiring an exodus from Arsenal, and Scholes and Gerrard were both playing catch-up to Chelsea, Lampard was setting the agenda.

It's why people speak of Diego Maradona in such glowing terms. He may not have won all of Lionel Messi's trophies, but without him there wouldn't be a Messi. That's right, I did just compare Lampard to Maradona: because without Lampard, the role of a midfielder now would be very different.

So, Vieira, Scholes, Gerrard or Lampard? It's not even a debate.

07 STEVEN GERRARD

LIVERPOOL

LEGACY Everybody forgets one thing about Steven Gerrard: it took a long time for the midfielder to win Liverpool's unconditional love.

For the first part of his career, the 'Stevie Me' nickname clung to the Huyton youngster. He was perceived as self-centred by some at Anfield, although the criticism was harsh. If anybody had a right to be egotistical it was Gerrard, but he was no big-time Charlie. He just understood that he was the one man on the pitch capable of transforming games that were slipping away from the Reds.

Gerrard's body language definitely didn't help – he often wore a concerned look on his face, with a furrowed brow. The frustration he felt with underperforming team-mates would show, but it was pretty easy to misinterpret. As a local boy, he just felt the pressure more keenly than the majority of his colleagues. He experienced the same exasperation as the Kop when things went wrong. Some would have buckled under the expectation. Instead, Gerrard rose to the challenge.

Of Liverpool's many legends, he stands out for his composure in a crisis. When the clock was ticking down and there was one final opportunity to save the day, he was the man you wanted with the ball at his feet. Gerrard soaked up responsibility. He could play in any position, too. If you were building a prototype Premier League player of the late-90s, they would have looked like the Liverpool captain. He was strong, quick and had a remarkable passing range. His technique was majestic, and all the more impressive because he did everything slightly quicker than everyone else on the pitch.

The turning point for Gerrard came in the summer of 2005, starting with what seemed like a stunning act of betrayal just six weeks after lifting the Champions League trophy. He agreed to join Jose Mourinho's Chelsea but, over an emotionally draining sleepless night of panic attacks, realised he couldn't walk away from his boyhood club. It was a painful time, but the reaffirmation of his relationship with Liverpool began a process that swept away any doubters. He would have won more medals at Chelsea, but instead became an icon for a city that cherishes football above almost everything else.

There were disappointments, though. He should have been part of a team that broke the title drought long before Jurgen Klopp's side achieved the feat. In 2008-09, with Gerrard playing in an adventurous role behind Fernando Torres, Liverpool finished second to a Manchester United side they had routed 4-1 at Old Trafford. Five years on, with a Premier League winner's medal almost in his grasp, Gerrard slipped against Chelsea – in that moment, the league was gone. The incident may haunt him, but it shouldn't: that failure in 2014 was one of tactics rather than individual errors. Poor management cost the Reds that title, not the stumble.

In turn, the Kop agonised for the captain; a man they knew personified the crowd. His greatness goes beyond his ability, even if he was the most talented English player of his generation. He symbolised Liverpool, the club and the city.

Gerrard is a Scouse colossus, remembered as a hero for as long as football is played.

06 ERIC CANTONA

LEEDS, MANCHESTER UNITED

Why did you leave Leeds? Were you looking for a move before the fabled phone call between Fergie and Howard Wilkinson?
I had a bad relationship with Wilkinson – we didn't have the same views on football. I am more like a Manchester footballer. At Leeds, football was played the old way – kick and rush. It was important to play for Leeds at first, because I learned a lot. But if I don't feel the environment is good, I don't want to be there. It's like with a woman. Sometimes you can't find love. Sometimes you can, but it's still not right. It's good to be in love, but you want more; you want to give, you want to receive. Sometimes that doesn't happen.

When did you start turning your collar up? Were you copying somebody else?
I put my shirt on. It was a cold day. The collar stayed up, so I kept it like that. We won, so it became a habit to play with my collar up.

How much of the Mancunian culture did you absorb? Did you ever watch *Corrie* and listen to The Smiths, Stone Roses or Oasis?
No, I didn't watch this programme. But I liked Oasis and the others... the Stone Roses. I liked The Smiths before I moved to Manchester.
I do miss Manchester, a lot. There's so much energy in Manchester in football, music and culture. Maybe it's because of the rain. Some cities have beautiful things to see and visit; in Manchester, they have energy. I could feel the energy from the history of the city.

What was going through your mind when you kung-fu kicked that Crystal Palace fan? If you'd landed on your feet instead of your backside, what would you have done next?
[*Long pause*] I did land on my feet, not where you said. That's why I went to hit him again. I didn't punch him strong enough, though – I should have punched him even harder.

What did you feel the first time you saw TV footage of you jumping into the crowd at Selhurst Park?
I didn't watch it, because I knew. All I had was journalists around my house. That's all I could see. My house was quite small. They blocked the light. But I played that moment, at Selhurst Park. It was a drama and I was an actor. I do things seriously without taking myself seriously. Even when I kicked the fan, it's because I don't take myself seriously.
I didn't think that I had a responsibility not to do it because of who I was. No, I was just a footballer and a man. I don't care about being some sort of superior person. I wanted to do whatever I wanted to do. If I want to kick a fan, then I do it. I'm not a role model. I'm not a superior teacher, telling you how to behave. I think the more you see, the more you realise that life is a circus.

Did you see the billboard at Old Trafford on your return, saying: 'We'll never forget that night at Selhurst... when you buried that 30-yard screamer'?
Of course. And I remember the goal – it was against Wimbledon. I liked the words on the poster, and I liked it when I was in court and the fans supported me. They travelled from Manchester, in the middle of the week, down to Croydon. I could feel that support, and the club also supported me, so I stayed.

05 RYAN GIGGS

MANCHESTER UNITED

"I remember the first time I ever saw him," recalled Alex Ferguson of Giggs in his 2013 autobiography. "He was 13 years old, and just floated over the ground like a cocker spaniel chasing a piece of silver paper in the wind." The Scot gave a 17-year-old Giggs his debut in March 1991, the Welshman becoming a regular the following season and repaying his manager's faith with back-to-back PFA Young Player of the Year campaigns. The pin-up boy's searing pace and dribbling paved the way for Fergie's other fledglings to make their debuts over the following years – he showed the Class of '92 what was possible.

Watching Giggs knock the ball past hapless opponents never got tiring – unless you were on the receiving end. His acceleration and close control kept the Old Trafford crowds on the edge of their seats for more than 23 years.

The most decorated footballer in British history, with 13 Premier League crowns, four FA Cups, three League Cups and two Champions League titles. He can't be touched.

His 1999 FA Cup semi-final replay goal against Arsenal is unbeatable, but in terms of Premier League high points, look no further than Giggs' sidewinding stunner at QPR in February 1994. As United powered to the title, their boy wonder fuelled his hype machine with a sumptuous solo strike which showcased his bursting talent.

Although he developed a teacher's pet reputation in his later years at Old Trafford, the Welshman didn't escape his manager's wrath. He and fellow United winger Lee Sharpe famously had their pre-drinks party interrupted by an irate Fergie as youngsters – tirade highlight: "Get these c**ts out of this house" – and Giggs was reportedly quick to answer back in the dressing room.

Giggs might be a contender for the greatest Manchester United player of all time – the midfielder racked up 963 appearances for the Red Devils, more than anyone else. He wasn't just a solid squad player, but consistently ace for the world's biggest club over two decades. Others may have had marginally more impact, but Giggs tore them apart. Again and again.

04 WAYNE ROONEY

EVERTON, MANCHESTER UNITED

Few players have made their English football entrance in more barnstorming fashion. Rooney's thunderous winner for Everton against Arsenal in 2002, aged 16, announced his arrival as an exceptional Premier League talent; later, his Manchester United debut featured a hat-trick in the Champions League. A boy who lived for the big stage, the 'assassin-faced baby' was a thrilling firebrand who feared nothing and nobody, but only added to his game as years passed by. He replaced Ruud van Nistelrooy as a superior all-round striker to help United continue their dominance in the face of new Premier League forces.

His spirited temperament was never better encapsulated than *that* thunderbolt volley against Newcastle in 2005, moments after sulking at the referee. Wazza could score any goal at any moment.

Rooney's mantelpiece is busy, too, featuring five Premier League winner's medals, one FA Cup, three League Cups and a Champions League crown.

Rooney's glorious overhead kick (below), which clinched a 2-1 derby victory over Manchester City in February 2011, goes down as perhaps United's best goal of the Premier League era. Forget the dash of shin, because the technical execution is sublime. It sent United eight points clear of their city rivals en route to a dominant title win.

Gary Neville once said that Rooney was such a handful on a night out, the then-United skipper would assign security guards to "man mark" him until bedtime. Rooney's love of a beer and boogie irritated Ferguson on more than one occasion. So did the forward's agent Paul Stretford, who a seething Fergie blamed for a 2013 transfer request just before the Scot's departure that May.

That Rooney became the Premier League's second-top goalscorer with 208 strikes is notable. Arguably more so, though, is the fact that he's also its third-highest assister. Versatile and unselfish, England's record marksman was particularly monstrous from 2009-11 for United, when he stepped up after Cristiano Ronaldo's move to Real Madrid. A special player taking great responsibility.

03 ALAN SHEARER

BLACKBURN, NEWCASTLE

Eras do not always begin and end when they are supposed to. The '60s arguably only came to life in 1962, when The Beatles released their debut single *Love Me Do* and Mary Quant unleashed the mini skirt on an unsuspecting establishment.

Liverpool are remembered for dominating the 1970s and 1980s, but their 18th league title actually came in the 1990s. The dawn of the Premier League, however, marked a clean break with the past; Manchester United, 26 years without a title, were champions in 13 of the first 21 seasons.

On the opening day of a new age, Blackburn drew 3-3 at Crystal Palace. Their 22-year-old debutant, the costliest ever signing made by a British club, netted twice. Viewed with 2022 hindsight, it's obvious Alan Shearer scored. Back then, though, it wasn't so inevitable that he would define a division. Shearer had made 118 First Division outings for Southampton, scoring 23 times. His return of 13 in 41 games of 1991-92 was perfectly respectable, but far from remarkable.

A rebranded league got a reinvented player – productivity replaced the promise. Shearer was a Premier League phenomenon. He was injured on Boxing Day after netting 16 goals for Rovers; without a cruciate ligament injury, he probably would have bagged the division's inaugural Golden Boot.

Instead, he became its record scorer in its second campaign. More than a quarter of a century later, he has never relinquished that status. Harry Kane could threaten it, but he's still more than 40 behind Shearer's tally of 260 at the time of writing. If Kane doesn't pass Shearer, then it's almost certain that no one will in the 2020s.

A REBRANDED LEAGUE ALSO GOT A REINVENTED PLAYER. PRODUCTIVITY REPLACED THE PROMISE

Shearer's relentlessness and ruthlessness brought him accolades. He's still by far the fastest to a Premier League century (in 124 games, 17 fewer than anyone else); still the only Englishman to scoop the Golden Boot three years in a row; still alone in scoring 30 in three consecutive campaigns; still alone in hitting 20 in seven Premier League seasons. He plundered 31 for a Blackburn team that came seventh and 23 for a Newcastle outfit that finished in the bottom half of the table. He smashed five goals in a fixture when the Magpies started the day in 19th place. No one else with a ton of Premier League goals for one team comes close to his ratio of 0.81 per game for Blackburn.

Throw in his 64 assists, and no one else has been involved in 324 Premier League goals.

Two factors make the bare statistics even more remarkable. Two cruciate ligament injuries forced him to evolve from an eager channel-runner who liked playing alongside a targetman, to the physical focal point who, aided by Sir Bobby Robson's advice, remained potent. Second: he turned down Manchester United in 1996 for the siren call of his native Tyneside. With the Red Devils' supply line, his 260 efforts might have surpassed 300.

Instead, after leading Blackburn to a first top-flight title in 81 years, he endured five lower-half finishes with his hometown club. Yet, as Kenny Dalglish – his manager at both Blackburn and Newcastle – informed Shearer, "It didn't matter who you played for, you always battered them in."

Brute force was often allied with finesse. Shearer's favourite goal, his cannonball volley against Everton in 2002, is a case in point. He was a wonderfully clean striker of the ball, but was also brilliant in the air: only Peter Crouch has notched more Premier League headers, and he has a seven-inch height advantage. Only Jimmy Greaves, Steve Bloomer, Dixie Dean and Gordon Hodgson have struck more goals in England's top flight.

Shearer retired with 283 league goals – and one celebration.

NEWCASTLE
BROWN ALE

vodafone
N'GOTTY
5

02 CRISTIANO RONALDO

MANCHESTER UNITED

It seems hard to imagine that Cristiano Ronaldo was not a household hame when he moved to Manchester United from Sporting Lisbon in the summer of 2003. Only 18 years old at the time, Ferguson and United pursued Ronaldo after the young winger embarrassed experienced Reds defender John O'Shea in a preseason friendly. Ronaldo then burst onto the Premier League scene during his debut by dismantling Bolton on the 16 August 2003, with United legend George Best describing his show as "Undoubtedly the most exciting debut performance I've ever seen".

This initial sparkle of brilliance – winning a penalty and providing an assist while constantly lifting the crowd with his blistering pace and dizzying step-overs – proved to just be a taster for the young phenom. Over his next six years at the club, Ronaldo went on to score 118 goals in 292 appearances, winning seven major honours. But as is often the case with young players, he did not immediately deliver on the potential he flashed in his debut against Bolton. In his first three seasons, he'd scored 27 goals in 137 games and won an FA Cup and League Cup, but failed to win a Premier League trophy as Jose Mourinho's Chelsea were dominant. Those seasons were promising but unspectacular, characterised by showy step-overs but a frustrating lack of end product.

The summer of 2006 is when Ronaldo took a leap. Ronaldo went through the controversy of knocking out England in the World Cup, having winked at the Portugal bench after drawing attention to clubmate Wayne Rooney's stamp on Ricardo Carvalho's nether regions to get him sent off. Media tensions were high, but Ronaldo and Rooney smoothed over their differences. And Ronaldo came back to United a changed player. "Physically, he changed from a boy to a man", teammate Gary Neville later recalled. "He left as a featherweight and returned as a light-heavyweight. That brought him a level of power he didn't have before."

And that change in power came with a change in mindset. "When he came to Machester United, he was a show pony," Rio Ferdinand later recalled. "He wanted to do skills, he wanted to show people how good he was... Then he realised it was about end product and to become the best player in the world it would be all about purely scoring goals... He forced himself to become that guy."

And "that guy" he became. Ronaldo drove United to the League title that season with 17 goals and 16 assists on the way to winning PFA Player of the Year, but his drive did not stop there. The 2007–08 season is when Ronaldo truly became dominant, taking that mentality shift to its devastating and frightening conclusion. He scored 42 times that season, winning another league title, the Champions League, PFA Player of the Year and the vaunted Ballon d'Or, the only man in Premier League history to win it while in England.

After a third consecutive league title in 2008–09, Ronaldo moved to Madrid in 2009 for a then-record £80m, having already cemented his legacy as one of the most talented players to ever grace the Premier League. He built on this legacy and more at Madrid, rivalling Lionel Messi on the way to five Champions League wins and five Ballon D'Or awards. After a stop at Juventus, an ageing Ronaldo returned to United in 2021, although there was no fairytale ending for him after a blockbuster interview with Piers Morgan led to his release in November 2022. Nonetheless, Ronaldo's legend remains as a Premier League giant.

HIGHLIGHT Being the only man to win the Ballon d'Or while playing in the Premier League is not a bad achievement, but if there is one iconic moment to sum up Ronaldo's United career it would have to be *that* free kick against Portsmouth in 2008. Straight run up, thump, swerve – top corner. Iconic.

01 THIERRY HENRY

ARSENAL

1. RAMS RAID FOR AILING TITI (1999)

According to legend, Arsenal vice-chairman David Dein gave Thierry Henry a videotape when he walked in the door. It featured clips of Ian Wright, with a note reading, "This is what you have to do." As if it were that easy.

In November 1999, after a tough initiation, the Frenchman moved Highbury to its feet for the very first time. Arsene Wenger was yet to start Henry and Dennis Bergkamp together at home, but did against Derby; fire and ice, youth and experience in delicate harmony.

The Gunners went one down before Henry shuffled into the spotlight. Before this game, there had been just two goals in 16 matches for a player bereft of confidence on the wing.

But Arsene always had his plan in mind. Two coolly taken goals snatched the narrative on a night where Henry displayed Wright's pace and poise from those crackly clips. On 72 minutes, he left the stage to a standing ovation. This was the moment Henry first held his adoring audience in the palm of his hand. He would keep them there for another seven exhilarating years.

2. FERGIE LEFT FLABBERGASTED (2000)

By October 2000, Henry wasn't only pouncing on opportunities – he was creating them from scratch. Thirty minutes into Arsenal's titanic tussle with defending champions Manchester United, David Beckham brought down Freddie Ljungberg. Sylvinho squared a simple pass to Gilles Grimandi, who found Henry lurking near the right edge of the penalty area, his back to Denis Irwin. United's four defenders were flat in front of Fabien Barthez: the drawbridge was firmly closed.

But where there was Henry, there was often a way. In a fluid movement, the Frenchman flicked the ball up and volleyed it over his left shoulder, like he had just pulled a pin out of a grenade and lobbed it at the castle walls. He peeled away in celebration while the ball was still mid-flight; it was arguably the most sumptuous goal in Highbury history.

"You can't really do anything about a goal like that," a baffled Alex Ferguson shrugged at full-time. He wasn't wrong.

3. GET THE BLOKE A STATUE (2002)

It's November 2002, around 3.12pm on derby day, and Henry is about to do something brilliant. When the ball lands at his feet, the score goalless, he's well inside Arsenal's half. It bounces, so he pirouettes 180 degrees and spins past Tottenham's Matthew Etherington. Now in the opposite direction, Henry cushions the ball down and slides into gear, leaning back and leaping away like a gazelle while prancing over the halfway line. As he hares towards the Tottenham penalty area, the Frenchman sidesteps three defenders as if they're not there.

This box-to-box explosion was the defining

> IT WAS AS IF SOMEONE HAD UNLEASHED A CAGED ANIMAL ON THE SPURS DEFENCE, YET THERE WAS SUCH GRACE TO HENRY

image of Wenger's early Arsenal sides. They played with such arrogance and elegance, power and balance: all encapsulated in their No.14's exquisite one-man counter-attack that afternoon. No one could get within five yards; the defence backed off like someone had unleashed a caged animal upon them. And yet, watching all of Henry's 6ft 1in frame skate across the Highbury grass, there was such grace and beauty to his movement. The greatest goals during Wenger's tenure felt choreographed like this.

To finish, Henry hammered home into the bottom corner, then legged the length of the pitch back again – shrugging off yet another defender en route, as Sol Campbell tried to embrace him. He slid on his knees in front of the travelling Spurs supporters, an enduring moment later immortalised in statue form outside the Emirates Stadium. The Tottenham faithful cursed, cussed and clamoured – but none of them could get near Arsenal's star man, either. Everybody else was more than used to the feeling.

4. PASS IT ON: 20'S PLENTY (2003)

Ruud van Nistelrooy would sulk like a PS5-less kid at Christmas if Manchester United won a game without his name on the scoresheet. However, when boss Ferguson used the word "selfish" to describe the Dutchman, he meant it as the highest compliment.

In 2002-03, Van Nistelrooy went toe-to-toe with Henry for the Golden Boot: two talismen, bullish in self-assurance. But when it came down to it, spearhead vs spearhead, Henry simply did what he usually did. He stepped out of the box altogether.

On the final day of the season, the strikers one goal apart, Van Nistelrooy netted a 25th at Everton to snatch the individual award. Henry, meanwhile, scored but also assisted Ljungberg three times against Sunderland – twice, when he could have taken a shot himself. "To me, the most beautiful thing is making the pass when you are in a position to score," he once said.

In a time before most people even looked at who had set up the goal, Henry finished with a record 20 assists that campaign – 18 of them from open play. Manchester City's Kevin De Bruyne only matched it in 2019-20.

For Van Nistelrooy, football was about the goals and nothing else. But for Arsenal and Henry, the game was about more than that. In a trophyless season, he may have lost the battle but carved out his own unique piece of glory in one of the English top-flight's finest individual campaigns. "None of the greatest goalscorers in history can compare with his assist record," declared Wenger.

How do you defend against someone who provides as willingly as he finishes himself?

5. THIS GUY LOOKS INVINCIBLE (2004)

In truth, Henry's hat-trick clincher at home to Liverpool in April 2004 was quite fluky. It was, though, the only moment all afternoon that he wasn't in abundant control.

Arsenal's equaliser was a mirror to Henry's first Highbury league goal against Derby, only less nervously placed – a first-time, left-foot strike. By now, however, such lethal finishing felt like vintage Thierry, rather than an Ian Wright

tribute act.

Arsenal trailed 2-1 to the Reds at half-time, their Invincibles status in jeopardy, but Henry seemed to slow down time by the touchline after the break; jogging, his right leg hovering like a magician's handkerchief over a dove, before passing to Ljungberg who looped Pires in to level proceedings.

A minute later, it was all over. Henry picked up the ball by the centre circle, then strode beyond Didi Hamann, bamboozled Jamie Carragher, folded Liverpool inside-out and buried home in the bottom corner. Henry had immense power but made football look weightless. He put Arsenal on his back and, even with Steven Gerrard dictating play like a swinging pickaxe, possessed the ability to take away everyone's breath – including that of the Merseysiders' defence.

6. THE GOODBYE KISS (2006)

Highbury was modest. A garden of a ground, with a well-kept lawn, traffic and train sounds overhead. It made the Invincibles look giant – like they could stretch into the clouds at their brilliant best – and certainly helped to fuel Henry's story.

Arsenal were losing 2-1 to mid-table Wigan when the Frenchman dug out a hat-trick for Highbury's final sign-off; the final goal at the beautiful old ground a penalty in front of the North Bank. When the ball struck the back of the net, Henry – Gunners captain and record goalscorer – dropped to his knees, kissed the turf and saluted the crowd.

It had to be him. No one else could close that chapter. We're all just stories in the end – but Henry's was one hell of a tale.

DESTINED FOR GREATNESS

The Premier League isn't just about talented oldies: these young stars are hunting down records and glory

TRENT ALEXANDER-ARNOLD

LIVERPOOL

The young career of Trent Alexander-Arnold is already worthy of legend status. A stalwart of Jurgen Klopp's Liverpool side since his breakthrough at only 18, Alexander-Arnold is a Premier League winner and third on the list of all-time assists by a defender. "The passing of Alexander-Arnold is just sublime," opined Gary Lineker. "He's on another level and has to play." Gary Neville said: "He's the best passer of a ball at right-back that I've ever seen." Praise indeed. Considered the best attacking full-back in the world, Alexander-Arnold's wicked crossing and pinpoint passing have been crucial to a legendary era of Liverpool football.

HIGHLIGHT Alexander-Arnold crushed Watford with three assists in a single game in 2019, becoming the youngest player ever to do so. "An outstanding game", said Jürgen Klopp afterwards. Understatement.

ERLING HAALAND

MANCHESTER CITY

The earliest player in his career to make our list, Haaland has come into the Premier League and already ripped it up. Haaland smashed the single-season scoring record with 36 goals in his debut season, with an eye-watering 52 goals in all competitions. With frightening power, pace and a predatory instinct to rival nature's best, Haaland will rock the Premier League for as long as he's around. His peers share this fear, describing him as "a force of nature" (Jürgen Klopp); "a one-man wrecking ball" (Owen Hargreaves); or "like a superhero in a cartoon" (Jan Åge Fjørtoft). A defender's nightmare. Haaland has won the treble in his first season comprising the Premier League the FA Cup and the Champions League.

HIGHLIGHT Haaland dominated from the get with City, scoring 19 goals from his first 12 games, a rate unprecedented in English football. He cooled off slightly from that, but not before smashing six hat-tricks over the season - a record only matched by Harry Kane and Alan Shearer.

DECLAN RICE

WEST HAM

Starting his career at Chelsea's academy, Rice swapped west London for east London at the age of 14 and has never looked back. The England international has captained since the age of 19, leading them to European qualification in 2021–22 with all-action midfield displays that earned him comparisons to Roy Keane from Jamie Carragher. "He's not just a holding midfield player, he drives forward with the ball. He is more than a sitting player," the Liverpool great said. The young Englishman is one of the most sought-after midfielders in Europe, and his legacy is only going one way: up.

HIGHLIGHT He doesn't score many, but Rice's goal and Man of the Match performance against Arsenal to lead West Ham to a 1–0 win in 2019 shows he can do it all.

SON HEUNG-MIN

TOTTENHAM

Trained rigorously by his coach father in South Korea, Son's deadly two-footed finishing has made him one of the best forwards in Europe. Since moving from Bayer Leverkusen in 2015, he has formed a formidable partnership with Harry Kane, the two of whom share the record for most goals provided to each other between a duo. Teamwork. An icon in his home country, he is considered by many to be the greatest Asian player of all time.

HIGHLIGHT Son has terrorised many a defence on his day, but his 2021–22 Golden Boot shared with the legendary Mo Salah has to be the best moment of his career.

BUKAYO SAKA

ARSENAL

With blistering pace, quick acceleration and a thumping left foot, Bukayo Saka has all of the tools to be a world-class right-winger. And Arsenal fans know he is. Still just 21, Saka leads the next generation of Premier League stars. Having started his career at full-back under Unai Emery, Saka found his home at the top end of the pitch and is equally capable of finishing or providing a killer pass. Saka has become Arsenal's main man at the ripe age of 21 and with the Gunners flourishing under Mikel Arteta, titles and glory look on the way.

HIGHLIGHT Saka produced a thrilling display against Liverpool at the start of the 2022 season, scoring twice in a 3-2 win. Taking down the Liverpool powerhouse announced Arsenal as real championship contenders, with Saka leading the way.

LEGENDS OF THE PREMIER

LEAGUE

Now we've given you our definitive, perfectly accurate top 100 list, let's dive deeper into some of the pillars of the Premier League who've made the English game the best there is

ERIC CANTONA
KING ERIC

They didn't make them like Eric then, and they still don't now. Unapologetically enigmatic, the Frenchman spent his career thrilling and befuddling in equal measure – no one in football history carries an aura like the King. Cantona wowed, warred and often wounded, but thank God he came here 30 years ago

Midway through the 1991-92 season, Michel Platini strode up to the boss of one of England's biggest clubs and began his sales pitch.

"I've got a player for you," he told the man stood in front of him, a fearsome Scot who'd enjoyed managerial success north of the border but had yet to steer his current team to a league title in England. Platini believed he knew just the person who could seriously improve their fortunes.

"He's a problem boy, but he's also really talented," said the French legend, then the coach of the national team. "He'd be perfect for your club."

Graeme Souness wasn't so sure. Liverpool were ninth in the top flight, their glory days fading to grey. That night, they'd beaten Auxerre at Anfield in the UEFA Cup, but that hadn't softened Souey's mood. The answer was an immediate no.

"Listen Michel," he said, "I'm fighting fires at the moment, trying to get some people out the door. They're resisting – I'm fighting a dressing room. The last thing that I need is another controversial figure in there."

Liverpool had just turned down the chance to sign Eric Cantona. A few weeks later, in December 1991, the France international announced his retirement at the age of 25. Banned for a month for throwing the ball at a referee, the Nimes forward responded to the disciplinary panel by approaching each member and uttering the word 'idiot' in their direction, one by one. When the suspension was then doubled, Cantona called it quits.

Thankfully, his retirement didn't last long. On 8 February 1992, a day after the expiry of his two-month ban, he was making his debut for Leeds United at Boundary Park against Oldham Athletic. Nine months later, he joined Manchester United... and the rest is history.

While Liverpool would go three decades without a league title, Cantona helped their biggest rivals end their own 26-year top-flight drought in 1993 and begin a glittering era of incredible dominance. Thirty years after his arrival on these shores, this is the inside story of the man who changed English football.

1966 WAS A GREAT YEAR...

Born in May 1966, he was raised in Marseille by father Albert – a painter of Italian heritage – and mother Eleonore, whose parents had left Spain during the Civil War. Cantona was a 14 year old turning out for his junior side Caillolais when he met his footballing mentor.

"Eric already had that way of standing very straight, that haughty stance," long-serving former Auxerre boss Guy Roux remembers as he talks to *FourFourTwo*. "He looked like a prince at a ceremony alongside the Queen of England.

"He came to my attention via someone I'd sent to a trials event in Aix-en-Provence. They told me about a phenomenon, tall and physically strong, who already had all the qualities needed. We immediately tried to get him to Auxerre. He'd already had a lot of trials, particularly at Nice, but agreed to come to our club with a dozen other kids.

"At the end of the ten-day training camp, we put him into a short eight-vs-eight match with our first-team professionals and he was excellent – even if some of them criticised him for dribbling too much. We could already tell that there was a fire inside him.

"I met him face to face and asked him if we could get him something he'd like. He told me about a jersey, so I sent him to the club shop where he was given a jersey, some shorts and socks. I later learned that he'd made the same request at Nice, and they'd charged him for it."

Cantona signed for Auxerre, initially staying in a lodge that once housed local monks near the city's cathedral. He didn't exactly live like a monk, though, even then.

"He was the most difficult [to manage]," Roux admits. "He had a late childhood and a turbulent adolescence. His training was under the guidance of Daniel Rolland, and we managed Eric between us.

"I remember an argument he had one afternoon with one of his best friends, Stephane Mazzolini. The two started chasing each other and they ended up in the dining hall, with Cantona trying to catch him. They jumped from table to table, overturning all the plates, cutlery and glasses. A massacre!

"Eric was the band leader – not of a mafia gang but of a cheerful little group who were mostly successful on the field. Later on, one match in Lens was postponed because of fog, so we travelled directly to Saint-Brieuc to prepare for a game at Brest. In the evening, we went to the town hall at Roscoff, a small town in Brittany twinned with Auxerre. At the end of a small ceremony with the mayor, I realised that seven players had disappeared. We sat down to dinner and I was facing a window, through which I saw them coming back. They were all around Cantona, who'd shaved his head – he had no more hair.

"Cantona was staying in a room opposite mine, and that night I heard him talking to his girlfriend, complaining that his head was cold. For their little night out, I sanctioned them two weeks without going out. But the next day, we played Brest and won."

Cantona's first-team debut came at 17, in 1983. He'd already appeared for France's under-17s, although the Foreign Office had to step in to defuse a diplomatic incident after he'd travelled to Leningrad for a youth tournament and spat at the referee – an officer in the Soviet army. As was mandatory for French teenagers back then, he also had to carry out national service, delaying his progress with Auxerre.

"He was in the Joinville battalion," Roux explains, referring to a special military unit for sportsmen. "One day, the colonel of the battalion called and told me that a general was coming for an inspection. He said that Cantona didn't shave well, and asked me what to do. The only solution we found was to send Eric to get potatoes and get him home late, so he didn't run into the general!"

Cantona returned for more brief first-team appearances in 1985, scoring his first senior goal against Rouen in mid-May before fizzing in a 25-yard thunderbolt against Strasbourg a fortnight later that confirmed Auxerre's qualification for the UEFA Cup. To gain more experience he was then loaned to Martigues, a few miles outside of Marseille.

"I'd learned that every Saturday night, he got into his car after Auxerre matches and went to see his girlfriend in Martigues – it was a 600km journey, and I was afraid it would end in a dramatic accident," Roux explains. "During 1985-86, Martigues were last in the second division, five points behind their rivals, but I thought a loan would be good for Eric, and he did too. He helped them stay up."

Cantona was also sent off twice – first for a tiff with one fan who'd insulted him, then receiving his marching orders again when Martigues were already safe from relegation.

"Martigues played Cannes – a friend of Eric's played for Istres, and if Martigues won then it helped Istres to stay up," Roux says. "He'd promised his friend that Martigues would win, but quickly he realised that his team-mates weren't playing very hard and got angry with them. One of the Cannes players told him to calm down, and Eric shot him an upper cut. He got a three-match suspension, which he had to serve at Auxerre because his loan was over. But I went to see the president of the federation, told him what had happened, and the suspension was overturned by a presidential amnesty."

Back at Auxerre, Cantona struck 17 goals in 1986-87. "He'd become an adult," says Roux, who managed the club for an incredible 41 years. "We often talk about Maradona's goal against England at the 1986 World Cup, but Eric did similar things with us. He'd start from midfield, dribble around everyone and score. He was already an exceptional player."

Above Guy Roux was Cantona's first footballing mentor, working hard to rescue his protégé from a few sticky spots

In August 1987, Cantona made his debut for France at senior level, scoring in a friendly against West Germany after starting upfront alongside Jean-Pierre Papin. "We lost 2-1 in Berlin, but Eric scored just after half-time," Papin tells *FFT*. "It was already Eric Cantona – we knew what he could bring to a team, and we quickly gave him the reins."

Briefly drafted back to the U21s for a vital European Championship semi-final against England, he darted from the halfway line, past Martin Keown & Co in the Three Lions defence, to score in a 4-2 win in Besançon. At Highbury in the second leg, he netted twice more – defeating Paul Gascoigne in the duel of the emerging mavericks, as Les Bleuets went on to become continental champions.

At club level, though, Cantona became embroiled in not one but two controversial incidents – the first with Auxerre's own goalkeeper. "One morning, there was eight centimetres of snow on the pitch, so I sent the players to clear it using the advertising boards," Roux says. "Cantona was pushing like crazy, but Bruno Martini was resting a little. The tone rose, then Eric ended the discussion with a nudge." Or, to put it less diplomatically, a headbutt.

In April 1988 in Nantes, an astonishingly high two-footed tackle on defender Michel Der Zakarian earned Cantona a red card and two-

month suspension. "Those two got into a dispute – I later learned they were from the same neighbourhood in Marseille," Roux says. "For Eric, it was OK to tease each other once in a while, but we're talking about a tackle at hip height! Sometimes it was hard to hold him back. After that tackle, he returned to the changing room and the stadium caretaker fled – he didn't want to bump into Eric..."

COVERED IN KETCHUP

Despite the controversies, Marseille shelled out a French record fee of around £2m to sign the 22 year old that summer. Everyone knew the talent the volcanic maverick possessed.

"All the big French clubs were interested, including Monaco, Paris Saint-Germain and Matra Racing," says Roux. The latter are now known as Racing Club and play in France's fifth tier but had just finished seventh in the top flight back then and were spending big to progress further. "Matra Racing invited him for dinner, and Eric asked me how he should dress. I told him not to put on his jeans with the four stab wounds at the knee, but a suit. He didn't have one so went to buy one. Matra Racing had a row of French-style guards to welcome him – he was excited.

"Then one evening, I got a call from Bernard Tapie at Marseille, asking if he could come and see my phenomenon. We arrived at

"ERIC DIDN'T SHAVE WELL. WE SENT HIM TO GET POTATOES SO HE WOULDN'T RUN INTO THE GENERAL"

Cantona's house at around 8 p.m., and Eric was painting. Tapie asked Cantona where he was born, and Cantona said Marseille. Tapie said, 'Well, that's it – you're coming to play in Marseille, then'."

OM got their man after outbidding their rivals and fending off late competition from Milan. "We needed players like Cantona," says Papin, who'd joined Marseille two years earlier. But Cantona remained sceptical of Tapie. "There were things about Marseille he didn't like," Roux says.

His time at the club started badly, too – left out of the France squad after a goalless first month, he responded by branding national team boss Henri Michel a "s**tbag", insisting he wouldn't play for Les Bleus again while Michel was in charge.

By January, Cantona was starting to forge a partnership with Papin, but his relationship with Tapie had deteriorated – then he threw his shirt away and marched off topless after being substituted during a charity match against Torpedo Moscow, arranged to raise funds after an earthquake in Armenia. Marseille banned him for a month and Tapie suggested Cantona needed psychiatric help, so the player boarded a plane to Barcelona, his grandfather's home city. He was loaned to Bordeaux for the rest of the campaign.

At the start of 1989-90, Cantona was again loaned out, to Montpellier, but then recalled to the France squad by new boss Platini, who was eager to harness his talent and salvage an ailing World Cup qualifying campaign. On Eric's return, both he and Papin bagged braces in a 4-2 win in Sweden.

"Platini knew football well, and he knew Eric and I could play together – we'd already done it at Marseille," Papin says. "I scored a lot of goals thanks to Eric, and he did too. We just complemented each other. It was never easy for the opposition to control him – he often had one or two defenders permanently on him, which allowed me to find space and use my speed."

Cantona bagged eight goals in eight games for France that season, even if Les Bleus still missed out on Italia 90. With ambitious Montpellier, he'd score 14 times and win the Coupe de France, despite a difficult start to the season when they were dragged into a relegation battle.

"There was talent in that team, but the atmosphere wasn't ideal," says their former midfielder Jean-Claude Lemoult. "A lot of responsibilities were given to young players, and that was complicated. Whether it's in a changing room, a movie or just in life, Eric is very prominent. He has ideas, views and he's not shy about expressing them. Reporters often came to talk to him, so he could say what he had to say."

With old foe Michel Der Zakarian now also a team-mate, perhaps another flashpoint was always inevitable.

"We lost 1-0 at Lille, and when we returned to the changing room I was talking to Michel," Lemoult says. "Cantona came over and got angry – I tried to calm him down by telling him that we weren't talking about him, but he threw a boot in my face and a fight broke out. The president wanted to fire him, but he met Eric a few days later, they had a chat and in the end he didn't."

Instead, it was manager Aimé Jacquet – later a 1998 World Cup winner with France – who was soon fired and replaced by Michel Mezy. Lemoult and Cantona put their scuffle behind them, and Montpellier went on to lift their first major trophy for 61 years.

"Eric had an important role in us winning the Coupe de France, particularly in the semis against Saint-Etienne," Lemoult says. "That fight between us was just the consequence of disappointment after a defeat, nothing more – we were separated and it ended there. I later became team-mates with him again at Nimes; it was Eric who advised the club to take me."

Cantona returned to Marseille for 1990-91, initially scoring regularly alongside Papin. "He was never the slightest problem in the dressing room," his strike partner insists.

Papin even got away with accidentally squirting an entire bottle of ketchup over him during a mealtime prank, of which Chris Waddle had been the intended recipient. Team-mates held their breath, expecting Cantona to explode, but instead he carried on eating as if nothing at all had happened. "Everyone who was there still remembers it!" Papin smiles.

Above Flying to the Coupe de France

Injury halted Cantona's progress, though – by the time he returned, Raymond Goethals had replaced Franz Beckenbauer, and boss and forward didn't see eye to eye.

Marseille won the league and reached the European Cup final, but Cantona didn't even make the bench having been frozen out from March onwards. OM were defeated by Red Star Belgrade on penalties after 120 goalless minutes of 'action'.

"It's a regret that he didn't play the final with us," Papin says. "I tried to use my role as captain to talk to the coach, but Goethals was a bit stubborn. The reason for Eric being sidelined wasn't sporting, even if the coach told us otherwise.

"But Goethals made it clear to me that he'd made his choices, and he didn't have to discuss them. We'll never know if we would have won that final with Eric in the team, but he never disappointed in big games. I think it could have been a very big day for him."

Cantona never played for Marseille again – he was sold to Nimes for around £1m and installed as their new captain. The French firebrand was reunited with old Montpellier boss Michel Mezy, but joining a promoted club was risky for a 25 year old who was still France's first-choice forward.

Nimes started the season poorly, and Cantona quickly grew frustrated. Platini sounded out Liverpool, attempting to find a better home for his key man, before the forward went nuclear. During a home game against Saint-Etienne in early December, Cantona grabbed the ball and hurled it at the referee after an innocuous free kick had been awarded against him.

"He left the field even before he was sent off," says Lemoult, his team-mate once more at Nimes. "I didn't see the incident coming, but Eric was unpredictable. Everyone knew it wasn't difficult to annoy him on the pitch – a lot of opponents did. He hated injustice and couldn't control himself."

A one-month suspension was dished out at his disciplinary hearing, then increased to two months after Cantona insulted the panel. As he later said, "They passed judgement on my life as a whole, not just the isolated incident, so I told them they were idiots, which was remarkably restrained for me."

"We didn't see him at the club for a while," Lemoult says. "He locked himself in his house, tormented by that episode. I went there to eat with him, and I also tried to make him understand that he had to keep going. But he wanted to end his career."

ERIC CANTONA'S INDOOR LEAGUE

A few days before Christmas 1991, Cantona announced his retirement from football. Only Platini's intervention changed his mind, after the French boss insisted that a transfer to England could be the solution. There, he was virtually unknown and could start afresh, without the past weighing him down.

So, in late January, Cantona travelled to Yorkshire for a stint training with Sheffield Wednesday on an artificial pitch because of freezing weather conditions. His only public appearance for the Owls came at the new Sheffield Arena, in a scheduled six-a-side Transatlantic Challenge clash against visiting US team Baltimore Blast of the Major Indoor Soccer League.

Part of a Wednesday line-up that also contained Graham Hyde, Chris Bart-Williams and American international John Harkes, grainy YouTube footage tells us that Cantona scrabbled around on a tiny

Above On loan at Montpellier

pitch, attempting to force the ball into a miniature goal from two yards. Perhaps unsurprisingly, Baltimore and the Major Indoor Soccer League both folded later that year.

Like Nimes, Wednesday had just been promoted to the top tier. Unlike Nimes, they doubted they had the budget to actually sign Cantona. "A former agent of mine asked if I'd do a favour to Platini, who was very keen to get Cantona back playing," Owls boss Trevor Francis later revealed to the *Yorkshire Post*. "He wondered if I'd have a look at him in training. I said, 'I don't really need another centre-forward, but as a favour, I'll do it'.

"I was surprised when he arrived – it was built up as if I was looking to sign him, which was never a consideration. He was here to do a few days' training, basically putting himself in the shop window. There was this indoor tournament – so I asked him if he wanted to play, and he had a kickaround.

"After those two days it was put to me, 'Are you going to sign him?' I said, 'Well, I don't think so, we'd like him to stay for a few more days for us to have a little look at him'.

"I think his manager took that as an insult – I don't know if it was a breakdown in communication, but they regarded it as he was Eric Cantona and he was not going to be on trial. The whole thing got messy, and he came to me and said, 'I've got a chance to go to Leeds'. He had my blessing."

Spearheaded by 18 goals from David Hirst, Wednesday went on to finish third, but then Cantona ended up as a champion at Elland Road, joining on loan from Nimes until the middle of April for £100,000, with the option to make the deal permanent for £1m.

"To begin with, I don't think any of us really knew who he was – these were the days before the internet," admits Jon Newsome, a member of that title-winning squad. "He was quietly spoken and didn't speak much English, but he joined in with things and his quality was there for everybody to see. Physically, you could see that he'd be able to handle the demands of the Premier League – anything that was thrown at him in training, he could deal with."

Leeds were already top when they travelled to Oldham in early February 1992, but they'd fallen behind at Boundary Park by the time Cantona was brought on for his debut and lost 2-0. With Lee Chapman and Rod Wallace already established as a strong partnership up front, the Frenchman only started one of his first six games – coming on as a sub to score against Luton. But when Manchester United moved two points behind Leeds with three games in hand after the Whites fell 4-1 at QPR in March, manager Howard Wilkinson trialled a new system that incorporated all three of his forwards.

The trio all scored in a 5-1 home win over Wimbledon, when Cantona wore the No.3 shirt, but the next three games delivered only two points; Manchester United took control at the top and Leeds' new signing returned to the bench. He responded with a sensational cameo at home to Chelsea, assisting Chapman before scoring a breathtaking effort of his own – juggling the ball one way and then the other before firing home.

"He turned the centre-half inside-out and then stuck it in the top corner," Newsome remembers. "He was incredible on his day."

Wilkinson swiftly confirmed Cantona's permanent signing – the Chelsea triumph kick-started Leeds' form as they overtook Manchester United again and won the title. Cantona had scored just three times, but he'd had some influence in the club's only league championship since 1974.

"A while back, I saw a Sheffield Wednesday fan say on Twitter that if they'd kept hold of Cantona, they'd have won the league because he went to Leeds, scored loads of goals and won us the title," Newsome says. "That was harsh on the lads who played 35 or 40 games that season, because Eric scored three goals and started six games. But he was the cherry on the icing on top of the cake, a little sprinkling of stardust, and on occasions he did something that changed the game.

"He was a good lad to be around. When we won the title, they built a stage for us on the steps of the city hall, and we stood there with the trophy – they reckon there were 250,000 there. Eric picked the microphone up and said, 'I love you – I don't know why, but I love you'. We all looked at each other as if to say, 'Where's that come from?' but that was him. He knew what to say and how to say it."

Below Cantona won the Charity Shield and First Division while a Leeds player

THE FORMULA 1 CAR ARRIVES

Cantona lined up for France at Euro 92 – the only major tournament of his career – but couldn't find the net as Les Bleus went out in the group stage, drawing 0-0 with Graham Taylor's England in their second match.

Back at Leeds, he scored nine times in his first seven appearances of the new campaign – netting a hat-trick in the Charity Shield against Liverpool, before repeating the feat in a home game against Spurs to become the first player to bag a Premier League treble. In the new Champions League, he scored in a September knockout tie against Stuttgart, later replayed at the Camp Nou after Leeds' German rivals were found to have fielded an ineligible player.

Within a couple of months, however, Eric was gone. While struggling to repeat their title-winning form, Leeds lost to Rangers at Ibrox in the second round of the Champions League – the Frenchman couldn't make an impact and walked straight down the tunnel after being substituted. He was dropped for the next match at QPR.

"Rangers was the start of his downfall," Newsome remembers. "History has shown that Eric was a very headstrong individual, and under Howard Wilkinson you all had your own roles to play on the field. If you didn't do what he asked you to do, it was quite simple: he'd get someone else to do it and you wouldn't be playing. It was things like the defensive side of the game, and not putting the ball at risk. But Eric wanted to do things his own way.

"Howard and Alex Ferguson are two very different people, and they handled him in two very different ways. By the time we played QPR, it was obvious Eric and Howard weren't seeing eye to eye. He went off early in training with an injury, and rather than seeing the physio, he went home. Then there was one pre-match meeting at the hotel he turned up late to and didn't have the correct attire. They were all statements by Eric to either annoy the manager or force his way out."

Cantona returned to Leeds' line-up for the second leg against Rangers and even scored, but the Whites went out anyway. Then they lost 4-0 at Manchester City in early November, slipping to 14th in the Premier League, before exiting the League Cup at second-tier outfit Watford. Cantona was dropped again and handed in a transfer request, demanding to join Manchester United, Liverpool or Arsenal.

Wilkinson tried to find a buyer in Italy, Spain or France, but he found no takers. Then came the most pivotal phone call in Premier League history, from Leeds' managing director Bill Fotherby to Manchester United chairman Martin Edwards, enquiring about signing Denis Irwin. By chance, Alex Ferguson was sat opposite Edwards and passed him a note that read, "Ask about Cantona."

Manchester United were only eighth in the league, nine points behind leaders Norwich, having hit just 17 goals in 16 games – fewer than three of the bottom four. Ferguson had missed out on Alan Shearer to Blackburn in the summer, then signed Dion Dublin from Cambridge, only for the targetman to break his leg in cruel fashion.

The Scot responded by trying to sign Hirst from Sheffield Wednesday, for what would have been a record fee paid by a British club. "I can still hear Alex now on my car phone, totally exasperated because he'd put in two offers that I'd knocked back," Trevor Francis said. "I refused £4m and Alex bellowed down the phone, 'Do you realise this is Manchester United Football Club, you're stopping a player going to Man United?'"

Cantona was a different type of player, arrived at almost by accident, but Leeds let him leave for just £1.2m. Or so Whites fans thought, anyway: Edwards later revealed on BBC documentary *Fever Pitch* that the fee was in fact £1m but publicly declared higher to avoid Fotherby getting too much stick.

"When he joined us, the club was a bit like a Formula 1 car – it just needed a Formula 1 driver to steer it, and Eric was that man," Gary Pallister tells *FFT*. "He was the final piece of the jigsaw, a perfect fit. The day he walked into the United changing room is still fresh in my memory.

"We were all a bit sceptical because of his reputation, wondering what kind of individual was joining us, but the moment he arrived, he had that aura – and it transmitted onto the pitch straight away.

"No one I can think of ever hit the ground running like Eric did. He had this real unique quality and understanding of the game, and gave us the imagination we'd perhaps lacked. From day one, he was outstanding."

"HE WANTED TO KILL THAT F**KER"

After making his first Manchester United appearance against Benfica in Lisbon, in a December friendly to mark Eusebio's 50th birthday, Cantona soon partnered Mark Hughes up front in the Premier League, with Brian McClair moved into midfield.

The Frenchman quickly scored four in four games – equalising in a draw at Chelsea, then bagging the leveller as they came from 3-0 down at Sheffield Wednesday. One goal and two assists in a 5-0 thrashing of Coventry soon followed, before a header as United hammered Tottenham 4-1. That was the day Cantona also delivered a sumptuous assist for Irwin, extravagantly flicking the ball over Spurs' defence with the outside of a boot, in a way that only Cantona could. He later claimed it was his favourite moment of his whole United career. In little more than a month, Eric had catapulted Ferguson's side to the top of the table.

"The way he played was different from anyone else – he was a genius," Pallister says. "But it wasn't just on the pitch that he settled in seamlessly. He really loved being among the lads.

"He was a different character – he'd talk about poetry and paintings, and also refer to a game as a blank canvas for him to perform a work of art. He was a bit different from the typical raggy-arsed footballer from a working class background! But the beauty of Eric was that he embraced all of our foibles, too.

"It's well known that the United lads had a bit of a drinking club going. We called them team meetings, and they often lasted until kicking-out time. A lot of foreign lads came to England and disapproved of that culture, but Eric absolutely loved it because he wanted to feel part of the squad. He gave as good as he got during those sessions – at the end of the night, he'd often be the one asking when we planned our next meeting..."

Cantona's lifestyle was relatively modest, as well. "Once, I remember one of the papers did an article on the houses we were all living in," Steve Bruce tells *FFT*. "I'm sure quite a few people were surprised to find that Eric lived in a little terraced house in Worsley and

drove a Honda Prelude – nothing flash. I remember him coming into training and asking, 'What's all this about? Why the fuss?' We said, 'Maybe they think you need a bigger house'. He said, 'Why? I have a house in Barcelona, I also have a house in Marseille – so I don't need a big house here'."

Cantona's return to Elland Road with Manchester United in March 1993 wasn't without incident – he spat at some home fans during the 0-0 draw and was fined £1,000 by the FA. Chasing their first league title for 26 years, the Red Devils dropped back to third, behind Norwich and Aston Villa, after a run of four matches without a win. In April, a trip to Carrow Road had the whiff of a title decider.

Cantona helped Ferguson's side destroy the Canaries on the counter-attack – playing in Ryan Giggs for the opener, then scoring himself to make it 3-0 after just 21 minutes. It began a run of seven straight victories that sealed the Premier League – Cantona had won the league for a third successive season with a third different club, and this time he'd been absolutely crucial.

The 1993-94 campaign would bring with it another Premier League title and 25 goals in all competitions – his highest ever tally. Arguably Cantona's best league strike was a missile of a free-kick at home to Arsenal as United surged clear at the top very early on.

Outside of England, things went less well. The Frenchman had scored in a 3-3 home draw with Galatasaray in the Champions League, then United travelled to Istanbul for the second leg, greeted by 'Welcome to Hell' banners at the airport. In an incredibly hostile atmosphere at the Ali Sami Yen, they drew 0-0 to exit the competition in November 1993, and Cantona was sent off after the final whistle for lambasting the referee. He was escorted off the pitch by a policeman, who then punched him in the tunnel.

"Eric went crazy in the dressing room," Roy Keane later said. "The rest of us just wanted to get out of there, but he was determined to go back outside to sort out the rogue cop. He insisted he was going to kill 'that f**ker'. It took the combined efforts of Brian Kidd and a few players to restrain him. Normally I wouldn't have backed off a fight, but even I wasn't up for that one. There were a lot of Turks out there."

A fortnight later, Cantona put France ahead in their final qualifier for the 1994 World Cup – his sixth goal of the group – only for Bulgaria to hit back and win 2-1 in Paris, eliminating Les Bleus. "Eric is one of the greatest players in French history – we scored a lot together during that qualifying campaign," Jean-Pierre Papin says. "Our partnership should have reached its full potential at the World Cup in the United States. Unfortunately, we missed out on getting there."

Cantona took third place in the Ballon d'Or, beaten only by Roberto Baggio and Dennis Bergkamp, then started to propel United to the FA Cup final – he bagged a stunning volley against Wimbledon at Selhurst Park, minutes after Vinnie Jones had almost cut him in half with an outrageous tackle. If he reacted with surprising calmness then, the same wasn't true in the Premier League at Swindon – Cantona was sent off for stamping on John Moncur after a tussle, before getting dismissed again at Arsenal three days later, this time for a second bookable offence.

United lost two of the three games he missed through suspension, as Blackburn drew level at the top – Ferguson's men had been 16 points clear of them at one stage. But Cantona returned with both goals in victory over Manchester City, and guided his side to their first ever double by scoring two penalties in the FA Cup final against Chelsea.

Before the first, Chelsea skipper Dennis Wise had wagered £50 that he'd miss. "£100," Cantona responded, before slotting the ball into the corner with trademark ease, having waited for Dmitri Kharine to dive. He offered Wise double or quits before the second one, then scored in identical fashion.

"He was a maverick, but he trained like a beast every day – and by God, he did the business, especially in the big games," Bruce tells *FFT*. "Cup finals, semi-finals... when you needed a goal, Eric came up trumps. The bigger the game, the more he enjoyed it."

FERGIE ON A HARLEY-DAVIDSON

Cantona became the first overseas star to win the PFA Player of the Year Award in 1993-94, although his summer was as eventful as ever. Not long after being appointed France captain by new boss Jacquet, he was arrested in the US, where he was scheduled to do media work, for an altercation about accreditation before Brazil's World Cup semi-final against Sweden. Then another miserable trip to Ibrox followed; sent off in a pre-season friendly, Eric would begin 1994-95 suspended.

Cantona was also banned for United's first four games in the Champions League group stage, following that Galatasaray dismissal. Thrashed 4-0 at Barcelona without him, the Red Devils lost at Gothenburg on his return and missed out on the knockout phase. In the Premier League, however, he struck 12 times in 21 games – an even better strike rate than the previous campaign.

Midway through January, in his first match alongside new signing Andy Cole, he bagged the winner against title rivals Blackburn, which hauled United to within two points of the top. But then came the fateful game at Crystal Palace, the red card for kicking Richard Shaw, and a kung-fu assault on the fan who hurled vitriol at him as he walked off.

"Sometimes when the red mist comes down, we all make mistakes, and he paid a high price for that one," Bruce admits. "I'm sure Eric regrets it – or maybe not! If you asked him if he'd do it again, he'd probably say yes."

True to form, the man himself once told *FFT* about his only regret from that incident. "I didn't hit him strong enough. I should have punched him harder," Cantona said. "If I want to kick a fan, I do it." Punch, hit, kick – same difference, eh?

He was sentenced to two weeks in prison but an appeal reduced his punishment to 120 hours of community service, which was spent coaching kids at United's training ground. That appeal verdict produced possibly football's most famous 14-second press conference. "When the seagulls follow the trawler, it is because they think sardines will be thrown into the sea. Thank you," he memorably declared, before getting up and strolling out the room.

Cantona's words baffled the world, his United team-mates included. "Our reaction was the same as everyone else – we hadn't a clue what he was on about!" Bruce laughs. "The papers were asking, 'Is he mad? Is he crazy?' We did ask him what it was all about, and to this day, I still remember his reply. He said, 'I don't know where it came from, but it was f**king good, wasn't it?'"

Left Cantona ended 26 years of hurt for Manchester United

Aimed at the media flock who'd followed his every move since that Selhurst flare-up, the Frenchman had written his line on a piece of paper beforehand after asking the club's baffled head of security what the correct English words were for a fishing boat and the small fish in the sea.

"Hundreds of journalists were there, and the club's lawyer wanted me to say something," Cantona recently explained, launching his new travel brand, Looking FC. "I didn't want to say anything, but he said, 'You have to'. I just said what came to mind. I could have said 'the sky is blue' or 'I saw a lion flying'. But I said that and left.

"I think the journalists were happy, and I was very happy because they all tried to understand what I'd said. They'd treated me like I was a criminal – I never killed anybody. Thousands of times, I'd heard fans say things and never reacted. This time I reacted – I'm not a robot, and I never wanted to be a robot. Sometimes I'm good, sometimes I'm bad. Sometimes I'm sweet, sometimes I'm s**t."

There was never any chance of his United team-mates ribbing him for his ostentatious quotes, though.

"No one took the mick out of him, ever," Bruce says. "Not because we were scared of him, but because he had the respect of the dressing room. He'd earned that with his performances on the pitch."

Cantona had also earned the affection of his manager, who'd already settled on a sensitive man-management style for the team's biggest star. Ferguson had previously enjoyed several conversations with Guy Roux about him, even visiting Cantona's mentor at Auxerre to glean information.

On the night of the kung-fu kick, the United boss directed his post-match hairdryers to Cantona's team-mates for letting a 1-0 lead slip, rather than balling out the Frenchman.

"The boss came into the dressing room and was fuming," Lee Sharpe said. "We look at each other, thinking, 'F**king hell, Cantona is getting it here!' He says, 'Incey, where the f**k have you been? Sharpey, my grandmother runs f**king faster than you! You're all a f**king disgrace. Nine o'clock tomorrow morning, I'm going to run your f**king balls off in training. F**king shocking. And Eric... you can't go round doing things like that, son'."

United moved quickly to suspend Cantona for the rest of the season, hoping it would be enough to prevent further punishment from the FA. It wasn't: Cantona was banned for eight months. Jacquet also stripped him of the national team captaincy – after 20 goals from 45 caps, he never played for France again, his lengthy absence allowing Zinedine Zidane to emerge as Les Bleus' new star. Without Cantona, United were pipped to the title by Blackburn in 1994-95, before their star man vowed to quit English football when the FA announced that they were investigating a behind-closed-doors friendly match against Rochdale, believing it may have contravened his ban. United insisted it was only a training game, but Cantona went AWOL, feeling the FA were being unfair.

Inter were interested in taking him to Serie A, but he agreed to return to Manchester after the FA relented and Ferguson dashed to Paris to track him down, riding around the streets on the back of a Harley-Davidson with Cantona's lawyer.

On 1 October 1995, Cantona made his much-anticipated return, setting up Nicky Butt, then converting a penalty in a 2-2 draw with Liverpool. "It was a long eight months for Eric – it was written in the stars that he'd score when he came back," Bruce smiles.

FAREWELL, FEATURING RICHARD KEYS

With Paul Ince, Mark Hughes and Andrei Kanchelskis all sold that summer, a young United side had famously lost the opening game of the season at Aston Villa, prompting Alan Hansen's famous declaration, "You can't win anything with kids." The Reds had also gone out of the UEFA Cup to Rotor Volgograd.

Manchester United trailed Newcastle by 12 points at one stage, but Cantona's return had provided leadership for the emerging Class of '92, before he struck the winner at St James' Park in early March 1996. Cantona scored in six consecutive matches – levelling in Fergie Time at QPR, then netting winners against Arsenal, Spurs and Coventry, plus a goal and two assists in a 3-2 triumph at Manchester City. In those six games alone, his individual contribution had earned United 12 points – enough to overtake the Magpies at the top.

Once more, he helped United to the double, firing in from the edge of the box in the FA Cup final against Liverpool to clinch a 1-0 win then lifting the trophy as captain in place of the injured Bruce. Before the presentation, though, he'd tried to persuade the centre-back to do the honours.

"A lot of words have been written to try to describe Eric over the years, and I'll give you two more – kind and considerate," says Bruce. "For me, that gesture at the cup final summed him up, and showed what a man he was. He'd just scored a late winner, but he approached me and said, 'Come on, you've got to lift the cup'. I said, 'Listen Eric, if anyone deserves to do that, then it's you. I've done it before – it's your turn now. Thanks for the offer, but this is your moment'."

Savaged by the press 16 months earlier, Cantona was named as the Football Writers' Association's Footballer of the Year and then appointed as captain on a permanent basis when Bruce departed for Birmingham.

On a visit to England, Roux saw how much Cantona was adored. "He was the King of Manchester," the 83 year old smiles. "I met him to make a documentary – when he stepped on to the pavement, there were 200 people around him. It was amazing to see."

United were playing catch-up again in 1996-97 – nine points behind Liverpool just before Christmas, when Cantona scored a sublime hang-it-in-the-Louvre goal in a 5-0 home win over Sunderland. After dribbling from the halfway line, he exchanged passes with McClair before brilliantly chipping keeper Lionel Perez, then stood arms outstretched, accepting the adulation as if to ask, 'Are you not entertained?' Maximus Decimus Meridius and *Gladiator* were still four years away, but Leeds fan Russell Crowe was taking notes.

"I can't think of another player who played with Cantona's swagger," says Pallister. "The way he played with his collar up, and that celebration against Sunderland. Imagine anyone else doing that – we'd never have got away with it. We'd have had the piss ripped out of us! But he carried it off superbly."

Cantona later said that the celebration was aimed at Perez, a former Nimes team-mate, who'd feared people might disapprove if he was too friendly with the United star before kick-off. "Before the game, I went over to say hello," Cantona said. "He didn't want to shake my hand, so maybe that's why I scored that goal. That's the biggest humiliation for a goalkeeper, and that kind of celebration, too. I just stand there. Look at me."

United fought back to win the league once more – Cantona's sixth title in seven seasons. It might have been seven in seven were it not for the kung-fu kick. But a day after they were beaten by Borussia Dortmund in the 1996-97 Champions League semi-finals, the King told Ferguson he would be retiring at the end of the season, aged only 30.

"I admire a player that can play at the same club for 20 years like Ryan Giggs, Paolo Maldini or Xavi," he later said. "I'm not that type of person. I get bored very quickly. I was very passionate about the game, and always said that when I lost that passion, I would retire. It just went like a light switch."

Cantona's retirement plan stayed a secret until the campaign was over. After providing an assist for Jordi Cruyff in a home win over West Ham, on the day United lifted another Premier League trophy, his last fixture as a professional came in a post-season benefit match for David Busst – Cantona scored twice against Coventry at Highfield Road on a night that also featured cameos from Gazza and, er, Richard Keys.

Then came the announcement of his exit. "Retiring at 30? Ridiculous!" says Bruce. "But that's Eric – he did things his way. Could we have won the trophies that we did without him? No, absolutely not. He was the catalyst, exactly what we needed. He was a great, great player. A born winner. In a way, we'd all like to be Eric Cantona."

Cantona packed more into his career than most other players combined. Before him, United hadn't won the league in 26 years. With him, they won it four times in five seasons, laying the foundation for nine more triumphs to knock Liverpool off their perch.

Eric Cantona was the man who started it all. Arguably, he's the most significant player in almost 30 years of Premier League history. Turns out Graeme Souness should probably have signed him after all.

Below Eric broke Geordie hearts in 1996

SERGIO AGUERO MODEL CITIZEN

In the summer of 2011, Manchester City signed a forward they hoped would help the club reach new heights. He would become one of the greatest foreign players ever to grace the English game

As the sky-blue confetti fluttered down onto the Wembley turf and Carlos Tevez raised the FA Cup into the afternoon sky with a roar, it seemed to the watching world that the Blue Moon had finally risen, decades of disappointment exorcised by the cold press of silverware. The hunt for a trophy was over, millions spent in recruiting a squad of stars vindicated by Yaya Toure's thunderous winner. And yet the sense that this team could be so much more remained, a belief that permeated through the corridors of power at City's majestic Etihad Stadium.

Despite ending the 2010-11 season in triumph, City had ultimately fallen nine points short of Premier League champions and bitter rivals Manchester United, been dumped out of the League Cup by West Brom in the third round, and seen their Europa League adventure ended in the last 16 by Dynamo Kiev.

In the league, City's attack had been spearheaded by future renegade Carlos Tevez, the Argentine netting 20 times. However, their next most prolific scorer was Toure with eight, a healthy return for a box-to-box midfielder, but not enough to alter City's domestic prospects. The likes of Mario Balotelli and Edin Dzeko (bought for £22.5 million and £27 million respectively) had only mustered a paltry eight Premier League goals between them. With the 2011-12 season looming, City desperately required the services of a ruthless predator if the momentum of their FA Cup win was to be harnessed and unleashed upon the league. They would find the marksman they needed in the form of a diminutive Argentinian plying his trade in Spain's La Liga.

NEW KUN ON THE BLOCK

Many of the finest players ever to grace a football pitch were at some point in their lives described as being born to grace a football pitch. Very few, however, were born to literally live on one. Sergio Leonel Aguero del Castillo was. Born to teenage parents into a world of abject poverty, the boy who would become affectionately known as 'Kun' (after his favourite Japanese cartoon character) was raised in ramshackle homes in Argentina's capital, Buenos Aires. Yet from the very beginning it seems young Sergio was destined for a life in football, for wherever the family moved, they always found themselves beside a potrero – an improvised football pitch. In fact, when the Aguero del Castillos relocated to Los Eucalyptus (in central Buenos Aires), their front door was a metre away from a corner flag. Naturally, Sergio began tottering out to participate in the games being contested on his doorstep.

Blessed with speed, a potent strike and a stocky frame that made him difficult to outmuscle, Sergio quickly made an impression, routinely scoring four or five goals a game. He was soon playing up to six matches every weekend for several teams, his devoted father Leonel accompanying him on his goalscoring tours of the city's rougher neighbourhoods. His exploits drew the gaze of various professional outfits, and when it came to deciding which team to join, the family's dire financial situation ironically proved to be a benefit. With no hope of paying to become members of a club (a demand many of Argentina's domestic sides made before admitting youngsters into their youth set-ups), Sergio's parents had few options. However, there was a club that was keen to take on the promising youngster, and they didn't require a membership fee: Independiente.

Joining the club at eight years old, Sergio worked hard to rise through the ranks, and in 2003 he finally achieved his dream of playing in Argentina's Primera Division when he became the youngest player to make his debut in the top flight. Despite a challenging start to his professional career that saw him wait nearly a year for another start, Aguero was determined to make his parents' sacrifices count (his father had enjoyed a promising football career of his own before hanging up his boots to support his son's progress). Eventually, his first goal for Independiente came, and over the course of three professional seasons another 22 would follow in just 54 appearances. Once more attracting the interest of numerous clubs, in May 2006 Atletico Madrid came calling, the Madrid club paying Independiente €20 million for a player who the year before had helped Argentina to win the U20 World Cup, a tournament illuminated by a tousle-haired attacker named Lionel Messi. The pair would repeat the feat at the 2007 U20 World Cup, in which Aguero would score six goals in seven games, and win Olympic gold at the 2008 Games in Beijing.

THE REIGN IN SPAIN

Any concerns that Aguero would struggle to adjust to a new life in Spain were rapidly dispelled by a number of dynamic performances, and Atletico's record-breaking acquisition would finish his first season with seven goals. A portent of things to come, Aguero would go on to score 101 goals for Atletico in 234 appearances, helping Los Colchoneros (the Mattresses) to Europa League glory, setting up both goals in a 2-1 win over Fulham in the final. A number of eye-catching displays served to elevate his profile further, including a man-of-the-match performance in a 4-2 defeat of Barcelona in 2008 and a brace against Chelsea in the 2009-10 Champions League. In his final season with the club he scored 20 La Liga goals, a target reached with the help of a first career hat-trick in his final game at the Vicente Calderon.

Despite signing a contract extension in January 2011 that would have tied him to Atletico until 2014, on 23 May Aguero asked to leave the club. Aggrieved at their star man's volte face, a segment of Atletico fans made their anger known by unfurling a banner informing the departing Aguero that they wished him dead. It had no effect, and on 28 July, Atletico's former charge was unveiled at his new club: Manchester City.

WELCOME TO MANCHESTER

Aguero's move to Manchester was a statement of real intent from City, who had parted with £38 million in order to sign the Argentine on a five-year deal that would see Agüero paid £52 million. The transfer made Aguero the sixth most expensive player in history at the time, an outlay that, despite his previous goalscoring feats, represented a tangible risk on City's behalf. Fortunately for both the club and its supporters, Aguero would pay the fee back with interest.

On 15 August 2011, City hosted Swansea at home in their opening game of the new Premier League season. With the hour mark approaching and City 1-0 up thanks to an Edin Dzeko strike, manager Roberto Mancini decided to introduce Aguero into the fray in place of Nigel de Jong. Sporting the number 16 shirt, Aguero jogged onto the pitch to a warm round of applause. Within eight minutes he would return the gesture.

Working the ball out to the right flank, the City midfield fed an onrushing Micah Richards, who dashed into the box and slipped a pass across the face of the Swansea goal. Aguero slid in to meet it and open his City account with a brave finish, and he was far from done tormenting the newly promoted Swans. By full time he'd set David Silva up with an audacious volleyed assist when the ball seemed destined to go out of play for a goal kick, and then rounded off his stellar debut with a sumptuous 25-yard drive to secure an

impressive 4-0 win. It had only taken half an hour of football for the City fans to fall in love with their new striker.

Aguero's rich vein of form continued in the early stages of the season as he plundered a goal against Tottenham, a hat-trick against a stricken Wigan Athletic, a brace away to Fulham and the third goal in a famous 6-1 demolition of Manchester United at Old Trafford on 23 October. Victory in the derby saw City move five points clear of the defending champions and sent shockwaves through the Premier League.

However, United were far from beaten, and as the season wore on they steadily closed the gap on City before overtaking them in March. By the time of United's visit to the Etihad on 30 April the Red Devils were three points ahead at the top of the table and closing in on another successful title defence. City knew they had to win. Cue a thumping header from captain Vincent Kompany to clinch a vital 1-0 victory to level the race with just two games to go.

Both sides followed the April derby with victories, thereby setting up a captivating final day in the title race. Armed with a vastly superior goal difference, City's task was simple: match or better United's result, and they would be champions for only the third time in their history and the first time in 44 years. With relegation-threatened QPR coming to the Etihad while United travelled to Sunderland, the destiny of the Premier League trophy seemed like a foregone conclusion. It would prove to be anything but.

CHAMPAGNE SUPERNOVA

It seemed initially that QPR would gamely follow the script on the final day of the season when Pablo Zabaleta fired City ahead. However, things turned upside down as QPR drew level shortly after half time and then snatched the lead on 66 minutes, despite having Joey Barton dismissed. Suddenly, City were staring into the abyss. They now had to score twice to wrestle the title from United, who were leading at Sunderland. For the next 25 minutes they would toil in vain until Dzeko levelled proceedings with a header from a David Silva corner in stoppage time. But 2-2 wouldn't be enough. Not now news of United's victory was filtering into a stunned Etihad.

Refusing to admit defeat, City continued to attack, and on 94 minutes Aguero received the ball on the edge of the QPR box. With seconds to go he fed a tumbling Balotelli, who returned the ball as Aguero skipped into the area. Collecting the Italian's pass, Aguero calmly sidestepped a lunging challenge to rifle the ball beyond Paddy Kenny in the QPR goal and unleash bedlam. Peeling off his shirt, Aguero raced away in jubilation, having scored the single most important goal in City's history to seal the most dramatic title win ever in the Premier League. "I swear you'll never see anything like this ever again!" cried Sky Sports' Martin Tyler as the stadium erupted. City had reached the promised land thanks to a goal that Aguero has since described as "the best moment of my life".

HITS AND MISSES

Unsurprisingly, after securing immortality, Aguero found it difficult to immediately reach such heights again. An injury-plagued second season reduced Aguero to 12 Premier League goals in 30 games during a campaign that saw United finish 11 points clear as league champions. To compound City's disappointment, Mancini's side contrived to lose 1-0 to relegated Wigan in the FA Cup final, a result that contributed to the Italian's dismissal just two days later.

City soon appointed former Malaga manager Manual Pellegrini, and the decision reaped instant rewards as the Cityzens won the 2013-14 Premier League title and the League Cup (the first of six League Cup victories for Agüero), their domestic campaign fuelled by 17 goals in just 23 appearances from Aguero.

In a strange twist of irony, Aguero's most prolific season for City then followed in 2014-15, but would be unaccompanied by silverware as City finished second in the league behind champions Chelsea despite the Argentine's 26 goals, a tally that secured him the Golden Boot award. Committed to the club until 2019 thanks to a new contract in August 2014, Aguero was now faced with his first trophyless season in England. His only reward in 2015 was being handed the number 10 shirt following Dzeko's departure to Roma. Thankfully for both Aguero and the club he had served so well, a new, pioneering manager would replace Pellegrini in 2016, a man whose arrival would herald the most golden age in City history: Pep Guardiola.

Supplemented by a host of new team-mates, including Ilkay Gundogan and Leroy Sane, and with Kevin De Bruyne beginning to

Left Aguero celebrates scoring his second goal for Atletico against Chelsea in the 2009-10 Champions League

fulfil his enormous potential, City clicked into place under the Spaniard's guidance. With Aguero leading the line, City finished third in Guardiola's first season before then embarking on an unprecedented campaign that saw them become the first team to win 100 points in a Premier League season, Aguero once more breaking the 20-goal barrier and helping his side to another League Cup win. City retained both titles in the 2018-19 season, again with the help of 21 league goals from their Argentine star. They also added the FA Cup to their bulging cabinet, completing the first English domestic treble in history.

Yet while domestic dominance was becoming almost routine for Guardiola's men, their efforts on the European stage continued to frustrate, most notably in the quarter-finals of the 2018-19 Champions League. Drawn with English rivals Spurs, City were awarded a penalty in the early stages of the first leg at the Tottenham Hotspur Stadium, only to see Hugo Lloris save Aguero's effort. The Argentine's miss would ultimately prove fatal as Spurs won an incredible second leg 4-3 to progress.

Closer to home, City's stranglehold on the league would end in the 2019-20 season as Liverpool romped to their first title in 30 years during a campaign bereft of fans due to the global Covid-19 pandemic. For the first time in his tenure, questions were being asked of Guardiola. Aguero, who for the first time had failed to score 20 or more goals in the league, but was by now the most prolific foreign player in Premier League history, would soon face his own personal questions too. His final season in Manchester was looming. He just didn't know it yet.

DON'T LOOK BACK IN ANGER

It's no secret that football can often be a cruel game, one devoid of any sense of sentiment. Even so, it seems especially unfair that Aguero's final season in England, a fact announced in late March 2021 by a grateful but cool-headed City, was so devastated by injury and illness. Reduced to just 12 league appearances (and four goals) by a combination of knee ruptures and Covid-19, Aguero was a shadow of his former lethal self, another Premier League and League Cup double and a Champions League runners-up medal offering little consolation to a player used to defining the biggest games. A lack of match fitness threatened to rob him of the chance of a final farewell at home to Everton on the last day of the season before his move to Barcelona, but thankfully he was able to make a brief cameo appearance, during which he netted twice to eclipse Wayne Rooney as the scorer of the most Premier League goals for a single club.

However, dejected as Aguero and his supporters may have been to see him leave, City's all-time record goalscorer will not be judged by his denouement. No, he will be remembered for transforming the fortunes of a club that before him had only harboured dreams of breaching the top six. Fans will recount his title-winning goal in 2012, the Manchester derbies he settled, the day he netted four against a bamboozled Leicester, having done likewise to Spurs a few seasons before. They will speak lovingly of the hat-trick against Aston Villa in January 2020 that elevated Aguero above all other foreign goalscorers to have graced the English top flight. They will reminisce about his 36 goals in the Champions League, including hat-tricks against Bayern Munich and Borussia Monchengladbach. Ultimately, they will cherish that beaming smile and a name that will forever be synonymous with their club. And they won't be the only ones.

When asked who the best striker in the world is, Guardiola was typically frank. "Messi. Messi is number nine, ten, 11, six, four. But the rest is Sergio." Neil Custis of the *Sun* newspaper was equally effusive when asked about Aguero's legacy. "If I was a manager and I had Aguero, I'd play him on one leg, never mind when he's nearly fit. He is the best foreign player ever to play in the Premier League."

When appraising Aguero's truly groundbreaking career in England it seems fitting to give the last word to the man himself, who upon the news of his impending departure going public was typically humble. "With the guidance of the owners and contributions of many players, we earned a place among the greatest in the world." That is true, Sergio, but nobody has earned the same place in the hearts of City fans, the boy from the potrero who never dared dream of Europe forever woven into the tapestry of a club that he called home.

Below Aguero slides home his fifth goal against Newcastle in just 20 minutes of play in the Premier League game on 3 October 2015

JURGEN KLINSMANN

JURGEN THE GREAT

Jurgen Klinsmann fought xenophobia when he arrived at Tottenham in 1994, but English football was soon in his thrall. The German hero tells FFT how his love affair bloomed – and why he wants another Spurs return

Jurgen Klinsmann's time with Monaco had come to an end, but there were two things he needed to buy.

The streets of Monte Carlo are lined with swish boutiques, offering some of the finest jewellery and *haute couture* on planet Earth. A World Cup winner and former Serie A superstar, Klinsmann could have bought pretty much anything he liked.

But he was about to move to England for the first time in his life, and he'd been warned that it could be difficult to survive there without two very important items: goggles and a snorkel. True, they're not the most obvious things that come to mind when you're about to set up home in north London, but when Klinsmann arrived for his opening press conference as a Tottenham Hotspur player, he made sure to take them along with him.

"I had them in a backpack, right next to me," the German tells *FFT* with a smile, as he thinks back to that 1994 unveiling.

In the end, the greatest prank in Premier League history never happened. Klinsmann never did don the snorkel and goggles in front of Fleet Street's finest that afternoon, as originally planned. Instead, he uttered a famous line that paved the way for one of the happiest periods of his life. "Maybe I can ask the first question," he began that day. "Are there any diving schools in London?"

Within weeks, he'd sealed his place in the hearts of Spurs fans forever.

THREE IS A MAGIC NUMBER

Klinsmann's road to the Premier League really began on November 14, 1987. The former bakery apprentice had progressed to German champions VfB Stuttgart after an impressive spell in the 2. Bundesliga with Stuttgart Kickers – and although VfB slipped to 10th in his maiden season in 1984-85, Klinsmann netted 17 goals. The following campaign, he netted five in a single match at Fortuna Dusseldorf.

Still, however, he had to wait for his first international call-up... until the goal that changed everything. At home to title holders Bayern Munich, in front of 70,000 supporters at the Neckarstadion, Klinsmann crashed in a superb overhead kick which sent Stuttgart on their way to a 3-0 victory. Curiously, he did it while wearing the No.3 shirt.

"That was the idea of my manager Arie Haan," says Klinsmann. "He was my mentor, I admired him, and he came up with all sorts of funny ideas. He said, 'Oh, I've got to switch your shirt' – maybe he was superstitious, as he never told me why!

"But it worked out great. That goal was my big door opener – it changed my life. Franz Beckenbauer, the national team coach, was in the stands, saw that goal and *boom* – he took me into the national team a month later. My debut was a friendly in Brazil. I kind of stole the spot from Klaus Allofs, who'd been Rudi Völler's striking partner. He never came back after my first game..."

It was Klinsmann who partnered Völler at Euro 88, having finished the season as Bundesliga top scorer – even if the dream of winning the tournament on home soil ended with semi-final defeat to the Netherlands. Soon he was named German Footballer of the Year and helped Stuttgart to the UEFA Cup final – Die Roten were beaten by Diego Maradona's Napoli, but Klinsmann's stellar displays earned a move to Serie A with Inter in the summer of 1989.

It meant the chance to play in what was then the world's greatest league, linking up with compatriots Lothar Matthaus and Andreas Brehme, who'd led the Nerazzurri to the Scudetto in the previous campaign. "Joining Inter was the biggest step in my life – the expectation was to win silverware," remembers Klinsmann.

Inter's main rivals were neighbours Milan and their Dutch triumvirate of Ruud Gullit, Frank Rijkaard and Marco van Basten, who eventually guided the Rossoneri to a second straight European Cup in 1990. Napoli won the Scudetto, leaving Inter potless.

But then came the World Cup on familiar Italian soil, pitting Klinsmann, Matthaus and Brehme against Gullit, Rijkaard and Van Basten once more. West Germany triumphed in the last 16 – the game became infamous for Rijkaard spitting into Völler's perm, before Klinsmann scored and produced one of the finest displays of his 108 international caps.

"The Dutch-German relationship was very intense in those years, stretching back to the 1974 World Cup Final when the Dutch felt they should have won," he says. "The 1988 semi-final was pretty much a home game for them, because they had 35,000 Dutch fans in Hamburg and won in the last minute through Van Basten.

"Then we turned things around in 1990. Rijkaard was sent off, Völler was wrongfully sent off too, and it opened up a lot of space for me – it was probably one of the greatest games I played for Germany.

"Luckily the relationship between Germany and Holland calmed down after that – I think the three of us at Inter and the three Dutch players at Milan helped, because we actually got on very well."

Klinsmann was soon featuring in a World Cup semi-final against England, although opted not to take a penalty in the shootout. "I was in a very angry state of mind, because I should have won that match already," he explains. "I'd had two really good chances – a header that was brilliantly saved, and one when I was through and hit a half-volley over the bar. When Beckenbauer asked me about taking a penalty, I said, 'Franz, I'm too emotional right now,' so I was probably sixth or seventh on the list – thankfully it was over by then! But it was a 50/50 match. We had a lot of respect for the English side."

Four days later, West Germany lifted the World Cup in Rome, defeating Argentina. "You can't comprehend it in that moment – you're just overwhelmed by the fact that you actually won the World Cup," he recalls. "It only comes to you after your career when people talk to you in the street and say, 'Hey, I watched that final'. Then you realise how many people around the globe you share that moment with, because World Cups are special for everyone."

When Klinsmann chats to Argentines, he admits that they often mention his role in Pedro Monzon's red card at 0-0. "Yeah, they do – and I mention a 10cm cut that he put into my leg..." he retorts. "But I've been to Argentina several times and people were always full of respect."

Even beyond South America, some sceptics believed that Klinsmann had used theatrics to get Monzon sent off – falling to the ground before throwing his legs high into the air, propelling his body upwards and crashing to earth again. The forward gained a reputation in that tournament for his dramatic reaction to fouls, although he insists he never dived during his career.

"No, I never did," declares Klinsmann. "But when I saw the video of that red card, I also thought, 'Why did you need to push yourself up when you went on the ground?!' It was just a reaction by my body, because it hurt – the guy really cut me."

CAPPUCCINO, WITH ADDED SUGAR

Klinsmann would win another trophy at the Stadio Olimpico a year later, as Inter beat Roma in the UEFA Cup final.

"When I first went to Inter, straight away we lost in the first round of the European Cup [to Swedish minnows Malmo], and that was bad – very bad," he says.

"In the second year, thankfully we won the UEFA Cup against Roma, because you lived with that expectation from people you saw in the street, when you went to the baker or the butcher. That's what you heard all day: 'Are we going to win this year?'"

Klinsmann lasted only one more year in Italy – a year in which Inter finished eighth in Serie A. "Giovanni Trapattoni left, Corrado Orrico came in and there were some internal arguments between players," he says. "Milan stole my strike partner Aldo Serena in the

Below Jurgen's Stuttgart form sealed a move to Inter

Above Tasting World Cup glory

1991 transfer window, so I ended up playing alone upfront with no support and scored very few goals. I asked the owner if it was OK if I moved on."

The striker headed for France to join Arsene Wenger's Monaco, and the experience was rather different. "You went from an 85,000-seat stadium with an incredible atmosphere, to 7,000 or 8,000 at league games," he says. "But it was a massive learning curve working under Arsene Wenger – we played very good football and reached the semi-finals of the Champions League. The two seasons I had at Monaco were special."

Klinsmann netted five goals for Germany at the 1994 World Cup, before he was on the move again for £2 million.

"I still had one more year on my contract at Monaco, but I'd made an agreement with Arsene that if a club came in for me after the World Cup, they'd let me leave," he reveals. "Then all of a sudden came a call from Alan Sugar on my phone. I was in my apartment in Monte Carlo, and he asked me if we could meet for a coffee. He said, 'I'm in my boat in the harbour'. I replied, 'Sure, that's 200 yards away from my place!'

"I walked down there, and pretty much in two hours we did the deal over a cappuccino. That afternoon I called Arsene, who was in his office at the ground – everything's walking distance in Monte Carlo, so we went over there and both teams agreed on the deal, a transfer fee, everything. It was done within a few hours.

"English football had always been on TV in Germany during the 1970s and '80s. Every German had a favourite English team – like most kids, I was a Liverpool fan because of Kevin Keegan and Kenny Dalglish. So when this opportunity came, I had no hesitation. I asked my wife, 'Do you fancy that, London?' She said, 'Sure, let's go!'"

Klinsmann would become one of the first overseas superstar arrivals of the Premier League era, but it was only after he signed that he found he wasn't entirely popular in England – harking back to Italia 90. "Later people said to me, 'Well we thought here and there in the semi-final against England, you were too extreme in your reactions', then I watched the game again and I could actually understand it," he says.

"But when I first signed, there were a lot of things I didn't know. I didn't know about the diver story, and I didn't know Tottenham was Jewish in a certain way – there were some comments being made about 'how can they sign a German player?' I learned to respond in the right way. A friend of mine in Monaco told me, 'With the English culture, one thing is important: never be offended by this type of humour – if you get provoked in a funny way, you have to figure out a way to top it'. He had the idea about the goggles and the diving school in London."

Fortunately, getting hold of his gear didn't prove too tricky. "I bought them in Monaco – when you're on the Cote d'Azur, you can find equipment!" he laughs.

Not that Klinsmann ever took them out of his backpack during his unveiling.

"Everyone laughed so much when I asked whether there was a diving school in London, and if I could take lessons, that it calmed everything down," he says.

"I thought, 'OK, you don't need to bring out the goggles now!'"

MISURA

"THEY STILL SHOW ON BRAIN SCANS"

With one joke, Klinsmann had won people over. Within a week, the club shop had sold so many replica shirts, they ran out of letter Ns and had to borrow some. From Arsenal.

The German headed home the clincher in a 4-3 win at Sheffield Wednesday on his debut and marked it with a tongue-in-cheek celebration, diving full length onto the turf, joined by his Tottenham team-mates.

"That came about because we drove up to the stadium before the game, and fans were holding up cards saying '5.8', '5.9', '5.7'," he chuckles. "The whole bus was cracking up, laughing like crazy, and Teddy Sheringham said, 'Jurgen, if you score today, we're going to do a dive, OK?'

"A week later, Teddy said, 'You've got to do it again,' because his son Charlie, who was a little boy then, had told him that all the kids were diving around in the parks after scoring. I said, 'If Charlie says so, we'll do it!' I scored again, and we did it again.

"For me it was fascinating to embrace the English culture, the humour, the atmosphere in the ground. When you come from Monaco to Tottenham, you have 40,000 fans singing behind the team, living and breathing every little situation on the field – a corner kick or a throw-in, it didn't matter. You saw the kids in the first row staring and smiling at you, and I just took all that energy for the entire season. I could have run forever – even after the final whistle I could have kept on running, because the energy created by the crowd in England is very special."

Klinsmann embraced the country like few foreign stars before or since. His beloved 1967 VW Beetle – driven all the way from Monaco to London by a Spurs staffer – was regularly spotted around N17.

"Just living in London was so special," he says, "getting to know that amazing city and the neighbourhood of Tottenham, going for fish and chips with team-mates on the High Road. All these things are really important, because it's the relationship you have with the club and the supporters, it just feeds you energy. I still feel it today when I go back there – I just want to go out there and run..."

Klinsmann plundered 10 goals in his first seven matches for Spurs, but results were inconsistent under gung-ho manager Ossie Ardiles. "Ossie was a master of attacking football as a player, and he only wanted to attack," remembers the striker. "He had us flying forward, but sadly that meant we also conceded a bit too much.

"But we had a fantastic time, and when Gerry Francis came in as manager midway through the season, he calmed down the defensive situation. We worked our way up the table and then had our run towards the semi-finals of the FA Cup."

That included a quarter-final at Liverpool, in which Klinsmann scored a late winner.

"I learned in that one-year crash course of English football that for Spurs fans, winning at Anfield was something quite unusual," he says. "When it happened in almost the last moment of the game, from a flick-on from Teddy, firstly you realise, 'Woah, we're in the semis'. Then right after the final whistle, we went to our fans and celebrated, I turned around and the entire stadium was giving us a standing ovation. They'd decided that on that day, we were the better team.

Left Lifting the UEFA Cup with Inter in '91

"I'd never experienced that before at an away stadium, that the home crowd gets up and says, 'You guys were better today'. Then in the dressing room afterwards, everybody was exploding with celebrations."

That memorable day came just two months after Klinsmann had suffered a head injury he was told could have killed him, after colliding with Mark Bosnich at Villa Park.

"I had two brutal experiences that season, although I don't blame anybody for them," says the 57-year-old, who has spent most of the past two decades based in California. "The first one was on my debut at Sheffield Wednesday – I had a knock with Des Walker at the end of the game, and I think it needed 11 stitches in my mouth. I woke up in the dressing room and the stitches were already done, it was a long concussion.

"LIVING IN LONDON WAS SPECIAL, SO WAS GETTING TO KNOW TOTTENHAM AND GOING FOR FISH AND CHIPS ON THE HIGH ROAD"

"Then I had the other one at Aston Villa, the clash with Mark Bosnich. I woke up in the dressing room and the doctor literally said, 'You're so lucky – if he hits you half an inch higher, you're not there any more'. Actually, I did some brain scans later on, because in America the whole brain situation is such an important topic with American football, and they can still see those two incidents on the scans. On both occasions, I think I was out for longer than 10 minutes."

Klinsmann netted 29 goals that season and was named the Football Writers' Association's Player of the Year, but Tottenham's FA Cup run ended in disappointment – with a 4-1 semi-final loss to eventual winners Everton at Elland Road. The Lilywhites came seventh in the Premier League, 11 points outside the European places.

Having still won a solitary major trophy in his club career, Klinsmann left that summer aged 30, having previously agreed a get-out clause that allowed him to depart after one season if he so desired.

"We should have won the FA Cup – I still believe that," he says. "A footballer's life is all about trophies. Then a call came towards the end of the season from Franz Beckenbauer at Bayern Munich. I still remember it today – I was sitting with my wife in our little mews house in Hampstead. When he calls and he wants you, you don't even talk money – you just think, 'It's Bayern Munich, and Bayern Munich means winning titles'. Pretty much the decision was made within two minutes.

"It was very difficult to leave Tottenham, because emotionally I felt so happy and so much at home at White Hart Lane. But I thought, 'Jurgen, you're running out of time here to win things, you're in the prime of your career'. Our team wasn't good enough to win the Premier League, we had to be realistic. I knew that there was no way we could beat the top four – we could beat them on one day, but not over the entire season. If I wanted to win a couple more trophies, I had to accept Bayern's approach."

Klinsmann's decision didn't go down well with Sugar. When the talisman offered him a signed shirt as compensation, the future *Apprentice* host infamously declared during a TV interview that he wouldn't even wash his car with the jersey.

"You had to understand the humour – I took that reaction as a joke," Klinsmann comments now. "At first he was angry, and I totally got that, but we had the deal that if I wanted to leave after a year, I could. I had so much admiration for him and the fighting spirit he always had for the club. What he did during his time there was outstanding – he gave it a solid foundation and then made it financially stable. We're good friends today – we're still in contact."

"THANKS FOR THE TROPHY, MA'AM"

Klinsmann finished second in the Ballon d'Or behind George Weah at the end of 1995, and his return to the Bundesliga delivered exactly what he'd hoped for.

"I won my first league title, and I won the UEFA Cup for a second time," he says. "I went back to Germany from Spurs with so much confidence – it felt like no matter what, I'd score plenty of goals."

He netted 15 of them in just 12 games en route to the UEFA Cup, a competition record until Radamel Falcao smashed 17 for Porto in the rebranded Europa League of 2010-11.

Then, Klinsmann returned to England to skipper Germany at Euro 96. He'd already netted three goals to help Die Mannschaft reach the semi-finals, when injury ruled him out of the showdown with the Three Lions.

"It was really horrible to miss that game," he laments. "But the atmosphere that night was unforgettable, with the entire stadium singing 'Football's Coming Home'. Even the Germans joined in. What the English fans created during Euro 96 was special for every player, and not only the German and English teams. Over the years I've met so many guys from other teams who said that was a very special European Championship."

Klinsmann was fit enough to start the final against the Czech Republic, before collecting the trophy from the Queen.

"I was so nervous to receive it from her, but it was about enjoying the moment – when else do you get a trophy from the Queen at Wembley?" he laughs.

The striker was enjoying success for both club and country, but a year later his time at Bayern was up. "I wasn't as happy there as at White Hart Lane," he admits. "I was at an amazing club with an amazing infrastructure, with people who had built that club like Franz Beckenbauer, Uli Hoeness and Karl-Heinz Rummenigge; great football people. But I was never on the same page as them – somehow, culturally it didn't match.

"Bayern are always in the spotlight and it's always about alpha animals. If alpha animals don't get along, you lose a lot of energy and that's what happened. I lost a lot of energy off the field with

Below "Come and get a whiff of these sweaty pits, your Maj..."

Above Near decapitation by Mark Bosnich

arguments and different opinions, so I went to Franz Beckenbauer and asked him if I could leave. The same thing happened many years later when I was the coach of Bayern – after a couple of months, you realised that culturally or socially, you're not part of it."

The goal-getter headed back to Italy with Sampdoria, though things went awry within months after the exit of Cesar Luis Menotti, Argentina's World Cup-winning coach from 1978. "I admired Menotti and only went to Sampdoria for him," continues Klinsmann. "But I damaged a ligament in my ankle and was out for six to eight weeks – he went to the club president and asked for two more players. The president said, 'No, I don't have the money, I'm sorry,' and Menotti left the next day – he took the first plane to Buenos Aires with the entire coaching staff! I came into the training ground the day after and asked, 'Where are the coaches?' People said, 'Oh, they're gone…'"

Sensing his relationship with new manager Vujadin Boskov would be difficult, and eager to be ready for the upcoming World Cup in France, Klinsmann made an emotional return to Spurs in December 1997, on a deal until the end of the campaign. He rejoined a club in the Premier League relegation zone under Christian Gross, but insists he never viewed his return as a gamble.

"No, I never looked at it as a risk – it was an opportunity," he explains. "You're stuck at Sampdoria with a coach you don't want to work with, and you get an opportunity to help the club you love. I spoke to Alan Sugar and Christian Gross, and the move worked for both parties – Spurs helped me because I was coming back from injury, and I could help them to get out of the relegation battle.

"I knew the team was far better than where they were in the table, and we were going to climb up the league sooner or later. In the end it was a little bit dramatic – it took a bit longer than expected!"

With three matches to go, a Spurs squad also containing David Ginola, Les Ferdinand and Darren Anderton sat 17th, two points above the bottom three. "Tottenham weren't used to fighting relegation, and a relegation battle is a totally different mental problem than if you're playing for the top eight," says Klinsmann. "It took a little while for everyone to realise 'we're in real trouble here' – that it wasn't about how beautifully you played, it was about getting results, point by point. The learning process took a couple of months, but once we appreciated that fighting and the result comes first, then step by step we can think about playing better football again, we made it work."

Klinsmann netted in beating Newcastle at home, before Spurs travelled to Wimbledon for their penultimate encounter. Klinsi scored four times in a 6-2 victory, to confirm safety.

"I had a feeling of relief that we'd get the job done, and scoring four goals made it even more special," he says. "I'd got myself back into shape and form, in a year when I was thinking about whether I should stop playing after the World Cup. Our son was born during our days in Munich, and I was wondering if it was time for the next chapter."

BERTI VOGTS AND A CAMPER VAN

Klinsmann hung up his boots after Germany's 3-0 defeat to Croatia in the quarter-finals of France 98. Six years on, after Die Mannschaft's group stage exit at Euro 2004, he received an unexpected offer to return while living in the United States, his wife's homeland. It was an offer that may not have arrived, had Berti Vogts not gone on holiday to California in a camper van.

"I'd done my coaching licences in 2000, then in 2004, my Euro 96 coach Berti Vogts was visiting California in an RV," remembers Klinsmann. "He was with his son and was driving from San Francisco to Los Angeles, then on to Las Vegas. I said, 'Stop by in LA and I'll make a barbecue'.

"During his visit, he said, 'What about you as the national coach?' I told him not to joke about these things, but he was serious and said he wanted to talk to the president of the federation. I said, 'OK, I'm open to talk, but I won't fly to Germany just to have a cup of coffee'. He made the call the next day, then the federation phoned me. A day later, we met in New York for our first meeting. That's when we decided to take on an adventure."

Klinsmann reinvigorated Die Mannschaft as a young, attack-minded team that thrilled home fans at the 2006 World Cup.

"I said, 'Things didn't work out at the Euros, and over the past few years we've struggled, so we can't do it the same way any more – you have to be open-minded'," he says. "The head of the federation was my ex-president at Stuttgart, Gerhard Mayer-Vorfelder, and he said, 'You have *carte blanche*'.

Above Enjoying one of his swan-diving goal celebrations for Spurs

"I JUST STARTED TO PUSH THE TRAIN, THEN IT GOT FASTER UNTIL 2014 WHEN IT WAS A BULLET TRAIN THAT RAN INTO BRAZIL"

"We chose to involve the whole team – the captain was Michael Ballack and we had an open discussion with the players about what type of football they wanted. It all starts with the culture of your country. What is it about? Germans are like the English: we want to be proactive, attacking, on the front foot, high tempo. We put the bullet points on a flipchart and came to the conclusion that, 'OK, if this is how you want to play and this is who we are, then we can go to work. We'll design every training session that way. We'll ask you to do a lot of extra work, things you're maybe not used to, but then we go at 200mph'.

"There were some moments in the process when it was in jeopardy – three months prior to the World Cup, some Germans wanted to fire me because we lost 4-1 in Italy. But our president stood firm and calmed everybody down. Even the chancellor Angela Merkel got involved – she called me and said, 'What's going on?' I explained to her and she helped to calm things down.

"Then everything we'd implemented over those two years, we showcased during the tournament. It built a massive partnership between the German population and its national team, because everyone identified with that style of football. It was four weeks of sunshine as well, which never happens!

"It became one enormous party – Germans really embraced hosting that World Cup, and football became the tool to show the world this was a new Germany, after reunification. Every time I go back to Germany, even now, they want to talk about 2006 because they feel like it changed the whole nation, and the reputation of Germany worldwide."

Glory ultimately eluded them as they lost to eventual winners Italy in the semi-finals, though they finished on a high by beating Portugal to seal third place. Klinsmann opted to step down after the tournament, turning down the offer of an extended contract. But he'd started a process that led to his assistant Joachim Löw taking over as boss, and guiding Germany to World Cup success in 2014.

"I'm just fortunate I had those two years to build a foundation, with the people that led Germany to the World Cup win: Jogi and his staff," he says. "I felt so happy for them, but all the work was done by the people who were there – it had nothing to do with me any more. I just started to push the train, then it went faster and faster with every year until 2014, when it had become a bullet train for that semi-final against Brazil."

Klinsmann's return to management with Bayern lasted less than a season, followed by five years in charge of the United States. He guided them to the last 16 of the 2014 World Cup, but lost his job after a poor start to the final stage of qualifying for the 2018 tournament. In 2020, he resigned 10 weeks into a spell in charge of Hertha Berlin.

"I would love to go back to management one day, with the right people at the right place, and hopefully at the right time," he says. "I work here in the US for ESPN every week and I follow everything in Europe, all the competitions."

After Jose Mourinho's exit from Tottenham towards the end of the 2020-21 season, Klinsmann contacted Daniel Levy to express his interest in the job. Levy spoke to a host of other coaches, and was rejected by most of them, before eventually hiring Nuno Espirito Santo, who lasted only 10 league games.

Klinsmann is diplomatic when asked if he was frustrated about never genuinely being considered for the role.

"They had different things, thoughts and people in mind already, and you just have to respect that," he says. "But at least you have an initial talk – I had that talk with Daniel, he said they wanted to go a different way, and that was fine. I told him, 'I have my fingers crossed for you,' like I always do anyway."

He admits that should things ever change in the future, it remains a job he covets.

"Tottenham is always something you'd love to do, because it's your club, you share so many emotional moments with them and you know lots of people who are still there," he says. "I'm still in touch with Gary Mabbutt and other people around the club, so who knows? Maybe one day."

Even if that ambition is never realised, the German's love for Spurs is unconditional. He lined up for them only 68 times, but his 38 goals forged a bond that means as much to him as the fans who worshipped him.

"The way people welcomed me at White Hart Lane, I'll never forget that, and all the experiences we shared together," he smiles. "That's the beauty of sport – it connects you. I had such emotional experiences with the club and I'll always carry them with me, no matter what."

Everything began on that August afternoon in Sheffield, with one of the Premier League's most memorable goal celebrations. All it was missing was the snorkel.

Below Joining in the fun of hosting the 2006 World Cup

ROY KEANE

THERE'S ONLY ONE KEANO

The unknown teenager Brian Clough called 'Irishman' was something special, a fearless and unforgiving leader who epitomised a glorious era at the Theatre of Dreams. There really was no one like Keano

"Roy Keane is the best player that I've ever played with," Denis Irwin, fellow Corkonian, Republic of Ireland international and Manchester United stalwart, admits to *FourFourTwo*. "My two favourite players who I played with were Robbo [Bryan Robson] and Roy. They were really similar, but I had a lot of time with Roy for United and Ireland. I saw him develop from being a box-to-box player to a holding midfielder.

"Our midfield in 1999 complemented each other. Scholesy was a magnificent footballer, partly because whenever he played alongside Roy it was the perfect partnership. Wide of them were Giggsy and Becks, but the driving force was always Roy."

Keane made 480 outings for United, putting him 12th in their all-time appearance chart, above George Best. Before that, the Irishman turned out 154 times for Nottingham Forest, scoring a surprisingly high 33 goals in three seasons at the City Ground. It was more than enough to show why Blackburn and United were prepared to smash the British transfer record to sign him in 1993.

Keane was a latecomer to the professional game, and an unknown teenager when he travelled across the Irish Sea to Nottingham in the summer of 1990.

"When he signed, I didn't really know him," Forest captain Stuart Pearce explains to *FFT*. "I was injured, and he ended up playing at Anfield against Liverpool [in Forest's second league game of the 1990-91 season]. I came in the next day and said to the physio, 'How was the game? Who played on the right side of midfield?' I was talking about Liverpool, expecting him to say Ray Houghton, but he said Roy Keane. I said, 'Who? I've never heard of him'. He said, 'No, he was playing for us'."

Keane, freshly signed from Cobh Ramblers in a deal worth up to £47,000, had awoken on the morning of the Liverpool game upset not to have started for Forest's reserves at Rotherham. He had spent most of the game sat on the bench and played only 10 minutes.

As he wondered why, Keane was called to Anfield in a car. There he was joined by boss Brian Clough, who handed him a pint of milk and said, "Here, Irishman, get this down you." Keane hated milk. He drank the lot.

On Merseyside, he tried to help the kitman, thinking he was just going for the experience. Except he wasn't: Keane was starting against the First Division champions, wearing No.7. His Forest team-mates didn't even know his name, merely 'Irishman'.

In Keane's own words, he played "OK". But when you consider that he said he had done "all right" after his greatest ever performance for United in Turin, "OK" was just fine.

Clough summoned him to his office a day later. He asked him to clean his shoes and for his name. "Roy," he replied. Their relationship would be unconventional but productive.

"When I walked into the dressing room after the game, Clough punched me straight in the face," recalled Keane, after an underhit backpass meant Forest's FA Cup third round tie with Crystal Palace was going to a second replay. "I was hurt and shocked – too shocked to do anything in response but nod my head in agreement. My honeymoon with Clough and professional football was over."

Yet Clough respected his best player deeply. In another match, after admonishing his entire squad by accusing them of being lazy and complacent, he turned towards Keane and said, "I love you, Irishman."

"Brian loved good players – managers tend to!" Pearce tells *FFT*. "Roy came over and had an instant impact – he was in the first team before you could believe it and he drove us. He helped get the team to the FA Cup final in 1991 and had a fantastic impact at the club. By the time he left for Man United, he was our standout player, without a doubt. He played in midfield, he played in defence – wherever he played he was outstanding.

"Roy always had a very strong personality – obviously he was 18 and I was 28 [at the start], so we were a decade apart, but you always knew that he had an edge to him. He backed his ability on and off the pitch. He'd have his say, even as a young man. We had a couple of years together – very successful years, as well.

"It was just the variation of positions that he'd play and still be the best player on the pitch. Cloughie dropped him into the backline and he was the best centre-half at the club. He could do a multitude of things and went on to become one of the greatest players the Premier League has ever seen."

Keane was actually heading to Ewood Park before United got involved, though: the Red Devils dispatched their ticket office manager to Manchester Airport, to pick up Keane in a battered old Ford Orion. A contact let the Irishman out of a back gate at the airport to avoid the press, and the midfielder looked for a double headlight flash.

"I met Brian Kidd and Alex Ferguson, played a game of snooker with them and had the usual small talk – they told me how brilliant I was and I believed them," revealed Keane. A British record £3.75m

CARLING
CARLING
F.A. PREMIERSHIP
CHAMPIONS
CARLING
CHAMPIONS
SHARP

transfer was agreed, outraging Blackburn manager Kenny Dalglish.

"I told Kenny that I was going to Cyprus on holiday with a few mates, and when I came back I was going to sign for United," added Keane. "He replied, 'I'm going to find you'. At every bar in Ayia Napa, I looked over my shoulder expecting to see Kenny Dalglish."

In his first campaign for champions United, Keane showed why he was the replacement for the player he's so often compared with: Bryan Robson. He was key as United won the league and FA Cup Double for the first time in 1993-94, playing 54 games in all.

"I saw myself as a goalscoring midfielder, working box-to-box, tackling, closing people down and grafting to win the ball back," was Keane's self-assessment of his first season at Old Trafford. "Offensively, I think I was at my most effective running onto the ball to finish moves, like the one which produced the winner at Maine Road [a 3-2 victory over Manchester City in 1993]. This left Paul Ince or Bryan Robson to drop deep and receive the ball from the back four, which I wasn't confident enough to do. But Robson insisted that it was something I had to do. Trust your own ability was the message."

"I WALKED INTO THE DRESSING ROOM AND CLOUGH HIT ME IN THE FACE. I JUST NODDED. MY HONEYMOON PERIOD WAS OVER"

Above With early mentor Cloughie

Right Having led the charge at Forest

His manager trusted him. Keane won seven Premier League titles at United, four FA Cups, the Champions League and Intercontinental Cup. He became their most important player after Eric Cantona retired in 1997 – the year Keane was handed the captaincy, by which time he had all but given up drinking alcohol.

That summer, media duties were added to his responsibilities. Keane gave fascinating interviews – and he could get straight to the point. On the 1997 pre-season tour to Hong Kong, this writer was at the press conference. I'd interviewed him several times on the tour and didn't ask him anything that day. Keane saw me later and wasn't impressed.

"Why didn't you ask any questions?"

"Erm..."

"What's the point of you coming if you don't ask any questions? I'm there for you to ask me questions."

I was in a Manchester bar with friends in the '90s when Keane entered. He came over and said hello, which was nice, but there was a sting in his presence. "You're not following me are you?" he asked, a verbal jab which led to a defensive, "I was here already." He just winked and went on his way.

Keane's relationship with Ferguson was – and remains – trying. "Two bulls in the same pen," was Andy Cole's view of a pair he still gets on very well with. Ferguson and Keane don't see eye-to-eye after an acrimonious 2005 exit from United. Keane feels he gave everything for his manager and played even when he was injured. Ferguson believes he was the boss and needed to discipline his midfielder like any other player.

"His Irish fire was fundamental to his value as a footballer, but his tendency to go beyond the bounds of acceptability would have to be curbed," said Ferguson of the 1995 Keane – but he was crucial to his team. When Keane missed much of the 1997-98 season due to a knee injury, United failed to retain the title, win a cup and went backwards in Europe by losing to Monaco. When he returned, he was integral to United's Treble-winning success, making 55 appearances in all competitions. No outfielder featured more.

"I didn't think I could have a higher opinion of any footballer than I had of the Irishman, but he rose even further in my estimation at the Stadio delle Alpi," beamed Ferguson after Keane's greatest United performance, when he helped them come from 2-0 down to beat Juventus 3-2 in the Champions League semis. A yellow card in Turin meant he had to miss the 1999 final against Bayern Munich. Again: Keane felt he had done "all right".

Unlike a number of old team-mates, Keane challenged, and regularly disagreed with, his master's voice. He even criticised United fans for a poor atmosphere at Old Trafford during a Champions League game against Dynamo Kiev in 2000. He was arguably

Below Keano led his team-mates to new heights in '99

absolutely right to do so – adding 'prawn sandwiches' to the football menu – and defended his right to be honest, compared to the bland, safe, plaudits given by other players.

"Some footballers nowadays are like robots when they speak to the press, because they have people working for them, and PR and all that," said Keane. "They want to know what questions they're going to be asked and all that crap. Ultimately, my comments were for the team. A week later, the atmosphere was different class."

It was Keane's team-mates who incurred such wrath on a daily basis.

"All the time, especially those who think it'll be easy for them," he insisted. "I do it in every game and training session. I can be a pretty critical guy, critical of myself and especially of the young lads who I can see have talent. Maybe sometimes I'm harsh, and I've left the training field feeling like I've been a bit out of order, particularly with the younger players. But if I wasn't trying to make a point, I'd feel like I was cheating them. If something needs to be said, then I'll say it.

"I think I have positive stuff I can pass onto the players from my own experiences. All I ask is that they are focused on what they are trying to do – that's part of my job. I'm not the only one who does it. Gary [Neville] does it. Giggsy does it."

That attitude was not without a price. "It has cost me certain friendships over the years with players, and some can be standoffish with me for United or Ireland," he revealed. "It's just part of my make-up and, in the long run, I think that's a positive thing. It's a short career and you have to be focused on what you do. The last thing I would want to think when I retire is that I hadn't been focused at a certain point in my career. To me, that's the biggest crime."

Irwin was a close friend. "Roy will contest this, but he wasn't the best footballer in the world – he left that to Scholesy," he tells *FFT*. "He was a combative player who could smell danger, read situations and tell where the ball was dropping. He was defensive-minded but could also break forward. He was a huge driving force in training and in being Manchester United."

Keane is now an outspoken pundit. His brutal honesty is a virtue, yet that may go against him in his hopes of managing a top club again. He found success at Sunderland, winning the Championship in 2006-07, but then failed with Ipswich.

Either way, he often has a point – although there's not one person in Manchester United history who divides opinion so much. Keane is an Old Trafford legend, and his stock in the city, where he has mostly lived since moving to England, is high.

But there's more than one side to him. In 2018, Keane led a group of ex-United players to organise a 40,000 sell-out match for Liam Miller, his fellow Corkonian who had tragically passed away from cancer.

"Liam was a very good player who played for United, Celtic and his country," said Keane. "A really nice guy, a quiet guy, very humble. But don't get me wrong, he was very strong. You don't get to the top in any sport unless you've got good confidence behind you and a lot of determination. Liam was no angel, but he knew how to play the game and he was a good guy."

He could have been talking about himself.

Right "Hey, hun, still hate you, too"

GIANFRANCO ZOLA
THE LITTLE MAGICIAN

Long before Roman Abramovich's billions and Jose Mourinho's opinions, there was a tiny Sardinian who transformed the face of Chelsea forever. For seven seasons, Gianfranco Zola weaved his magic as English football watched in awe.

It was almost 11pm in Cheshire when the helicopter fell from the sky. Matthew Harding was making his way back to London, having watched his beloved Chelsea slip to defeat at second-tier Bolton in the League Cup. He never made it home. Along with four others, the Blues' vice-chairman died on that fateful October night in 1996.

Harding was a figure of hope, following an awful quarter-century for Chelsea. Between 1971 and 1996, the club won no major titles and finished outside English football's top 10 on 21 occasions. Without their investor, their prospects seemed uncertain once more.

A fortnight after Harding's death, a new figure of hope arrived at the crucial moment. Gianfranco Zola was just 5ft 6in tall, but he changed everything. In the 25 years since the Italian's arrival, Chelsea have never finished outside the top 10 and celebrated 20 major trophies. Few players have altered the course of history in such pivotal fashion.

If Zola was special, it was because he learned from the grand master. He was an unpolished diamond, still competing in Italy's third tier in his native Sardinia when spotted by Napoli in 1989, aged 23. He was welcomed to Stadio San Paolo by one Diego Maradona. "Finally," the Argentine told him, "they've bought a guy even shorter than me!"

Zola played only a fringe role as the 'Little Donkeys' secured the 1989-90 Scudetto, but spent as much time with Diego as possible.

"'El Pibe' was so important for Gianfranco," says Massimo Crippa, who played alongside the Italian for Napoli, Parma and the national team. "They had similar characteristics, and Zola gained so many outstanding skills from Diego's technical knowledge.

"They'd spend a very long time together on the training field, trying different free-kicks. Gianfranco was a bit shy at the start but he had great qualities. Even though he wasn't very tall, he was hard to mark and so strong. When Maradona left the club in 1992, Zola was given the No.10 jersey and then played extraordinarily well."

In 1992-93, Zola scored 12 Serie A goals and provided 12 assists, the joint-highest tally in the league. As Napoli began to struggle financially, Parma swooped with a £6m bid. He netted 18 times in his first campaign at the Stadio Ennio Tardini, but disappointment was to follow at USA 94.

On July 5, Italy trailed 1-0 to Nigeria in the last 16 when Zola was introduced from the bench for his first tournament appearance. Eager to make an impact, and believing he had been denied a penalty after falling inside the area, he had an uncharacteristic rush of blood – charging after Augustine Eguavoen and chopping a boot across the defender to win possession back. Eguavoen went down and Zola was shown a red card, responding by kneeling on the pitch, arms folded like a crestfallen child. He's the only player to be sent off on his birthday in World Cup history. It could have cost Italy, had Roberto Baggio not bagged a brace to rescue the 10-men Azzurri. Zola was available from suspension by the time they reached the Rose Bowl final, but he wasn't called upon.

The following season, he hit back with his highest ever goal tally, scoring 28 times as Parma challenged for a first league title and won the UEFA Cup. Hristo Stoichkov's arrival soon altered Zola's role, however, before he suffered more tournament misery – missing a decisive penalty against Germany as Italy exited Euro 96 at the group stage.

Months later, Zola decided to leave Serie A, after new Parma boss Carlo Ancelotti began to play him on the left of a rigid 4-4-2 system.

"Ancelotti had other intentions for him – he preferred to use that kind of player as a wide midfielder, but it wasn't Gianfranco's role so he decided to consider proposals from other clubs," Crippa tells *FourFourTwo*.

"I was really surprised when he moved to England, but Chelsea were quite an Italian team at that time, with Gianluca Vialli, Ruud Gullit who'd played in Serie A, and Roberto Di Matteo. Seeing what he did at Chelsea, it was the perfect choice."

It seems implausible now, but there was scepticism in the Chelsea squad when Zola joined for £4.5m in November 1996.

"When he first arrived, John Spencer was in the team and playing very well," ex-Blues defender Michael Duberry tells *FFT*. "Everyone loved Spenny, so Gianfranco came in and we all wondered, 'Why do we need this guy?' He wasn't one of the biggest names coming out of Serie A. When he started training though, I thought, 'Wow, all is forgiven, he can play... I love Spenny, but this guy is unbelievable'."

Already 30, Zola was desperate to make an impact. He was handed a debut at Blackburn in November and was Premier League Player of the Month by the end of December, after netting five goals in six games. By February, he had scooped BBC Goal of the Month after collecting the ball near the byline at home to Manchester United, then bamboozling Denis Irwin and Gary Pallister to somehow work his way into a position to fire home.

Zola's long-range stunner helped Chelsea come from 2-0 down to

AUTOGLASS
AUTOGLASS
20

beat Liverpool in the FA Cup fourth round, then a brilliant piece of skill outfoxed the Wimbledon backline as he scored in the semi-finals at Highbury. By the end of the campaign, Chelsea had secured sixth place in the Premier League – their first top 10 finish since 1990 – and another clever Zola flick laid on an assist for Eddie Newton as the Blues beat Middlesbrough 2-0 in the FA Cup final. Finally, the 26-year major trophy drought was over.

Before that, Zola had been named Football Writers' Association Player of the Year – he's still the only man to win the award despite arriving in England partway through a season. Hard work complemented his talent.

"Gianfranco would be one of the first on the training field and one of the last off," recalls Duberry. "There was one time when the boss, Ruud Gullit, said to the young English players, 'You lot aren't technical enough, so you're going out half an hour early to do some skill exercises'. There was Jody Morris, Andy Myers and myself, and we saw it as a punishment. Why were we having to do that when Frank Leboeuf and Roberto Di Matteo were in the changing room sipping espressos, watching us from the window and laughing?

"Zola sensed that. He'd say, 'Dubes, come on, I'll come and do them with you – it's not punishment. See it the other way, as a way to better yourself'. He and Vialli both came out. When you could see Gianfranco getting something out of it, everyone else changed their approach. He was only around 4ft 2in, but was a mammoth of a man – his gravitas, his warmth. When people ask me to name the best I ever played with, I don't hesitate – it was Zola."

During his debut Premier League season, the forward struck a winner for Italy against England at Wembley, in qualifying for the 1998 World Cup. He began to assist Chelsea in Europe, too. Already League Cup winners in 1997-98, the Blues reached the European Cup Winners' Cup final thanks to three Zola goals en route. Struggling with injury before the showpiece against Stuttgart, the Italian was named on the bench – then hammered home the only goal of the game within 30 seconds of his introduction.

Season after season, the magic continued. In 1998-99, Zola helped Chelsea come third and seal Champions League qualification for the first time. He was still at his dazzling best as the west Londoners reached the last eight, thumping Galatasaray 5-0 at the infamously intimidating Ali Sami Yen in the group stage courtesy of a Gianfranco masterclass.

"Before the game, Galatasaray supporters smashed the windows on our bus," Gus Poyet told *FFT*. "But we had Zola. When he came off after 80 minutes, those same fans stood up and applauded him."

At the start of that 1999-2000 campaign, Zola had pondered calling time on his career come the season's end, but thankfully didn't. He bookended it with an audacious scooped assist for Poyet to score a flying scissor-volley against Sunderland on the opening day, and a teasing set-piece which produced a David James error in the last FA Cup final at the old Wembley against Aston Villa.

Above Franco (front row, third from right) learned from Diego (middle row, third from right) at Napoli

The Italian wasn't exempt from dressing room banter, though – unsurprisingly, Dennis Wise was at the heart of it. "Gianfranco was reading a John Grisham book, a cliffhanger where it all came together in the very last chapter," remembered Graeme Le Saux. "Our captain decided it would be funny to tear out the last chapter and Gianfranco didn't realise, so we watched him getting closer to what he thought was the end of the book, until one day in the dressing room, he got there. That was the first time I saw him lose the plot – he was going around accusing everyone of stealing the pages, demanding them back!"

Zola turned 34 in the summer of 2000, but still he kept producing. His football brain, his biggest asset, was as sharp as ever.

"He was a footballer who wasn't dominant physically, but gained his advantage through intelligence and innovation out on the pitch," says Mario Stanic, who played alongside Zola during the Italian's final years at Stamford Bridge. "He saw things before anybody else. He showed that with a professional attitude and the correct mentality, you can continue to play dominantly in your 30s. We shared a dressing room for three wonderful years – he embraced new players and made us feel part of the team.

"I'm still in touch with him today. The two of us would play football-tennis all the time at training – he used to arrive an hour and a half early so we could play. It was always full of laughs and crazy tricks."

Breathtaking skills were never far away when Zola was around, his most notable coming in Chelsea's 2001-02 FA Cup run. That season, the veteran was beginning to face a battle for his starting place, as Claudio Ranieri tried to lower the team's average age by pairing Eidur Gudjohnsen with Jimmy Floyd Hasselbaink upfront.

He hit back by reasserting his class at home to Norwich, meeting a low corner at the near post and flicking a backheel volley into the net. Only an artist like Zola could have scored a goal like that.

"It was a wonderful goal, although it wasn't surprising for us as team-mates," Stanic tells *FFT*. "It's understandable that it looked great to everybody else, but when you saw what he did every day at training, that was just an ordinary day for him. What made Gianfranco so fantastic was the ease with which he did flicks and tricks like that. He was an individual who always put the team first, a quality that is extremely rare for players as good as him. But he never doubted his own ability."

Remarkably, that continued belief allowed Zola to regain his spot in 2002-03 and notch 16 goals – the best haul of his Chelsea career, earning him their Player of the Year award. In the closing stages of the final game of the season, the 36-year-old schemer tormented a defender some 11 years his junior, turning Jamie Carragher inside out and sending the Liverpool stopper tumbling, before darting past two more bamboozled Reds in a sumptuous piece of skill.

It would prove to be Zola's final act in blue. His displays at Stamford Bridge had played a significant role in tempting Roman Abramovich to purchase the club, but days before the Russian billionaire's takeover was completed, Zola decided to return home and play the remainder of his career in Sardinia. Desperate to keep the out-of-contract Italian in England, the incoming owner upped the terms of the new deal on offer at Chelsea, but Zola had already agreed to join Cagliari. Abramovich was said to be so disappointed, according to unconfirmed reports, that he swiftly made an offer to buy the Serie B side.

"Gianfranco was iconic at Chelsea – he was part of the attraction," says Duberry. "It's like if you're buying a new house – you think, 'Oh, I thought I was getting that nice lampshade. They took that as well? Why didn't they leave that in there?' The timing of him going was a shame, because maybe Abramovich would have invested in Gianfranco for a little longer, and we could have seen him lift the Premier League trophy even if he played a supporting role. Ian Wright got to lift the trophy towards the back end of his Arsenal career – it would have been lovely for Gianfranco to have that iconic moment, too.

"But what he did at Chelsea was great as it was, and the club did win things during that period. It was the influence he had on other Chelsea players like Frank Lampard, too. The attention to detail, to practise and work hard – it rubbed off on anyone who joined the club. People talk about Jose Mourinho putting that mindset into Chelsea, but Zola had already been doing it. He had such an impact there. He transformed the club."

Legacies don't come much better than that. Chelsea's successful era began back on that autumn day in 1996, when Gianfranco Zola walked through the door at Stamford Bridge.

Below Galatasaray fans applauded the Italian's excellence in Chelsea's 5–0 away win in the Champions League in October 1999

DAVID GINOLA THE FRENCH ACE

David Ginola arrived in England with journalists asking him who he was. After four campaigns of thrilling wing play, they were clambering over one another to vote him the league's best player. Oh, he was worth it all right...

Over 26 years on, David Ginola can still remember the bafflement he felt at his first press conference in English football.

Ginola had just joined Newcastle from Paris Saint-Germain for £2.5m – a considerable sum in 1995. He had reached the semi-finals of the Champions League months earlier and been targeted by Europe's biggest clubs. He was poised to become the second Frenchman to play in the Premier League, after Eric Cantona. But not everyone was aware of his talents.

"When I arrived at the first press conference, a journalist said, 'Can you tell us who you are?'" says Ginola, smiling as he reminisces to *FourFourTwo*. "In Paris, we'd won the league title, we'd won the cup twice and I'd been French player of the year. But I was completely unknown to the English press, which surprised me.

"I replied, 'What do you mean, who am I?!' The English press didn't know much about French players then – now, they know everything about them. But I was a surprise for them, a discovery, that 'Oh, this is a great player'."

Ginola was Premier League Player of the Month just four matches into his time at Newcastle, and would become one of the biggest stars of the next few seasons – named both PFA and Football Writers' Association Player of the Year after moving on to Tottenham in 1997.

With his good looks, musketeer locks and swashbuckling dribbling, the French left-winger stood out so much that he sometimes resembled the lone pro on the field, carving his way through a rearguard of over-matched amateurs. Few could dazzle quite like David Ginola.

THE CRUYFF U-TURN

Newcastle was not Ginola's dream move in the summer of 1995 – initially, at least. Having helped PSG eliminate Barcelona from the Champions League, the 28-year-old looked set to link up with his childhood hero Johan Cruyff at the Camp Nou.

"I had two posters in my bedroom when I was young – one of Cruyff and one of Diego Maradona," reveals Ginola. "Cruyff was my inspiration – the way he played, the way he behaved. I met him at a golf tournament in Tarragona, south of Barcelona, and he told me I was his priority that pre-season. Barça under Cruyff played some of the greatest football ever, so it would have been something magic.

"Everything was organised, but he said he had to get rid of two foreign players before signing me – Hristo Stoichkov and Gheorghe Hagi. They couldn't find clubs for them, and I got a call from Cruyff saying, 'I'm sorry, we can't make the move'."

Soon, Ginola discovered that Kevin Keegan wanted him at Newcastle. "I found that very attractive," he says. "When I was about nine years old, I told my dad that I wanted to be a footballer. I said that while I was watching Liverpool vs Saint-Etienne in the European Cup, when Keegan was playing for Liverpool. I had a good phone conversation with Terry McDermott, the assistant at Newcastle, and said, 'OK then, let's do it'."

Newcastle weren't the only English team interested. "I gave my word to Terry in the afternoon, then around midnight I got a call from David Dein at Arsenal," recalls Ginola. "He asked, 'Have you signed for anybody?' I said, 'Well... why?' and he said, 'Because we want to sign you'. I said, 'Actually, I gave my word to Newcastle, sorry – the deal is done'."

Had Dein's call come a day earlier, Ginola admits that he might have been tempted to choose the Gunners.

"Arsenal were one of the biggest clubs in the country, while Newcastle had just moved from the First Division to the Premier League and still had to prove they were a great side," he says. "The decision would probably have been different. But when I called my dad and said, 'I'm signing for Newcastle and working with Kevin Keegan,' he was happy."

Ginola was joining an ambitious outfit, just as he had done twice before in France, albeit with limited success. He had moved to Matra Racing from Toulon in 1988, only for the club to suffer financial problems and relegation to the amateur leagues.

He rocked up at recently promoted Brest, who finished 11th but were kicked out of the top flight because of their own money woes. Months into the 1991-92 season, they filed for bankruptcy, permitting Ginola to join PSG as a free agent, where his obvious talent was harnessed in the quest for titles.

At Newcastle, he experienced none of the issues he'd had with Matra Racing or Brest. Although he was surprised to be employed on the left flank, having often operated as a No.10 in Paris, 'Le Magnifique' loved every second of his time under Keegan.

"He got the best out of every player," says the Frenchman. "He said, 'David, I know what you're capable of – just do what you're good at. I don't want you to defend much – give me your best in attack and put

PSG
Liptonic

as many balls into the box as possible for Les Ferdinand'.

"I tried to entertain and be very positive in every match. In England, the game was a lot quicker; it was intense, exciting, instinctive. I liked it. That's how we played at Newcastle – instinctive football."

The August 1995 Player of the Month prize soon dispelled any doubts that Ginola would succeed. In the third game of the campaign at Sheffield Wednesday, he smashed home a stunning long-range strike to extend the Magpies' winning start.

"The media in France said English football wouldn't suit my game, and I always wanted to prove people wrong," he says. "I remember that game against Sheffield Wednesday. Our players were taking the mickey out of me, as I was coming from Paris with my fashion, and they said, 'David, do you know much about Sheffield?' I said, 'Er, no, not really'. They said, 'You'll see, it's a very tough place'. I replied, 'That's OK, wherever we play, it will be fine'.

"I tried to do my stuff during that game, and it was appreciated. On the way back to Newcastle, we had a drink in town with the lads to celebrate, and the Newcastle fans were falling on their knees! I didn't experience that in France – it was good there, but not that much. The reception I always received at St James' Park was like being at home with your family – they cheered when you did things, and they expected a lot from you. It was great, to be honest. It was great playing for Newcastle."

"I TRIED TO ENTERTAIN AND BE POSITIVE – AT NEWCASTLE WE PLAYED INSTINCTIVE FOOTBALL"

By mid-winter, Ginola's performances had helped Newcastle surge clear at the top of the table. "I'd call my mum and she'd ask, 'How's the weather there today?'" he reflects. "I'd say, 'The weather is grey and it's pouring down with rain'. She'd say, 'David, the sun is in your heart and in your soul'.

"I went to training every morning with that in mind – give sunshine to people. If you do that, you usually get something back. Then we were top of the league and 12 points clear – it was out of the blue. Nobody had expected Newcastle to do quite so well, and so quickly."

In the end, the title race pivoted on a battle against his compatriot Cantona.

"It was a big rivalry set up by the press, but it wasn't the case," insists Ginola. "Eric was playing very well for Manchester United, and I tried to help my team. His goal at St James' Park [in United's 1-0 March win] was key. We were disappointed, as we played so well, we entertained so much, and I think we deserved to win the league that year.

"Maybe we could have done some things differently, managing the last 20 minutes of matches when it was 1-1 or 1-0. Sometimes 1-0 is enough. It was a lack of experience. It was a shame, because to arrive in England and win the league in my first season would have been something amazing."

Newcastle briefly led the league again the following season, after Ginola scored another cracker as Manchester United were thrashed 5-0 on their St James' Park return.

"In the dressing room after the game, we thought, 'We've just done something great there'," he says. "We had incredible players – Alan Shearer had joined that summer, plus Les Ferdinand, Peter Beardsley and Faustino Asprilla. Many of the players I'd never heard of when I first arrived but realised were great, like Lee Clark, Steve Watson, Keith Gillespie, Robbie Elliott, John Beresford, David Batty, Darren Peacock, Rob Lee... I can't name all of them, but brilliant players."

Ginola was awarded BBC Goal of the Month for a sensational UEFA Cup effort at home to Ferencvaros in October, when he juggled the ball outside the penalty area before volleying it into the top corner. But his stay at St James' Park lasted just two seasons, having grown unhappy under new manager Kenny Dalglish following Keegan's shock mid-campaign exit in January 1997. It had been Keegan who'd blocked another opportunity to join Barcelona before the start of 1996-97.

"Keegan called me and said, 'David, we're not going to sell you'," explains Ginola. "I said, 'Gaffer, if you were in my position at 29, this is the last chance for me to go to one of the biggest clubs in the world – you have to sell me'. He said, 'Last year I let Andy Cole go to Manchester United and was almost killed by the fans – if I let you leave now, it's going to be a massive issue for me'.

"I could understand it, and told him that because I felt great at Newcastle, I'd carry on working like I did in the first season. But at the time I thought the decision was a selfish way of thinking, especially because he left six months later.

"Newcastle without Keegan was different – the way we trained and the approach. Kevin is a kind and gentle person, putting an arm around your shoulder. Dalglish was colder, and I soon realised that I wasn't the type of player he'd sign or keep."

SUGAR SWEETENS A DEAL

Ginola's departure from Newcastle would be sealed thanks to a mad speedboat ride on the Mediterranean. He was back in the south of France for the summer – having grown up a few miles from Saint-Tropez – when Spurs' £2.5m offer was accepted.

"[Chairman] Alan Sugar said, 'I'm anchored in Villefranche-sur-Mer, just outside Monaco – can you come and see me on my boat?'" continues Ginola. "I was going to make the deal on the boat but it was July 14, which is a national holiday in France. A lot of the roads are busy, so I thought, 'If I drive by car from Saint-Tropez to Monaco, it'll take ages – three or four hours'.

"I called a friend and said, 'I need to go to Monaco as quickly as possible'. He said, 'Give me an hour,' then called back and said, 'I've got a boat'. We left Saint-Tropez in the boat, going at 40 knots [45mph] on the sea. It was wild! In 58 minutes, we arrived.

"Sugar was standing on the side of his boat – 50 metres long, a big thing called Louisiana – and kept shouting at us. I couldn't work out what he was trying to say, but he was making lots of arm gestures. I thought, 'What's going on? Maybe he's changed his mind!'

"He was really annoyed about the noise of the speedboat, but then he spotted me and said, 'Oh, it's you!' I asked him why he'd been shouting and waving at us and he said, 'I've just spent a week with

Above On the run with the Magpies

my grandchild. I need some quiet now!'

"I went on his boat and he told me about Tottenham, then after dinner it was dark and he said, 'You're not going back to Saint-Tropez on a speedboat tonight, it's dangerous. You're a Spurs player now, and you can sleep here'. We talked more and he made plans, saying, 'You're going to arrive at White Hart Lane and we'll make a bottle of Gin Ola.'"

Tottenham had finished 10th prior to the Frenchman's arrival and slipped to 14th in his first campaign at the club, battling against relegation for much of the 1997-98 season. Despite that, he was a star player for his new side and knew he had made the right move.

"Even if the club wasn't pretending to win things, I tried to be very consistent with my performances," he insists. "I felt great there. Maybe it was the fact the players, the staff and the fans were relying on me a lot. I liked that pressure – it gave me even more power and I felt that from the beginning. I thought, 'Let's make the club better'.

"I'd speak to supporters after games, and some people cried, saying, 'David, thank you so much. We're playing such bad football but you're giving us something to cheer us all up'. Wow, when people are crying, that's a huge responsibility. My family travelled to see some of my games and said, 'When the ball comes to you, there's a silence in the stadium – we can sense the anticipation building because the fans expect you to do something great'. I enjoyed that – I always knew I needed to do something on the pitch."

That summer, Ginola had to watch on as France won the 1998 World Cup Final in Paris, believing he had the talent to be a part of it. He had been blamed by some – including former boss Gerard Houllier – for Les Bleus' failure to qualify for the 1994 tournament, when he had opted not to protect the ball in the corner for the closing seconds of a vital game against Bulgaria.

In 1998-99, however, Ginola emphatically displayed his ability, despite the early-season arrival of renowned disciplinarian George Graham as manager. "The press said George Graham wasn't suitable for me – he wasn't the coach who'd give me the opportunity to express myself in the team," he remembers. "But that was wrong. They didn't know the person I was. That season was something magic, as I worked even harder in training under George, just to prove everyone wrong. I ended the season with the League Cup and PFA Player of the Year award. What else was there to say?"

Arguably the finest moment was Ginola's individual goal at Barnsley in March 1999, where he picked the ball up on the left flank, rhythmically darted both right and left like a slalom skier, then nonchalantly stroked the ball home from inside the penalty area. "It was the perfect illustration of the season," he says. "It's 0-0 in the quarter-finals of the FA Cup. Everyone is watching you, expecting you to do something amazing, and then you do your stuff. I can't really explain how you construct a sequence that will end up with a goal. Everything was just very fluid, and it turned out perfectly."

With Tottenham fans delirious behind the goal, what did that moment feel like? "Crap, it feels crap..." he replies, mischievously trying to stay deadpan, before he's unable to suppress the laughter any more. "It feels amazing! It feels amazing because you've just scored, it feels amazing because you know you've just scored a great goal, and it feels amazing because you win the match 1-0. The whole thing put together meant a lot."

In the season when Manchester United won their famous Treble, 32-year-old Ginola became the first player of the Premier League era to win the PFA award without playing for a top-two team – Spurs finished 11th. Gareth Bale (twice, also for Tottenham) is the only other player to win the award for a side that didn't finish in the top four.

"When I got to Grosvenor House for the awards ceremomy, I bumped into [PFA chief executive] Gordon Taylor and he said, 'David, how are you doing?' with a tiny smile," recalls Ginola. "I asked him, 'Why are you smiling?' He said, 'You'll see...' It was a surprise when my name was announced – I went on stage and didn't know what to say. We had a party afterwards – Nicolas Anelka won the Young Player of the Year award, and he came up to me and said, 'You're an inspiration'. I wasn't sure about those moments, because some people said David Ginola was an individual on the pitch, but I was a team player. I'd rather have changed it for the league, but it was great anyway.

"To win it at 32 years old was an explanation to people who said David is more focused on his modelling or advertising for L'Oreal. That wasn't true – you can't be player of the year at 32 if you're not 100 per cent committed to your job."

Ginola won the Football Writers' Association prize, too. That year, Cruyff also hailed him as the best player in the world.

"That was the best award of all," enthuses Ginola. "When you're 10 years old and you're a massive fan of a player, then one day he wants to sign you, that's some achievement. If you add what he said in 1999, I'm not sure how to explain how I felt, because it wasn't a question about me. He was just asked, 'For you, who's the best player in the world right now?' and he said David Ginola. Wow, thank you very much."

MR BLOBBY FIGHTS BACK

Just a year later, Ginola was shocked to be made surplus to requirements at Tottenham.

"I would have loved to end my career at Spurs," he says. "Alan Sugar called me in the summer and said, 'I have something to tell you – you're going to be on the transfer list'. I said, 'What?! What do you mean?' He told me that George Graham didn't want me any more. I said, 'You're going to have to explain this to the fans, because I'm not saying it's David Ginola's decision'."

After an unexpected meeting with Aston Villa chairman Doug Ellis

Below Ginola doing what he does best for Tottenham

while on holiday in Mauritius, a move to the Midlands was sealed. "We had a nice lunch and he said, 'We'd love to have you at the club one day'," remembers Ginola. "I said, 'Well, funnily enough, I'm on the transfer market...'"

But his 18 months at Villa Park were largely unhappy. The most notable moment was a blockbuster strike against Manchester City, when the Frenchman removed his shirt and flexed his muscles to prove a point to gaffer John Gregory, who had claimed the winger was out of shape. He looked anything but.

"It was a very weird relationship with John Gregory," explains Ginola. "You arrive in the morning, there's a newspaper, and you see all the players laughing in the dressing room. On the back page, it showed my head on the body of Jimmy Five Bellies, and the headline was John Gregory saying that David Ginola is Mr Blobby. When you're trying your best to get into shape, it was a humiliation, so when I scored that goal I wanted to say, 'Look at me – you're saying I'm Mr Blobby?'

"I need to like my manager and respect him. If you don't like me, don't expect me to like you. I thought, 'No, I'm making my effort and if that's not good enough for you, it's not going to work'."

After seven brief appearances at Everton in 2001-02, Ginola retired at 35. "I lost the little flame – it's within your soul," he says.

When he looks back on his career, there's plenty of pride, but also a feeling that he was capable of even more.

"That's what I think, if I look in the mirror," admits Ginola. "If I'd played for a team like Barcelona, I probably would have played at Euro 96 and the 1998 World Cup. I never got to play at a major tournament, which is a big shame, because playing for France at a World Cup, and winning it, really would have been something amazing. And I think... well, I don't want to say it, but I think I deserved to be in that 1998 squad."

His spells at Newcastle and Tottenham may not have earned him a spot at a tournament, but they established a bond that will always remain special to Ginola.

In the years since his retirement, the Frenchman has worked as a TV presenter and an actor, as well as briefly standing for FIFA president in 2015. The move was perceived as a gimmick by some, partly because of the backing from Paddy Power, but Ginola insists he had genuine plans.

"It wasn't taken seriously by most people because you need a certain background – if you're not from that background, you're not taken seriously," says Ginola, whose former PSG team-mate George Weah did move into politics and is now the president of Liberia.

"I wanted to bring football back to the fans and give the money back to the people. For example, when you award the World Cup to Brazil, you're not saying to them, 'Well, if you want the World Cup, we're not going to pay tax'. No, we'll pay the tax and make sure the money is then used for social work, so that the poorest people in the country get the money from football. The game is for the people, so the money it generates has to be given back to the people. When you saw Sepp Blatter and Michel Platini, all those issues, it's not acceptable.

"I called federations in some places around the world and they said, 'Mr Ginola, we'd love to have you as president because we know we're going to be respected, but if I give you my vote, I'll be destroyed by the system, as the system is made by people for themselves'. Unfortunately it won't change, unless we all want to see things change."

Ginola has longed for change at Newcastle too, after years of misery for fans under Mike Ashley's ownership. He turns 54 in January and remains hopeful of a return to football, believing he has something to offer, perhaps as a sporting director. He would jump at the chance if an opportunity ever presented itself at Newcastle, to help re-establish the bond between club and supporters.

"I would love to, because Newcastle was my first club in the Premier League and they deserve better," reveals Ginola, who made a quick recovery from a heart attack in 2016. "Geordies deserve one of the biggest clubs in the country, in Europe, in the world. They've got the potential, but for many years things have been done in very weird ways that haven't made the club better. I want to see Newcastle being very successful and not only in terms of results, but its stability and how they work with the academy. There were Geordies in our side and they gave us something crucial – the heart of the club, the passion. I have so many ideas and I'd love to put something in place – the way I see football, with everyone aiming for the same thing, like a family. You need to explain to the supporters, 'We have a project, and I'll tell you exactly what it is'.

"If I worked for Newcastle, it would be so easy to say, 'I'm going to buy a Spanish guy, a French guy, an Italian guy, a German guy and I'll make the team great'. That's an easy way: you've got the money and you buy all the best players around. But I'd want to bring the academy players to the first team, a bit like Barcelona under [president] Joan Laporta with Messi, Busquets, Pique, Xavi and Iniesta. When you're a foreigner and you arrive at Barça, you see that most of the players were at the academy, and they're the soul of the club. You need a soul – that's what's going to make you win titles."

Titles eluded Ginola and 'The Entertainers' in 1996, but they came agonisingly close. The Frenchman was arguably the biggest star of the best Newcastle team in more than half a century, then became one of Tottenham's greatest players of the Premier League era.

"Can you tell us who you are?" journalists asked when he first arrived on English shores. During seven years in the Premier League, he left no one in any doubt. By the time he hung up his boots, everyone knew David Ginola.

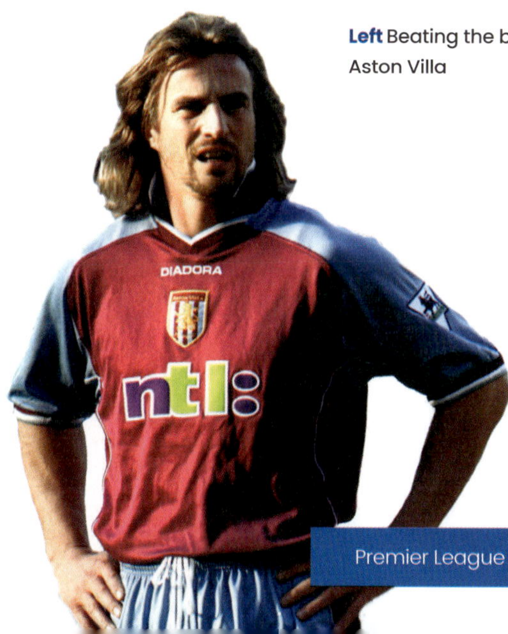

Left Beating the bulge at Aston Villa

JUNINHO BORO'S BRILLIANT BRAZILIAN

In 1995, Juninho arrived at Middlesbrough with big ambitions and an even bigger suit. Now, Brazil's pint-sized former No.10 reminisces about his Teesside love affair featuring hot-headed team-mates, heartbreak and a very happy ending.

Whenever I look back at my career, Middlesbrough will always spring to mind – it was a marvellous moment for me, professionally and personally. The club, town and fans welcomed me so warmly from day one that my family and I felt at home there… even if we wouldn't have been able to point at it on a map beforehand. It was in the 1995 Umbro Cup that I first grabbed Boro's attention. At 22 years old I was already Brazil's No.10, plus a Copa Libertadores and Intercontinental Cup champion with Sao Paulo from 1993. The latter title came in an epic 3-2 win against Fabio Capello's Milan, where Tele Santana put me on during the second half in Tokyo.

If I'm honest, I played really well in the Umbro Cup, and scored when we beat England 3-1 in the last match of the tournament at Wembley. Bryan Robson was Terry Venables' assistant, as well as player-manager of Boro, and liked what he saw that day, not only technically but also in my behaviour. I got kicked all over the pitch but kept going despite being only 5ft 6in. Back then, the Premiership was still a very physical league, so I think that courage counted in my favour.

After that, Boro showed a real interest in signing me. However, I still hadn't played the minimum amount of games for Brazil to grant me a work permit in the UK, so Bryan had to wait a while until I achieved that number. When that eventually happened, Boro approached Sao Paulo to negotiate with them.

I wasn't expecting to leave Sao Paulo that soon. My international career had only just begun, but two factors were key for me accepting Middlesbrough's offer. First, my contract was coming to an end, and there was a big gap between what I wanted and what Sao Paulo were willing to pay to renew it. Cafu had recently gone through something similar and it took him two months to agree a new deal with the club. As a result, he spent 60 days only training.

With that in mind, I didn't want the same thing happening to me. The second and most important factor was the project presented to me by Middlesbrough. Robson and chief executive Keith Lamb flew to Brazil and told me how they were planning to transform the club – to bring it up to a higher level, become a medium-sized Premiership club and play European football. Truth be told, I didn't know much about English football, as few matches were shown on Brazilian television – Italy's Serie A was far more popular, for instance. Some of my friends said to me, 'Eh? English football?' They started watching matches on TV and wondered how I'd be able to succeed in England, given that it was a more physical game than the one we played in Brazil. As I was skinny and small, they asked if I was sure about it.

Bryan brought me several VHS tapes of Boro matches so that I could see them play, and underlined his idea of playing good football – not using loads of long balls. His exact words were, 'I want the ball on the floor'. The club had just been promoted from the second division, but that didn't concern me at all. My focus was on whether I'd be playing regularly and how the coach could help me improve my game.

I was lucky to find good and honest people in charge of the club, too. In chairman Steve Gibson, I was confident Boro would be financially safe in the long term, and that convinced me it was the right decision. There were rumours about Arsenal being interested in me as well, but Middlesbrough were the only club to put a bid on the table. I believed in them, took the offer and never had a reason to look back.

On the way to Teesside, we stopped in London where the chairman's private plane was ready to take my mum, dad and I to our new home. 'Are we going to fly in that?' asked my dad, who's a little frightened of flying. Thankfully, it was a very safe trip! When we landed at Teesside Airport we soon spotted some Brazil flags, and then there were about 5,000 fans waiting for me at the stadium. They showed me so much affection, it was rather beautiful.

Looking back, I still ask my parents today, 'How did you let me dress like that for my unveiling?' Oh my God. I look at the photos, and that giant suit I bought myself could easily fit two Juninhos in it. I should have been a laughing stock!

As I didn't speak a word of English, the club provided an interpreter for me. My first press conference went really smoothly and the Italian translator came across well. However, to my surprise, I was later told that the guy didn't translate a single word of what I'd said. I became good friends with a Brazilian family who lived in Middlesbrough, and they said he'd just made everything up.

It wasn't the only time that interpreter put me in an embarrassing situation. Before my debut at home to Leeds in 1995, he translated everything that Robson had said for me, plus some instructions that were written on a board – the time we were all due to meet the next day, for example. He didn't say anything about a dress code, though.

Matchday came, and Bryan couldn't believe his eyes when we met on the stairs leading up to the players' lounge – I was wearing a denim jacket and trousers while everyone else was in a suit and tie. As soon as I entered the lounge and my team-mates saw me, everyone burst out laughing – I didn't have a f**king clue what was going on! It was as embarrassing as it was hilarious. Another time, I told the translator that I'd like to eat some beans – *feijão* in Portuguese – and he brought me a pheasant, which is called *faisão* back home.

As you can tell, the language barrier was difficult at first, so I took an intensive English course. On top of that, Jaime Moreno – a Bolivian player who was already at the club when I arrived – helped me a lot, and I learned Spanish and English. While I didn't pick up the language completely, I communicated with my team-mates through gestures in the dressing room. Both sides tried to make ourselves understood, and I got along with them after some persistence.

As everything was different to me and my family, we learned loads of things each day, lived a new life and only saw the positives of what was going on. We were quite happy with what we were experiencing, so I didn't care much about the bad weather. The cold could be a pain sometimes, but we were totally fine with our surroundings. All around town, people welcomed me with open arms and affection – wherever I went, they treated me like a king. When I first arrived, my house was just on a regular street, so people in the community would often come and ask me for autographs. From time to time, kids turned up playing football, so I'd join in and offer them tips.

I've always been a guy who prefers to stay at home, although I was single back then and liked to go out after matches. I knew a few good places, like Italian restaurants, and there was also a bowling alley in town that turned into a casino later on – I went there to have a bit of fun. I visited a few nearby towns such as Whitby, which is famous for its fish and chips, but something I regret not dedicating myself to was seeing historic places across the country. I'm quite interested in that sort of thing now, but back in the day I was still very young and a little bit ignorant! I found all that stuff pretty boring, but I honestly regret not doing more of it.

Robson played a major role in me settling relatively quickly too, and it was a pleasure to cross paths with him. His human side is the most remarkable characteristic of his personality. He's such a generous man that whenever he had to tell someone off, his lips started to

Above Helping Sao Paulo upset Milan.

tremble – aggressiveness isn't part of his make-up. It didn't mean that he wasn't a demanding manager, though. On the contrary: he never accepted anything less than 100 per cent from everyone and always wanted to play good football, which suited me perfectly. I liked English football from the start actually, because I had space. It was quick, for sure, but I knew how to position myself on the pitch so that I had plenty of room to play my game.

I always tried to think about what I'd do before getting the ball. As English football was so fast, thinking ahead of the defenders gave me an edge. With those great pitches, I only needed one touch to control the ball. I used that first season to adapt to the conditions and style of the league, and it paid off given that I stood out during the second season. My feet were inflamed for a period in the first year – perhaps because of the cold – and that hampered my game a little bit. I had to put newspaper in my boots to warm them up!

Boro had some good personalities in their team, including guys like Nigel Pearson who also played a key role in helping me to settle and understand the dynamics of our dressing room. He's a fantastic guy but was really tough, too. One day he headed the post and my mouth fell wide open – it was such a loud noise. He was crazy trying to head the ball in from so close to the goal, and my immediate thoughts were, 'When I get tackled by this guy, I'm f**ked'.

After coming 12th in 1995-96, Fabrizio Ravanelli and Emerson joined us in the summer. Those ambitious signings were already planned in the project that I was shown back in Brazil, and the impact they had on our team was clear. In the beginning, though, my partnership with Ravanelli was quite tense. He scored a hat-trick against Liverpool on the opening day of the season, but was mad because he felt I should have passed the ball to him on several occasions. We argued a lot on the pitch that day, and it continued in the dressing room. Emerson had to take my side, as I was at a disadvantage due to my size! Luckily for me, no fight happened. I wasn't jealous of Fabrizio at all – for me, the more top players we had, the better it would be for the team.

Robson had to call a meeting between the three of us. Ravanelli still didn't speak English, so he was arguing in Italian. I didn't speak it very well, but I could pick out the odd word – whenever I didn't like what he'd said, I confronted him in Bryan's room. Although it was tense, we cleared everything up and our partnership clicked after that.

Below Rocking up at the Riverside in his gigantic suit

Ravanelli was such a clever forward moving between the lines, which perfectly suited my playing style to carry the ball from midfield and wait for the right moment to assist him.

Arguments are a normal occurrence in football when they involve ambitious players, like both of us were. That's why I enjoyed working under Bryan so much – he brought in those characters who were so demanding with each other. No one wanted to lose a thing and we had a great team spirit. Even though that squad was very competitive, we let things go after every defeat and believed we could win the next game; that things could work out whenever we wanted.

Unfortunately, everyone remembers our match against Blackburn in December 1996. My English wasn't the best at that time, so I wasn't fully aware of what was happening. There seemed to be a bad illness spreading through the squad, but I wasn't affected. The club claimed that we wouldn't have enough players to play the game, so called it off. We never expected to be deducted three points because of that, though – which would ultimately lead to us suffering relegation. We needed to beat Leeds at Elland Road in our final game of the season, but could only draw 1-1. It wasn't enough to keep us up. I felt so bad for Boro because I knew what it meant to the town. By then I'd already become a true fan and couldn't hold in my tears – I was heartbroken.

Either side of that devastating day, we got to two cup finals. In April, we were moments away from lifting the League Cup at Wembley, but Emile Heskey equalised for Leicester late in extra time. In the dressing room, you wouldn't have known there would be a replay – we already felt like we had lost the second game at Hillsborough. Ten days later, Leicester won 1-0 after extra time.

The FA Cup final against Chelsea came too quickly after the massive setback of relegation. Unconsciously, it got in the way – we were really down the week before, then had to get ready for a final in such a sad atmosphere. We knew we had to forget everything else and focus on the final, but those bad results had a bad impact on the team. Roberto Di Matteo scored his brilliant goal after only 42 seconds, which didn't exactly help us much.

After that came my decision to leave Middlesbrough. I was still quite impulsive at 24 and didn't fully understand the big picture. I only have good things to say about Atletico Madrid, but with hindsight I might not have left Boro – or I could have tried something else like going on loan to another Premiership club. The 1998 World Cup was just around the corner, and I wanted to remain at the highest level possible to be an option for Brazil boss Mario Zagallo.

I was actually flying high with Atletico in the 1997-98 season when a serious injury – a broken fibula – wrecked my World Cup dreams in February. I managed to come back before the end of the season and play a few matches, but it was too late: I didn't make Zagallo's squad. When I didn't see my name on the list, it felt like I was injured all over again. I was destroyed inside.

Many things didn't go right for me in the year and a half after that. Shortly before the opportunity to return to Middlesbrough on loan for the 1999-2000 season arose, my confidence was very low and I wasn't getting along with Atletico coach Arrigo Sacchi. As soon as the chance to rejoin Boro cropped up, I didn't think twice. I needed to feel at home to boost my game, and Robson was there for me again – he showed me the affection I needed at that time.

To be honest, my second spell at the Riverside Stadium didn't go the way I expected it to. I wasn't in my ideal shape and didn't really click with the new squad that Bryan had assembled. We had Paul Ince and Paul Gascoigne, but I wasn't in a good moment. That's why Boro didn't use the option they had to buy me at the end of the season.

That feeling of unfinished business stayed with me. Two years later, the England team's assistant manager came calling once again. While Robson was Venables' No.2 when he spotted me in 1995, it was Steve McClaren – assistant to Sven-Goran Eriksson – who contacted me after England lost 2-1 to Brazil at the 2002 World Cup. I already knew that Atletico didn't want me back after my loan moves in Brazil with Vasco da Gama and Flamengo, so I accepted McClaren's offer. I felt that my career in England shouldn't be about failure and relegation.

Below Juninho was "treated like a king" by Boro fans

Above Emerson always had the Brazilian's back when Ravanelli rowed; but they soon cleared the air and clicked.

When I went back, I suffered a second serious injury straight away, but at least managed to play the last 10 matches of Boro's 2002-03 season. There was a more collective playing style than in my previous stints, and it seemed like McClaren didn't want me in the spotlight all the time. I noticed that the club had even changed the order in which the starting line-up was announced at the Riverside: before, I used to be last followed by a huge ovation, but that was no longer the case. McClaren had his own psychologist in the backroom staff, and I guess it was their decision to portray me as just one more player to underline the team spirit. But I can't deny that decision didn't upset me slightly.

Setting that aside, I believed that we could be champions – perhaps not of the Premiership, but I trusted our team to do well in the cups. We had high-profile players including Bolo Zenden, George Boateng and Gaizka Mendieta, and an incredible captain in Gareth Southgate. First and foremost, he's a fantastic person – a true gentleman. Second, he was an exceptional leader who managed to unite the group, and absolutely everyone respected him.

Despite not being at the same level as I was in my initial spell, I still scored at Highbury in the first leg of our 2004 League Cup semi-final victory over Arsenal. That was crucial in our campaign – just look at what our opposition did in the league that season.

The atmosphere in Cardiff for the final against Bolton was amazing – I got goosebumps as soon I stepped on the pitch. We were confident, and a more solid and experienced team compared to the other two finals I'd played in with the club. I was so glad about the result [a 2-1 win] and it was full of emotion – I was delighted to see Steve Gibson in the celebrations. We had to throw him in the air because of his belief in the project, as he had given us the conditions to achieve what we wanted – to play in Europe. I wanted to stay, but McClaren said I was free to look for another club. In other words, he was telling me, 'You can leave because you're not in my plans'. Boro ended up reaching the 2006 UEFA Cup Final and losing to Sevilla.

I remember saying back then that, regardless of the League Cup's relevance, winning it with Middlesbrough made me as happy as when I won the 2002 World Cup with Brazil. It was something very genuine – a challenge I accepted at the beginning of my career – and a dream come true to lift that trophy. For the giant clubs it may not mean as much, but for Boro it was our Champions League.

In this final note, I'd like to tell Boro fans that I feel like one of them – I still support the club and hope the team can get back on their perch again. I might not watch all their games, but I often look out for what's going on there and their results. They will always be in my heart after everything I went through on Teesside.

MICHAEL OWEN THE BOY WONDER

Years before Lionel Messi and Cristiano Ronaldo raised the award's profile forever, Michael Owen was crowned Europe's best player in 2001. He and Jamie Carragher talk FFT through his annus mirabilis, and ponder why he never got the credit he deserved.

Michael Owen has never been one to shout. At his absolute fresh-faced turn-of-the-century peak, there was no swagger, no smug look-at-me celebration – just the sense of someone going about his job to the best of his considerable ability, banging in goals for club and country.

In 2001, Owen was irresistible. He picked up six trophies that year: the FA Cup, League Cup and UEFA Cup treble, plus the Charity Shield and UEFA Super Cup – and then, just three days after turning 22, the Ballon d'Or. He remains the last Englishman to win the award.

The gong came on the back of 31 goals for a Liverpool side desperate to reinstate itself as a force domestically and in Europe. The bigger the game, the better he played. A highly intelligent footballer with brilliant movement, he could time his runs to perfection. He was also, despite his youthful stature, an absolute fiend to get off the ball.

Owen was blessed with a ruthlessness as well; a single-mindedness worthy of Roy Keane. Today, as he sits down to talk with *FourFourTwo*, the former marksman shrugs when we ask him for his memories of that incredible year. Despite all of the silverware, he rarely stopped to think about what he was accomplishing.

"To me, if you sit back and think about what you've just achieved, it's a weakness," says Owen. "To be very good, and consistently very good, you need to be greedy, and it has to become an obsession. It's not so much about the enjoyment of winning something. It's more about the pain of watching someone else take what should be yours."

That 2000-01 Liverpool vintage has somehow slipped through the cracks, lost between the white-suited Spice Boys era of the mid-90s and the dramatic triumph of Istanbul. Owen's old room-mate, Jamie Carragher, reckons the treble-winners were a much better team than the one that saw off Milan in the 2005 Champions League Final.

"It was definitely my favourite season," the ex-defender tells *FFT*. "If you win three cup competitions and also finish 3rd in the league, it means you won most of the games you played. And we did. That's probably the one team I look back at and think, 'I was playing with all my mates'. Michael was there, Robbie Fowler, Danny Murphy, Steven Gerrard, Didi Hamann, Jamie Redknapp – people I'm still close with now were in that team. Sharing those things together is special."

That particular Reds outfit wasn't the easiest on the eye. The path to victory was often built on frustrating the opposition and grinding out results. With Manchester United and Arsenal frequently operating on a completely different level to everyone else, Gerard Houllier's charges worked within their limitations, making the most of counter-attacking opportunities and a dogged team spirit. "We were a tough side, with a fantastic back four," recalls Owen. "Sami Hyypia, Stephane Henchoz, Carragher – they were like trojans in every single match they played. We had Hamann and Gerrard too, of course. We had guts, and no one played more games than we did that season. We played every game that was available to us, and that in itself is no mean achievement."

The first half of that mammoth 63-match campaign had been fairly humdrum, with little to suggest what was to come. Owen, unable to help England out of their Euro 2000 group, hit seven goals in his first six league appearances of the season, including a hat-trick against Aston Villa, but then scored only once in his next 13. A seven-month period from October to April brought him two Premier League goals.

Liverpool weren't pulling up any trees, either, losing to Ipswich and Middlesbrough in December. Then, something began to spark around the turn of the year. A lot of that was down to Owen clicking into gear. "In that season, with Owen, Fowler, Emile Heskey and Jari Litmanen, we possibly had the best set of strikers in the world," says Carragher. "Michael didn't really have a great first half of the season, but as soon as he got his form back, it was scary."

Owen actually didn't feature in the first of Liverpool's trophy wins that season: he was an unused substitute as Houllier started Heskey and Fowler in the League Cup final at Cardiff's Millennium Stadium. They eventually beat second-tier Birmingham in a penalty shootout.

But while Fowler started in Cardiff, he found himself falling down the Anfield pecking order. Houllier clearly preferred the pairing of Heskey and Owen. The Frenchman had been steadily building his team since arriving on Merseyside in July 1998, initially as joint-manager with Roy Evans. Like his countryman Arsene Wenger, Houllier was something of a footballing Anglophile, keen to marry a Gallic eye for detail with classic English strengths of teamwork, resilience and belief.

"He really dragged the club into this new era of how you look after yourself and prepare," explains Owen. "We were looking at Arsenal and they were mind-blowing. We were thinking, 'These buggers don't get injured, they run faster than us, they run longer than us, they're never resting players – what the hell are they doing?'

"Houllier was the first to introduce those ideas at Anfield. He could never tell Gerrard how to pass a ball, or me how to finish, or Carragher

Reebok

Above Owen took Roma apart on their own turf

Owen went into the game in peak form: in his previous two matches, he'd scored three goals against Newcastle, then two against Chelsea.

Liverpool faced a Gunners side above them in the league table, and Wenger's side dominated for the most part. Arsenal had three shots blocked on the line – one by Henchoz's hand, which went unnoticed by the match officials – and once Freddie Ljungberg had rounded Sander Westerveld to put Arsenal in front with 18 minutes remaining, time was rapidly running out for the Reds. Nobody was prepared for what happened next – except perhaps one man.

In the 83rd minute, McAllister launched a free-kick into the penalty area, Markus Babbel nodded the ball down and Owen found space in the crowd to fire in the equaliser. He looks back on that moment now with something approaching reverence; that it was meant to be, even when playing rope-a-dope in the blazing Welsh sun.

how to defend, but what he was really good at was judging players. Tactically he was very astute. He was good at motivating and getting us working as a unit. He was a very good leader of people."

After lifting the League Cup, it was full steam ahead on all fronts, with the UEFA Cup proving a particularly potent platform. The club sensed that it was back on the European stage once again, free from the long shadows cast by events at Heysel and subsequent ban from Europe. "The UEFA Cup was massive back then," continues Owen. "We played Barcelona, Roma, Porto, Olympiakos – and that's before we got to the final. It was a really difficult competition to win."

Owen had scored twice against Fabio Capello's in-form Roma at the Stadio Olimpico in February. Liverpool's quarter-final tie against Porto began with a goalless draw in Portugal, but two quick first-half goals at Anfield from Murphy and Owen, heading in a Gerrard corner, gave Liverpool a comfortable lead that they protected without much grief.

Barcelona awaited in the semis, live on the BBC. Incredibly, kick-off for the first leg at the Camp Nou was put back to 8.10pm at the Beeb's request, to avoid clashing with *EastEnders* and the revelation of who shot Phil Mitchell. Presumably all of Barcelona wanted to find out, too.

But there was little drama on offer in Catalonia as the Reds defended in numbers to thwart a Barça side featuring Rivaldo, Luis Enrique, Pep Guardiola and Frank de Boer. The return leg brought a famous victory, with 36-year-old Gary McAllister scoring the only goal from the penalty spot following a Patrick Kluivert handball. It was to be Liverpool's first European final in 16 years. "We could always take big scalps," smiles Carragher. "That was the great thing about that team – we may not have been the best, but we could beat the best."

They were also repeating the trick domestically, working their way to the FA Cup final against Arsenal, back at the Millennium Stadium.

"ALL I THOUGHT WAS, 'IS THERE TIME FOR A WINNER?' IT WASN'T 'IF', IT WAS 'WHEN'"

"Once I scored that first goal, I jogged back to the halfway line and this feeling came over me: I just knew," he reveals. "It was like the Ali fight when Foreman was smacking him on the ropes and it seemed impossible, but suddenly, one punch and I knew that Arsenal were gone. They were gone. The only question in my mind was, 'Have I got enough time to score before the final whistle goes?' It wasn't 'if', it was 'when'. I'd never had that feeling before, and I've never felt it since."

Was there time for a winner? Barely five minutes later, Owen had his answer. He latched onto a long pass from Patrik Berger, shrugging off Lee Dixon, before one touch took him away from Tony Adams. On his weaker foot, Owen coolly dispatched a shot into the small goal-bound gap just beyond David Seaman's outstretched left hand. Michael Owen had won the FA Cup. The forward-flip goal celebration; the screaming, wide-eyed delight; the mayhem in the stands – it all belonged to him.

"It was such a magical day," he says. "It's funny: good things happen and you get caught up in the joy of winning for your team-mates and fans. There's nothing bad about it when you have a day like that."

Days were becoming a precious commodity at Liverpool. They had only three of them between the FA Cup showpiece in Cardiff and their third final of the campaign, against Alaves in the UEFA Cup. The club from Vitoria-Gasteiz, capital city of the Basque Country, were the big surprise package of the season: they had triumphed 2-0 at the San Siro against an Inter team boasting Christian Vieri and Clarence Seedorf, before shellacking Kaiserslautern 9-2 on aggregate in the semi-finals.

Although Liverpool's players were now feeling the strains of a long season, they were quickly 2-0 up in Dortmund thanks to Babbel and Gerrard. Alaves pulled a goal back, but Owen tumbled in the box and McAllister converted the penalty. Houllier's side led 3-1 at the interval.

"I always remember coming into the dressing room, looking around and almost giggling," Owen admits to *FFT*. "Some of us were thinking, 'How good is this? It's almost a gimme'. You're expecting the final to be hard, and at half-time I was thinking that they were so easy to beat. Never, ever have I been so wrong. We almost blew it."

Six minutes into the second half, the score was 3-3. Liverpool's solid defence was suddenly a shambles. Fowler put them back in front, only for Jordi Cruyff to glance home another Alaves equaliser in the final minute of normal time. "On the way to the final, everyone was saying we were boring – lots of 0-0s and 1-0s – and then it all just went mad in the final!" recalls Carragher with a laugh.

In the end, Liverpool and Owen were able to complete their treble. Alaves had two men sent off in extra time, then Delfi Geli's own goal gave the Reds a dramatic 5-4 win via the short-lived golden goal rule. It was the club's first European trophy since Rome in 1984.

"It was where the club needed to be," explains Owen. "It was such a buzz. The fans were amazing – it felt like we'd taken a million of them to Dortmund." It was also an important moment for Houllier. "He was desperate to win the UEFA Cup, to put us back on the European map," adds Owen. "He understood the club's history and values."

After two knackering cup finals, there was still a final Premier League match to play in May. Win at Charlton, and Liverpool would be in the Champions League for the first time, back in Europe's elite competition for the first time since that fateful night at Heysel.

Three days after the UEFA Cup final, Liverpool emerged 4-0 victors at The Valley. Owen set up Murphy to net the third, and scored the fourth himself. The Reds had come 3rd in the table, 11 points off champions Manchester United but down from 24 the previous campaign. "We'd won all those trophies that season and went away that summer proud as punch," says Owen. "We just needed one or two more

Below An FA Cup winner, having turned the final on its head at the last gasp

Above Winning the penalty for old man McAllister to convert in the UEFA Cup final

players to get a bit better. We wanted to win the league with Liverpool so much. Me and Carra used to speak about it all the time. The desire within us was almost unbearable."

Owen had the same desire to achieve something with England. With the summer over, and the 2001-02 season only one month old, the national team travelled to Munich to take on Germany in a World Cup qualifier. Trailing to a sixth-minute Carsten Jancker goal, Sven-Goran Eriksson's men were soon back on level terms, with Owen finding the empty net after Nick Barmby had beaten Oliver Kahn to a high ball. Gerrard put England in front and then Owen ran riot, lashing a strike past a flat-footed Kahn before charging clear to wrap up his hat-trick. It confirmed the 21-year-old as Europe's most dangerous marksman.

In December came recognition of that fact, as Owen was named the winner of the 2001 Ballon d'Or. He received a total of 176 votes from a panel of sports journalists across UEFA's member countries. Raul was second with 140 votes, Kahn third with 114 and David Beckham fourth with 102. Francesco Totti, Luis Figo, Rivaldo, Andriy Shevchenko, Thierry Henry and Zinedine Zidane filled out the top 10, but none of them received even a third of Owen's total votes.

Owen may not have been able to call himself the best player in the world – only in 2007 did the Ballon d'Or become a global award – but he could officially proclaim himself the best player in Europe. He was only the fourth Englishman to receive the honour and the first since Kevin Keegan, a back-to-back winner with Hamburg in 1978 and '79.

Back in 2001, however, there was very little fanfare about Owen's prestigious achievement. In England, the cult of the individual had yet to take hold. Lionel Messi and Cristiano Ronaldo had yet to emerge. Owen wasn't even presented with the award at Anfield until April, on the pitch a few minutes before a run-of-the-mill 2-0 win over Derby. Owen scored twice that day, but that was as far as the celebrations went. No gala ceremony. No garish designer tux.

"I believe I don't get the sort of credit that other people would get for winning the Ballon d'Or," Owen admits today. "It's never been that important in our country. When I was in Spain, they said I was a hero for winning it. I'm immensely proud of winning it. I look down the list of names, and I still have it saved on my phone – a photo of the points system and who was second, third, fourth and the rest of it.

"You look at that list and it's awe-inspiring. That's all I ever wanted as a kid. I didn't just want to be a footballer; I wanted to be the best footballer. Winning it feels better now than it did when I was playing. You're 22 – it's just another trophy, and now I've got to win it again."

He never did, of course. Injuries, bad luck and Liverpool's below-par signings didn't help, as finishing runners-up to Arsenal in 2001-02 was followed by a slide down the table. "We brought in El Hadji Diouf, Salif Diao and Bruno Cheyrou – guys who were expected to propel us, and it just went totally the opposite way," says Carragher.

Owen and his team-mates struggled to push on from that cup treble of 2000-01 and Houllier eventually departed in 2004, having appeared to run out of ideas. When the chance of a fresh start presented itself to Owen that summer – and at Real Madrid, no less – the 24-year-old was ready to listen.

"The last thing I thought was that I was going to leave Liverpool," says Owen. "We were on a pre-season tour in America and my agent phoned me while I was in my room with Carragher, who got wind of what we were talking about. I put down the phone and he said, 'Pffft, don't go. They've got Raul, Ronaldo and Fernando Morientes – you won't get a game!' I was 50-50, but I just had this overriding feeling towards it – and I'm blaming Ian Rush, actually! I thought, 'If I do go, then I've already played for Liverpool for a long time and, hopefully, I could always come back, so just go and sample it – the Galacticos; that white kit, where everyone prances out like an angel; that amazing stadium; a different culture'.

"Eventually I agreed. But do you know when you sign something and think there's no going back? When you think, 'Oh my God, what have I done?' I remember crying my eyes out as I went off to the airport, thinking, 'What am I leaving behind?'"

Owen stops short of using the word 'regret', but leaving Liverpool still weighs heavily on him – as does the rather mixed opinions of some on the Anfield terraces towards their former player. His fine international career possibly didn't help, never quite shaking the sense that he was England's Michael Owen rather than Liverpool's Michael Owen. Nor did that squeaky-clean image, with all of the rough edges smoothed out by PR firms and agents.

John Gibbons, of Liverpool fan site and podcast *The Anfield Wrap*, thinks that it's probably down to sheer numbers – that, and signing for Manchester United in 2009.

"We've always been spoilt for strikers," says Gibbons. "We've found it a lot more difficult to find a decent left-back over the past 20 years than a centre-forward. That allows people to discard Michael Owen too easily. Robbie Fowler was more loved, but Owen was brilliant for Liverpool. He would always put so much into it when he was on the pitch. You could tell that he was desperate to win.

"I can understand why he gets so frustrated, because he probably sees players spoken of a lot more fondly when they didn't put in half the work he did. A lot of it is about what happened afterwards. Going to Real Madrid didn't go down very well, then when he came back to England and joined Newcastle, it was a surprise. But it was signing for Manchester United that really severed all ties."

Carragher believes his former room-mate's heroics of 2001 should place him alongside the Anfield greats; that he should get more love from the club's fanbase. "I think in time that will come," he suggests.

While Virgil van Dijk came close to getting his hands on the trophy in 2019, finishing runner-up to Lionel Messi, and Mo Salah may fancy his chances in the future, for all of their legends, for all of the club's European glory, only one player has ever bagged the Ballon d'Or while playing for Liverpool. Michael Owen.

Below Owen had mixed emotions about his move to Madrid

CARLING
ARSENAL

DENNIS BERGKAMP THE DUTCH MASTER

It almost started with a scuffle at a petrol station, but ended with a statue. In 2020, 25 years on from his Highbury arrival, FFT spoke to the Arsenal legend who transformed a club forever.

Dennis Bergkamp is smiling, as he remembers Clacket Lane services on the M25.

Just the merest mention of his visit, and the Dutchman is already getting flashbacks to the summer of 1995. "It was unbelievable..." explains Bergkamp, chuckling as he chats to *FourFourTwo*.

He isn't talking about the service station's facilities, as impressive as they undoubtedly were 25 years ago. He's talking about the moment when fate intervened – the moment he knew his Arsenal career was bound for glory.

A day earlier, Bergkamp had completed a £7.5 million deal to join the Gunners, following an unhappy spell at Inter in Serie A. Driving back home to the Netherlands from North London, he unwittingly took a much longer route than planned, ending up on the southern section of the M25 motorway.

Briefly stopping to fill up his BMW at Clacket Lane, just south of Croydon, he noticed the man behind him in the queue growing ever more agitated, frustrated that this rookie to the world of British petrol stations had parked in a position that blocked others from accessing the next pump. Eventually, the angry man jumped out of his car. It was Ian Wright.

The pair had never met. Soon realising it was Bergkamp stood in front of him, a suddenly joyous Wright sprinted over to give his new strike partner a hug.

"I've spoken to Ian about it a few times since, and it's ridiculous that we could have met in that petrol station, at that service station," says Bergkamp now. "How many people are there in London – about 15 or 16 million?! But you meet up on the day after you sign the contract for Arsenal, in the summer holidays – it was absolutely crazy. If that's not a sign, I don't know what is."

The duo would go on to form one of the best double acts of the '90s. Together, they would propel Arsenal to Premier League title glory, but Bergkamp had only just begun.

The Dutchman would prove the defining player of a sublime era for the club; the star who did more than anyone to transform the Gunners from the dour outfit that struggled through the final Premier League years of George Graham, to one of the greatest attacking teams of modern history. Along the way, he scored beautiful goals for both club and country. Few footballers could paint pictures on a football pitch quite like Dennis Bergkamp.

DENNIS THE LION TAMER

For Bergkamp, British football has always meant something special. Born in May 1969, he was named after the top scorer of that season's European Cup: Manchester United forward Denis Law. As a teenager, he idolised the poise and technique of Glenn Hoddle.

He had to wait until the age of 23 for his first senior appearance in England. That night, the Netherlands travelled to Wembley for a 1994 World Cup qualifier. The Oranje were third in the group, having played a game more than both Norway and Graham Taylor's England. Within half an hour, they were 2-0 down and in big trouble.

Then Bergkamp changed the course of history. Jan Wouters dinked a pass to the edge of the penalty area, and his colleague needed just one touch on the volley – the subtlest of lobs to lift the ball over Chris Woods and into the net. The Dutch fought back to draw 2-2 thanks to a late Peter van Vossen spot-kick, and England's campaign unravelled.

Six months on, Bergkamp would put an end to the Three Lions' World Cup hopes, netting the Netherlands' second goal in a 2-0 Rotterdam win. The Dutch would accompany Norway to USA 94.

"I always had a connection with England, so you could understand that those games were very special to me," Bergkamp says now. "When I was a kid, I admired English football. Once a week, I'd watch highlights from the English league on television. Those qualifiers were special moments. I was more motivated, more intense."

Just as Marco van Basten was succumbing to injury, Bergkamp was emerging as the Netherlands' new main man. As a youngster, he had learned from the greatest of them all: Johan Cruyff.

"I first met Johan when I was in Ajax's youth team," says Bergkamp, thinking back to that moment aged 12, after Cruyff had returned for a second spell as a player. "He was with the first team, but sometimes he'd come over to the academy and coach part of a training session. I remember he did that for our age group – he turned up and did a few exercises, we'd all follow him and copy, then he went again. He left an amazing impression on everyone.

"He was the first-team manager when I was 17, and took me from the youth team to make my professional debut in December 1986. He was like a connection throughout my career, and in Holland we call it a red thread. We'd always meet up – it could be a month apart or four years apart, but we'd always have contact."

In his first season, Bergkamp was a substitute in the European Cup

Winners' Cup final as Ajax beat Lokomotive Leipzig. Cruyff left midway through the next campaign but Bergkamp came off the bench again in the Cup Winners' Cup final, where this time Ajax lost to Mechelen.

A finisher as much as a provider in those early days, he topped the Eredivisie scoring chart in three straight seasons at the start of the '90s – netting a career-high 33 goals in all competitions in 1992-93, a year after winning the UEFA Cup. Bergkamp also scored three times in four matches at Euro 92, sharing the Golden Boot with Karl-Heinz Riedle, Tomas Brolin and Danish midfielder Henrik Larsen.

In the summer of 1993, a couple of months after that goal against England at Wembley, it was time for Bergkamp to take the next step in his career. As he made a decision over his future, he spoke to Cruyff – then in charge of Barcelona.

"Funnily enough, he never asked me to join him," reveals Bergkamp. "But he had a certain way of speaking like, 'All right, why would you go to that team or that team? That club isn't good enough, and the other will give you these problems'. He never actually asked me to join Barça, but of course I knew that he wanted me to go there!

"In those years, though, you were only allowed four foreigners and only three could play at one time. I remember Ronald Koeman, Romario and Hristo Stoichkov were there. Big names. I wanted to make a name for myself, and I always wanted to go to Italy, so I decided to join Inter."

Below "I always had a connection with England, so games against them were very special to me"

In 1993, Bergkamp would finish second in the Ballon d'Or and third in the FIFA World Player of the Year votes, having been third in the Ballon d'Or 12 months earlier. However, his move to Inter didn't go as planned.

Bergkamp joined the Nerazzurri after promises that they were planning to implement a new attacking style. Those plans were soon shelved and they plummeted to 13th in Serie A, avoiding an unthinkable relegation by a point.

"At Ajax there were a lot of young players – I wouldn't say it was like a playground, but it was based more on technique and having fun," continues Bergkamp. "As a striker, you'd have five or six chances to score in a game. But then you have to make the next step, and Italy was the total opposite of what I was used to. As a striker, you'd only have one chance a game and you had to make sure you scored, because there was a lot of pressure on you.

"If I hadn't moved to Inter, I wouldn't have become the player I was in England, because it was a learning experience. Sometimes in Italy, though, I saw football as going to work. You'd turn up at 9am and go home at 5pm. It was more intense – much more was expected. It was more serious, much bigger than the Dutch league.

"My wife and I had recently got married, so privately our two years in Italy were like an extended honeymoon, but in football it was work sometimes, battling hard to get some acknowledgement."

Bergkamp netted just eight times in his first Serie A season, although he scored eight more to become joint-top scorer in the UEFA Cup where the matches were more open. Inter went all the way

Arsenal
CHAMPIONS 2001-

– seeing off Norwich en route to the final against Austria Salzburg – and Bergkamp collected a third European trophy at the age of 25.

But that wasn't enough to convince everyone at San Siro, and his second campaign delivered a paltry four goals. His relationship with coach Ottavio Bianchi deteriorated, and even the journeys to and from away games added to the Dutchman's stress. Inter often travelled in small propellor planes, and Bergkamp became ever more scared of flying after a series of uncomfortable trips.

"It was a psychological thing that grew on me, to the point where it was interfering with my football," he says. "For away matches, I was focusing on the journey after the game more than the game itself."

In the summer of 1995, Bergkamp made two significant decisions. After meeting up with the national team ahead of a Euro 96 qualifier in Belarus, then realising he couldn't face the flight to Minsk, he pulled out of the trip and decided his flying days were over. "I didn't want to do it any more," he tells *FFT*. "It was a difficult decision, but it made me a better player and better person. I could leave it behind. Yes, I missed one or two games that I didn't want to, but mentally I was free to be a better player. It helped me."

He also decided to leave Inter. "At the end of the second season, my agent asked the club what their intentions were for the next year," he explains. "A lot of promises had been made but they hadn't followed up on them, so again we asked some questions about the squad and manager. They couldn't give us any straight answers, so both parties agreed, 'Let's move on'. That was very late, May or June, and then we had to focus on finding a new club really quickly. I said straight away that I wanted to go to England."

He wasn't short of options. "I think my agent mentioned there were three or four clubs in England," reveals Bergkamp. "I'm not sure if one was Manchester United, or if in London there were one or two – maybe even Tottenham, I don't know."

It was Arsenal, though, who grabbed his attention. He had already been intrigued by an article he read about the club in Dutch magazine *Voetbal International*. "Arsenal had won the Cup Winners'

Cup around that time and there were a lot of stories about them, which I'd been digging into," he recalls. His agent had connections with the club, too, after fellow countryman Glenn Helder moved to Highbury from Vitesse Arnhem months earlier. "Arsenal contacted my agent, and I spoke to David Dein and Bruce Rioch on the phone. They told me their plans and I had a good feeling about it. That was within one week of deciding to leave Inter, so there was no room for other teams any more. That's the way I work – when I make a decision, I stick to it."

NOT BAD FOR A CARLOS KICKABALL

Arsenal may have lifted the Cup Winners' Cup after victory over Parma in 1994, but Bergkamp was arriving at a difficult moment for the club. League form had tailed off badly after their last title triumph in 1991: they came 10th in 1992-93, when they were the lowest scorers in the entire division, then 12th in 1994-95. George Graham had been sacked in February 1995, after receiving a payment from an agent. The team had reached a second successive Cup Winners' Cup final, before being embarrassed by Nayim from the halfway line against Real Zaragoza. Rioch arrived that summer, with plans to transform the Gunners' style.

"It was some sort of a gamble, but it turned out well," the Dutchman says of his decision to join. "I didn't really know about 'boring Arsenal' when I signed – I only heard that throughout my first couple of years at the club, when people told me about it.

"They had the intention to build something around me, and to play attacking, attractive football. They lived up to their promises. I wanted to change something in the team. That was the reason I went to Inter, and that was the reason I went to Arsenal, too – to play my own part in that philosophy."

"IF I HADN'T MOVED TO INTER, I WOULDN'T HAVE BECOME THE PLAYER I WAS IN ENGLAND. IT WAS A LEARNING EXPERIENCE"

But his first seven games for the club didn't produce a goal. Unable to find the net in a League Cup tie at fourth-tier strugglers Hartlepool, one national newspaper called him a 'Hartle-Fool' on their back page. Spurs chairman Alan Sugar made pointed remarks about big-money overseas signings, dubbing them "Carlos Kickaballs", and Stuart Pearce suggested that Arsenal should have bought Stan Collymore instead.

Thankfully, most of the criticism passed Bergkamp by. "Me and my wife were in a hotel, Sopwell House, and she was pregnant which was another step in our lives," he says. "We were in the hotel, sometimes desperate to make our own food, because after several weeks you're fed up with the hotel menu!

"We never noticed that the papers were writing that stuff. My main focus was to do well for the club and my new team-mates. They were expecting me to score and make a difference. I thought those first few games went OK, but that wasn't good enough. It was only after six or seven that I heard there was some talk about me. I think other players and managers had a go at me – even chairmen from other clubs, who said I was just coming to collect my money and then disappear again. I only realised that after one or two months, so maybe it was for the best or it would have been more difficult. I knew I had to improve, even though it wasn't that bad at the start. But once I scored, it was a relief for many people – including myself."

Bergkamp broke his duck at home to Southampton on September 23 with two goals in a 4-2 win: the first an expertly-controlled volley, the second a sensational strike from outside the box. He scored 16 times that campaign, guiding Arsenal back into Europe thanks to a stunning late winner in the final match of the season.

Left Despite UEFA Cup glory, his Inter career didn't take off

But days before 1996-97 got underway, Rioch was sacked following a breakdown of his relationship with the board. "When Bruce was fired, that was a strange time for me," admits Bergkamp. "A year earlier, I'd joined Arsenal based on the plans they had. Now I was thinking, 'OK, what's this? Is it going another way? Is it some sort of Italian approach again, promising things but not doing them?'

"But soon enough, I heard that Arsene Wenger was going to become the manager. When I played at Ajax, there were only two teams in the world who played a 4-3-3 formation – one was Ajax and the other was Monaco, where Arsene was the manager. So I thought, 'This actually might turn out all right – he's got an attacking philosophy which could suit my game'. Then he came in and started talking to all the players. I understood what his approach to the game was, and we were on the same level from day one."

Wenger also got the best out of Wright at Highbury. "Our partnership worked," says Bergkamp. "We could learn from each other, on and off the pitch, and it seemed to help us both reach a higher level. I learned a lot from the English guys like Ian, and they were eager to learn from my philosophy of the game – they used to mention that many times. It all came together."

"MY FAVOURITE? THE ARGENTINA GOAL"

In 1997-98, Bergkamp and Wright fired Arsenal to the Premier League title. Bergkamp scored 22 goals, his best tally in English football. That August, he became the only player ever to have finished first, second and third in the same BBC Goal of the Month competition. One came at Southampton, the other two on a remarkable evening at Leicester, when he bagged all three in a 3-3 draw. Foxes manager Martin O'Neill described it as "the best hat-trick I've ever seen".

After a curling effort from outside the box, then a dinked finish which looped off goalkeeper Kasey Keller and just underneath the crossbar, his treble was completed in the 92nd minute. Brilliantly pulling David Platt's ball from the sky with the outside of his right boot, Bergkamp instantly flicked it past Matt Elliott with his second touch, then coolly side-footed into the far corner with his third. All of it was delivered in one breathtaking moment.

"I knew I could do those sorts of things," he says. "Everyone I played with knows what kind of level was reached in training sessions, and it all came together against Leicester. The first goal was special because that was a trademark of mine, curling the ball into the far corner. The second had a little bit of luck, but the third goal was so satisfying, as it's something you've got in your mind. You want to do that move, go to the goal and score.

"It was very similar to my last-minute goal against Argentina at the World Cup. The ball is coming from a long way behind you, and in that one or two seconds you decide what you're going to do. If it all comes together, that's so satisfying."

Indeed, it was striking just how alike that winner against Argentina was, in the France 98 quarter-finals, ten months later.

"You practise five or six times a week for those moments," he adds. "You know you can control the ball, have a good first touch, another touch and finish, but it's a matter of doing it at the highest level. All of those little fragments have to come together."

Given the magnitude of the match, that stunner to down Argentina is his favourite goal. "I'd say so, as it was on the world stage," he says. It also took him past Faas Wilkes as his country's all-time top scorer. "It was amazing – a quarter-final against a team like Argentina, then making history. You still see the goal a lot. I can only be proud of that."

In that season ahead of the World Cup, Bergkamp had been voted Premier League player of the year by both the PFA and Football Writers' Association – finishing third again in the FIFA World Player of the Year poll, this time jointly with Zinedine Zidane. Like Zidane, he played the game with an incredible beauty, honed from an early age.

"I spent hours playing on the streets and always admired a certain way of playing," he says. "The way I moved, the way I controlled balls and my technique probably made it look beautiful. You've got to have elegant players, and some who play a different way with more tackles, working hard. That's nice to see, too. Beauty was more my style, but it wasn't that I didn't want to make ugly goals or bad tackles."

Bergkamp could certainly stick up for himself when required: he was sent off four times during his time at Arsenal. "I learned especially in England to defend myself, because it's a very physical game," he says. "You can moan and complain about it, but you can also do something about it yourself. Sometimes it looked a bit silly and wasn't the right way to do it, but you have the mentality that you want to win, and that could all go down to one battle with a player who wants to take the ball away from you. The mentality kicks in and says, 'OK, I don't want that', and sometimes you do mad things. But I could handle myself."

"OF COURSE HE F**KING MEANT IT"

After Ian Wright, came Thierry Henry. Bergkamp had suffered the pain of missing an FA Cup semi-final replay penalty in 1999, before Ryan Giggs' solo goal put Manchester United firmly on course for the Treble. Months later, Henry arrived and another formidable strike partnership was formed. While Bergkamp was once the main goalscorer at Ajax, he was largely content to supply at Arsenal.

"I enjoyed trying to provide for the other striker, to make you strong as a couple," he says. "It suited my game and it suited theirs – most of the time they were the finisher and I was the one preparing the goal. I could adjust myself to many different players. Thierry was probably the most complete player I ever played with – you can't really say that he had some flaws, or something he wasn't very good at. He also had a super mentality. He was a winner."

Bergkamp brought an end to his international career after Euro 2000, to focus on club football. In any case, travelling to the 2002 World Cup in Japan and South Korea would have been impossible without flying.

He rarely featured in European away games for the Gunners, having agreed when he signed that he wouldn't be required to fly. Sometimes they missed him – Arsenal's Champions League form was often not as impressive as their league form, but when possible he would travel to matches in Western Europe by car.

"I'd go with my wife and her father," reveals Bergkamp. "He did the driving, so it really wasn't an issue. I was used to road trips from when I was 18, and I enjoyed it. It meant that I could go to the games and

Above "Now you see me, Nikos..."

play – I had to cover a few more miles than the rest of the squad, but they were good memories."

For the 2000 UEFA Cup Final against Galatasaray, he ventured as far as Copenhagen: a 16-hour drive from North London. Sadly his journey didn't end in victory, as the Turks won 4-1 on penalties. But Bergkamp would lift the FA Cup four times, and a second Premier League triumph came after another moment of genius.

Earlier in that 2001-02 campaign, Bergkamp had memorably helped Arsenal beat Juventus in the Champions League, twisting and turning to provide a sublime assist for Freddie Ljungberg at Highbury. But the Gunners sat third in the Premier League in early March, ahead of a key fixture at second-placed Newcastle. Eleven minutes in, Robert Pires fed Bergkamp on the edge of the box, and the Dutchman scored what was later voted as the Premier League's greatest goal.

Collecting the ball with his back to goal, Bergkamp brilliantly flicked it around one side of Nikos Dabizas, pirouetted past the Greek defender on the other, then coolly stroked it past Shay Given's despairing dive. So seemingly impossible was the move to pull off, a debate has raged ever since about whether he actually meant to score in the way he did. "I saw Dennis do stuff like that in training – of course he f**king meant it," was Ian Wright's blunt assessment.

"The week after that goal, 'Did you really mean it?' was the question everyone was asking me," chuckles Bergkamp. "I couldn't understand what people meant by the question. I didn't see the goal on television for several days, and so many people were asking me that I thought, 'OK, I have to see what they saw'. I watched it back, and then I could understand what they meant. The pass from Pires was slightly behind me and I was adjusting myself to the situation, because I wanted to go through on goal with one touch. I touched the ball, but my body was already turning the other way, so it looked quite good! For many goals, players just decide at the last moment what they're going to do. That was the same with me. I'm glad it looked like that, and that everyone is still talking about it today."

Arsenal won 2-0 at St James' Park that night, ending the season with a further ten consecutive victories to overhaul Manchester United and claim the title. Two seasons later, Bergkamp was involved in one of the most remarkable teams in Premier League history.

There had been speculation about the Dutchman's future ahead of the Invincibles campaign: out of contract, the 34-year-old only agreed a new deal just three weeks before the start of the 2003-04 season. He insists, though, that he had no intention of leaving.

"In my mind, never," he says. "I decided very soon into my Arsenal career that I'd like to finish in football there. I always had in my mind that 33 or 34 would be the end of my career – it was actually 37, which shows what a great time I had.

"In that final period of my career, my contract was extended by one year maybe two or three times. Before the Invincibles season, that was maybe the biggest battle with the board to get my contract extended, because at a certain age you have to take a pay cut and won't play as often. But I always took care of my body and knew I had a few years left in me; that I could be important for the team. I must admit, when you have such a good time it's hard to battle with people you respect, but you do it for yourself and your future. In the end, though, we both made the right decision."

Bergkamp treasures every moment of the unbeaten Premier League campaign that followed.

"The word says it all – invincible," he smiles. "You felt like that going onto the pitch. You knew you were going to win – it was just a matter of how, and by how many goals. You'd look around the dressing room and think, 'Jeez, what a team'. We were better than our opponents in every single area.

"We were all friends, too. We'd go to dinner with six or seven players, or meet up at someone's house with the wives and girlfriends. Maybe you need to be a team of friends to be successful. It was a great time and it went down in history. It's hard to beat – there have been some fantastic teams since then, quite recently with Manchester City and Liverpool, and they find it really difficult to do what we did. Every year, it makes me more proud. It was a tremendous achievement."

THE LAST TANGO IN PARIS

The 2005-06 campaign would be Bergkamp's final season. Fittingly, his last goal arrived in an April fixture designated 'Dennis Bergkamp Day'. Supporters wore special T-shirts and a number of Ajax fans were in attendance, as the veteran came on as a substitute and found the net against West Bromwich Albion.

"A few months ago, I saw it again with my family because we read that 'so many years ago today, it was Dennis Bergkamp Day'," he says. "We discussed it and I only realised then, 'Oh, it's quite amazing that I scored my last goal that day!' It's special to put that down in history."

His last appearance came in the Gunners' final match at Highbury, against Wigan – but he would have loved to sign off in the Champions League final against Barcelona, even if he had only played a small role in that European campaign.

"I didn't play a lot that season because my Achilles were worn down, so physically it was difficult," he admits. "I spoke to Arsene before the Champions League final and he said, 'I'm not playing you in the game, but obviously I want you to come with us – you're in the squad'. I knew I wasn't going to play, so it was respectful of him to tell me. It was like, 'I know in those years that we've grown as a club, you've played a big part in it, and now here we are on the biggest stage in club football'. Arsene more or less said, 'Maybe we owe you to play in this game, but I just can't do it'. I truly respected that and I understood, because of course others would start in Paris.

"I was only hoping to come on and maybe make a difference in my last game, but that went down the drain after 20 minutes when Jens Lehmann got sent off, and then it was a very different game. I'm sure Arsene had it in his mind to put me on at the end if everything was OK, but after the red card it didn't work. I was so happy for the club to get to that stage, though. I knew I'd helped to develop the team."

Bergkamp's immense contribution would be recognised again, when Arsenal opened the Emirates Stadium by playing Ajax in a testimonial for the Dutchman. A few years further down the line, a letter arrived. Another significant honour was about to come his way.

"I knew I'd done something for the club, that the respect had been there from day one, but when I got a letter asking if it was OK – if I'd agree! – to have a statue outside the Emirates, I couldn't believe what was happening," he says, laughing at the politeness of the request to immortalise him. He was never likely to object.

"It was an amazing gesture, something for the big names at a club. I was part of Highbury for 11 years, but to still be part of the Emirates as well is fantastic, and shows how much Arsenal think I contributed in their history. It's one of my biggest achievements."

Bergkamp returned to his old club Ajax in 2008, remaining on their coaching staff for nine years before departing in December 2017 when the Eredivisie side decided to make changes.

He admits he would consider returning to England. "When the time is right, I'd love to go back and get a role somewhere," he reveals. "At the moment we're great in Holland. I've got a young family and have been out of coaching for a little while now. But I must admit, I have the urge to go on the pitch again and help, whether it's with the technical or coaching staff. It might be a bit too early, but you never know. We'll see what comes my way."

Have Arsenal ever mentioned a return? "At the moment there hasn't been any contact about that, but as soon as I make my decision, let's see what happens," he says. "Of course it would be ideal at Arsenal, as I spent 11 years there and have a good feeling with the club."

Given that Thierry Henry and Patrick Vieira have both managed, with Montreal Impact and Nice at the time of the interview, does he dream of going back to the club with one of his old team-mates some day? "I follow how they're doing from afar," says Bergkamp. "It's a shame that MLS stopped after Thierry took a job there, and Patrick is doing well at Nice.

"I'm really interested in Mikel Arteta and how he's doing at Arsenal, as there have been signs that he wants to change their philosophy. It looked good in the few matches I watched earlier in the year. But my future, who knows? In football, one day is not the same as the other."

Whether he ever returns to North London or not, his Arsenal legacy is secure. Just as he intended when he first arrived at Highbury in 1995, Bergkamp guided the Gunners into an era of success and transformed their style of play into one admired around the world.

"That's probably the one thing I'm unbelievably proud of, because it says you were important for a long period," he reflects. "You don't change a team or philosophy in a year or two. I was there for 11, and even now, people see Arsenal as an attacking team – definitely nowhere near a boring team. I believe I helped to change that.

"When I finished my career, the biggest compliment I received was from Bob Wilson. He said, 'Just remember one thing, Dennis – you were the one who changed this team, this club and this philosophy'. He was someone who had played a big part at Arsenal previously, and coming from him it was quite special. Even after all the moments, the trophies and the goals, that was one of the biggest compliments anyone could have given me. It made me realise 'OK, I've done something right'."

Right Dennis' testimonial in 2006 was the first match at the Emirates

Fly Emirates
Fly Emirates
Fly Emirates
Arsenal

CARLING
asics
McEWAN'S
LAGER

ALAN SHEARER GEORDIE BOY

Alan Shearer has topped the Premier League goal chart for 28 years, despite three major injuries and four seasons in the old First Division. Even then, his record may never be broken – but how? *FFT* salutes a scoring phenomenon

On December 18, 1993, a seven-yard toe-punt extended Blackburn's lead over Manchester City. This marked the last time Teddy Sheringham, or anybody else, had the most goals in the nascent Premier League era – an era then encompassing 16 months. That afternoon, and every day for over 28 years hence, Top Premier League Goalscorer was the sole domain of Alan Shearer.

In 2023 , despite his 260 Premier League strikes for Rovers and Newcastle remaining an unfeasibly high benchmark for imitators, Shearer's goalscoring record is unfairly normalised in our collective consciousness. In fact, 'record' should read 'records': the fastest to 100 goals (124 matches, 17 fewer than anyone else) and the joint-most scored in one match (five). These aren't normal statistics. Second in the Premier League goals chart, across 30 seasons, is Wayne Rooney on 208. To match Shearer, Rooney would have had to plunder another quarter of his career tally again.

Rooney departed the Premier League at 32, whereas Shearer retired aged 35, so it's tempting to attribute the latter's exploits to longevity alone. Tempting, but wrong. Firstly, Shearer would hold the record even if he'd retired at 32. Secondly, while 14 campaigns is some haul for a player who suffered three career-threatening injuries – especially as that doesn't include more than four years with Southampton in ye olde First Division – 441 Premier League appearances is only the sixth-most among strikers. A ratio of 147 minutes per goal ranks among the division's very best, even today.

And, unlike Rooney and the league's other leading scorers – Andy Cole, Sergio Aguero, Frank Lampard, Thierry Henry – Shearer spent most of his career playing for a team that was quite rubbish quite often. Newcastle had some heady days with Wor Al, but recorded bottom-half finishes in five of his 10 seasons.

How, then, did Shearer score so often? The short answer is ruthlessness, adaptability and penalties – 56 spot-kicks in all, 13 more than any other player. But statistics don't tell the whole story.

In 1992, a rebranded league brought with it a rebranded Shearer. When *Stars In Their Eyes* was the Saturday night entertainment before *Match of the Day*, it was as if a bushy-haired Southampton wannabe had entered the door marked 'PREMIER LEAGUE', then re-emerged through the dry ice wearing a Blackburn shirt and holding the match ball.

Up to then, there'd been no suggestion of a record-breaking career. Shearer turned 22 on the eve of the 1992-93 season; we forget that he'd surpassed 150 senior appearances before that. In April 1988, he'd become the youngest ever scorer of an English top-flight hat-trick, netting thrice on his full debut as Southampton beat Arsenal 4-2 – although there wasn't much danger of the 17-year-old living off it. Arsenal manager George Graham called his strikes "soft goals" that "he didn't really earn", and the following day Shearer was cleaning the first-teamers' boots again. He didn't score for another 18 months.

He joined newly promoted Blackburn for £3.6 million with 23 goals in 118 First Division games for Saints. But before the new Premier League logos had dried, the workhorse with a one-in-five rate was replaced by a stallion who found the back of the net virtually every week. Shearer's opening 13 Rovers fixtures produced goal returns like the mic check of a particularly thorough roadie: 2, 1, 0, 0, 1, 2, 0, 2, 1, 1, 1, 2, 2. The first Golden Boot of the new age went to Sheringham, with 22 goals. Shearer had smashed 16 by Boxing Day, plus another six in the League Cup.

Boxing Day brought unhappy tidings, as a cruciate ligament injury against Leeds ended his campaign (it wasn't Leeds' fault, but he nonetheless took revenge by notching 20 times in 19 Premier League matches against them). Somehow, Shearer bounced back with three consecutive 30-goal league campaigns – and yes, these were 42-game seasons, but his scoring rate translated to 30-plus across 38 games. The new-look league had a new-look star and he looked... quite boring.

Let's start with the iconic goal celebration: a simple hand raised in the air, as if to alert anyone keeping score. His title celebrations in 1995 involved creosoting a fence (years later, he confessed that he'd just helped his father-in-law do it, which is somehow even more dull). Together with the liberal use of his elbows, the ready-salted image of Alan Shearer means he's remembered less fondly than his exotic peers from France, or Italy, or even Guernsey.

But what's wrong with ferocity over finesse? Shearer's shooting technique was torn from the pages of a comic book: you could almost see a whooshing white line tracking the ball from laces to net. Not for Alan the dink, the chip or the stroke – not when he could hit the ball really, really hard. His favourite goal was a thunderbolt volley for Newcastle against Everton in 2002, struck so sweetly that the footage seems to shift into fast-forward. But for the net, that ball would still be travelling.

If that was Shearer's best Premier League goal, then his best Premier League season, with apologies to Geordies, was 1994-95: nearly a half-century of goals (34) and assists (13) as Blackburn clinched the league crown. Kenny Dalglish's side had served Manchester United notice: in April 1994, they beat Alex Ferguson's charges 2-0 at Ewood Park and went into the final few weeks level pegging, before finishing second. Their first goal was indicative: an eight-pass, seven-player move ending with Shearer. They were no one-man team, but all attacks drew inexorably to their No.9. A streak of 17 league games between September 1993 and January 1994 brought Rovers 26 goals – Shearer applied the finish for 22 of them.

That summer, Rovers paid Norwich £5m for Chris Sutton. Though it's spurious to claim Jack Walker 'bought' the title given Dalglish's starting line-up cost less than Ferguson's, replacing the broken-legged Kevin Gallacher with Sutton did create football's 'SAS', as he and Shearer shared 49 goals between them. Shearer scored or assisted 25 league goals before Christmas – still a record – as Rovers set off like a train. When that train ran out of steam, their final 14 fixtures yielding just one win by more than a single goal, his ruthless finishing proved crucial. United fluffed their lines at West Ham on the last day. Blackburn won the league. Alan creosoted the fence.

Jack Walker loved Shearer. He did not love Ferguson. After Manchester United lowballed their Lancashire rivals with a £12m bid for the striker, Blackburn's owner snapped, "When someone says no, it means bloody no," and made a £4m offer for Eric Cantona that was dripping in sarcasm.

NOT FOR SHEARER THE DINK, THE CHIP OR THE STROKE – NOT WHEN HE COULD HIT THE BALL REALLY, REALLY HARD

Shearer *was* leaving, however. His Euro 96 Golden Boot had followed another 31 league goals in 35 matches, even as Rovers finished seventh, netting five hat-tricks in six months (only 13 players have hit five in their Premier League careers). Before finally giving into the inevitable, Walker offered his chief marksman a player-manager role. He was 25.

Against today's signing-on fees and loyalty bonuses, Shearer's contract demands back in 1996 seem quaint, as suitors in the proposal parlour were told he must take penalties and don the No.9 shirt. Newcastle shrugged, paid a world-record £15m and whisked him to his homeland; the returning hero was unveiled outside St James' Park to a Geordie chorus of "Shearer's coming home", and later that week he faced a spurned Ferguson in the Charity Shield. Manchester United won 4-0.

Shearer's decision looked a lot better three months later when the Magpies routed the Red Devils 5-0 for a seventh straight league win. The previous six had all been by a single goal, but here their title rivals were rocked by superb strikes from David Ginola and Philippe Albert, with Shearer slotting home the fourth goal after providing assists for both Darren Peacock and Les Ferdinand.

That was as good as it would get. Shearer finished the 1996-97 season with 25 goals in 31 league games and Newcastle in second place, having struggled during his occasional absences with minor injuries. But then came the big one.

It happened, of all times, in the last minute of a pre-season friendly. On the same day that Newcastle sold Ferdinand to Tottenham, Shearer caught his studs in soggy Goodison Park turf and left his ankle ligaments behind. At 26 he'd already had two hernia operations, as well as knee surgery after that Yuletide injury in 1992. That time, despite a blood clot in his knee, he'd returned as strong and fast as ever. This was different.

Surgery cost Shearer vital acceleration – the "push," he'd later call it, "where you get the power from for that first yard". It was a painful realisation. He was used to cutting through defences like a knife; now a knife had cut through his defences. Hard work and sheer bloodymindedness helped him steer Newcastle to the first of back-to-back FA Cup finals, and he even ended the campaign as their top scorer in all competitions – as he did in each of his 10 seasons there – despite that 1997-98 tally including just two league goals. More importantly, he evolved. He rebranded.

Albeit never lightning-fast, Shearer had previously escaped markers through quick movement: anticipation, then acceleration. He was a dogged all-round threat, finding and making space, creating goals as well as scoring. Now he adapted, becoming a focal point and averaging four assists per season instead of seven. His game gained another

Below Al's goals sealed title glory with Blackburn – his solitary trophy

dimension: height. Armed with a prodigious leap and a seemingly titanium forehead, he dominated defenders and elbowed his way to the front of set-piece queues. Nearly 25 per cent of his Magpies goals were headers.

He was no mere poacher, however. During Bobby Robson's emotional first home game managing a dropzone-dwelling Newcastle, against Sheffield Wednesday in September 1999, Shearer was everywhere; running the channels, whipping in crosses and capping a hard-working creative display with a goal. OK – five goals. United romped to an 8-0 win and an overwhelmed Shearer breathlessly told the BBC, "We mustn't get carried away."

Understandable. Shearer fired Newcastle to most of their highest post-war league finishes and their only two cup finals since 1976, yet they're without a major trophy since lifting the Inter-City Fairs Cup back when the Inter-City Fairs Cup was a thing. Still, there's glory in being a local hero. When the talisman of Tyneside notched his 201st Newcastle goal to break Jackie Milburn's club record in his final season, the Gallowgate roar could have woken Milburn from eternal sleep.

"He's the greatest," said Fiorentina legend Gabriel Batistuta in 2003. "To maintain your performance as a top-class goalscorer over a long period takes phenomenal dedication, self-belief and willpower. Throw in a number of serious injuries – how many? Three? – and to still be producing at the highest level is an amazing feat." Batigol added that Alessandro Del Piero was a fan of Big Al (who had indeed suffered a third career-threatening injury in 2000); after Newcastle beat Juventus 1-0 in the 2002-03 Champions League first group stage, Juve boss Marcello Lippi told Del Piero, David Trezeguet and Marcelo Salas to study videos of Shearer's display.

Though Andy Griffin scored the winner that night, Shearer then netted five in two games against Bayer Leverkusen and Inter, and two seasons later he top-scored in the UEFA Cup with 11. That Premier League record wasn't in a vacuum. Once you throw in cup games, First Division appearances and his one-in-two record for the national team – featuring less stat-padding against minnows compared to England's other marksmen – Shearer's career tally passes 400. If you consider 1992-2022 an arbitrary time period, he's fifth for all-time English top-flight goals, and second post-war.

Yet, for club and country, Shearer's solitary trophy was that single league title. Individual gongs are meaningless, some say – perhaps even Shearer himself – but he did win the PFA Player of the Year award twice, after bagging the FWA prize in a different season, as well as Premier League Player of the Year, three top-tier top-scorer accolades and a Euros Golden Boot. The latter came in the same year that he finished third in the Ballon d'Or, as one of only six Englishmen with a top-three place since the start of the 1980s.

His legacy is goals. Though Shearer's cause was helped by longevity and undroppability (unless you're Ruud Gullit before a Tyne-Wear Derby), his early hit rate bears repeating: 112 goals in 138 league matches with Blackburn. Despite playing only three and a half seasons there, Blackburn's Shearer ranks 23rd in the Premier League's top scorer list. Newcastle's Shearer is 12th.

His record surely won't be broken – even Harry Kane, nearing 30, still has lots of work to do to reach it. All hail Alan Shearer: king of the rebrand. Erling Haaland is coming up fast in goal scoring and at 22 years old has already broken the season record.

Above "Hands up if you love the Toon Army"

PAOLO DI CANIO SAINT PAOLO

Paolo Di Canio was never boring at his first three British clubs. Incendiary at Celtic, infamous at Sheffield Wednesday and wonderful at West Ham, the Italian's imperfections made him a terrace charmer.

Few players ever told Sir Alex Ferguson to "f**k off" and got away with it. But when the Manchester United manager calls you up on Christmas Day out of the blue, what's a guy supposed to do? With Paolo Di Canio, though, there's usually a simple explanation.

The Italian required plenty of them in a career littered with hot-headed outbursts and tittersome flashpoints. Yet there was one common thread which ran throughout: the infectious passion which made him a terrace hero no matter where he went in British football, having joined Celtic from Milan for £1 million in July 1996.

These days, Di Canio works as a pundit and commentator on Premier League matches for Sky Italia, and lives a quieter life in the Olgiata district of Rome's countryside. Not that he wouldn't leap at the chance to return as a manager, mind you, after dugout spells at Swindon and Sunderland. When *FFT* picks up the phone to let the 53-year-old know of our cult heroes special, he's all too happy to reminisce on the happiest period of his life.

"Let's say that my homeland is Italy, but honestly my first football homeland is England," he beams. "Although I was born here, probably in another life I was English."

The feelings are mutual, especially at the first two Premier League clubs that Di Canio represented. During six campaigns with Sheffield Wednesday and West Ham, Di Canio's personality, panache and sporadic ref rage illuminated stadia across the land – but Scotland was first on the receiving end...

"I WANTED TO TAKE HIM..."

Di Canio ended his solitary season at Celtic with the Scotland PFA Player of the Year prize – received in full Highland regalia, naturally – after scoring 15 goals in 37 games. As debut seasons go, it was rather good... if you ignore everything that happened around it.

In a campaign where Rangers collected their ninth consecutive title and won all four Old Firm league encounters for the first time since the Scottish Premiership was formed in 1975, Di Canio frequently flip-flopped from ace to anarchist. For a game-changing debut at Kilmarnock and Yuletide wonder goal at home to Aberdeen, there were also diving accusations and suggestions of a Protestant conspiracy among referees.

It all came to a head against the Gers in March 1997, when the Italian became embroiled in a bitter war of words with Ian Ferguson and, according to the midfielder, "said he was going to break my legs". Just five months later the prickly Paolo was gone, following fellow objectors Pierre van Hooijdonk and Jorge Cadete out the exit – much to the satisfaction of chairman Fergus McCann, who'd sarcastically dubbed them the Three Amigos. In his place had already arrived a little-known Swede called Henrik...

How do you look back on your experience at Celtic now?

I went to Scotland with great enthusiasm, because Celtic came from my childhood when I played Subbuteo with them. They had a very special shirt that you didn't see much on TV – it had always fascinated me because it was completely different from the standard jerseys, with all those horizontal stripes. Not knowing the Scottish league, my choice was cultural, too – I wanted a life experience, so went with my three-year-old daughter and wife. Especially in those years, Italian players didn't really go abroad. Years later, I recall my time there with so much joy – you're lucky to have these experiences, getting well paid for the work you like, but then to do it in such an important place?

The welcome was unbelievable. [Manager] Tommy Burns was truly an extraordinary person. At first, my wife and I settled into a hotel, but then moved into a house. One day after training, I heard the doorbell ring – it was very cold, I went to open it... and it was Tommy. I didn't speak any English, but I remember he walked in and sat on the sofa.

I wasn't used to that kind of thing! In Italy, a coach had never come to my house. We spent an hour talking – or gesturing, really – and he offered us his support. We lived two blocks away, in an area of cottages. "We're here for anything," he told me. "Tomorrow, my wife will come around to take your wife shopping." Immediately, that filled my heart. The Scots are fantastic, warm people.

Can you tell us what happened in that last Old Firm match against Rangers in March?

We lost 1-0 to Brian Laudrup's goal. I didn't score, but I hit the crossbar. It weighed us down, unfortunately. Ian Ferguson provoked me, of course, because of my character and the situation – I wanted to take him! He was the symbolic player of Rangers, the gritty one. I'd scored when we beat them 2-0 in the cup quarter-finals 10 days earlier, and was the quality player of Celtic with a bit of character. Ferguson had been a fool with some of the other players, then he'd done it a little with me – a foul from behind, pulling the collar of my shirt, trying to provoke me. From that moment, I wanted to go and get him. Then he was mocking our supporters at the end of the game. I even wanted to take him in the dressing room. [*Laughs*] It was full of people, though, and they separated us.

How much did you enjoy playing in Old Firm games generally? You got booked in nearly all of them!
I remember it as being incredibly emotional. I'd heard so many stories, but didn't imagine it could be like it was. The tension, the love, the songs... I was really impressed. We know it goes way beyond football, and this makes everything much stronger: at the stadium you could feel this positive anger that sometimes became negative outside it.

There was a competitive charge that we players had to pour in, in an intelligent way, on the field. Having been a [Lazio] fan, I was more sensitive than others about games like that: I appreciate them, admire them, and above all understand their meaning. When you play Rangers, there are no distractions – if my family were there, I would totally forget about them! I was so into it that we warmed up in -5 degrees and I still didn't feel the cold, despite being short-sleeved! I thought, 'I'm in Scotland, I'm among Celtic's warriors and I have to put my qualities in'.

Why didn't you stay there for longer? If you could do it all over again, would you leave in a different way?
I remember the three-hour discussion to negotiate a contract with the chairman who said, "We want you at all costs." We agreed that at the end of the season, if I did well, we'd renew at the agreed figures and with an extra year. Everything is relative in football, and everybody has their own idea about the performance of a player, but I was voted the best player in Scotland.

Instead, the chairman called my attorney and told him, "Paolo played well, but for us he had to do much more." I knew something was wrong, so in the end I just said, "Look, it's better that I leave. I'm sorry because here, for the love and the way I am, I would have stayed for life." I was 28 – I would have done five or six more seasons there and been fine.

Even Di Canio probably wasn't expecting England to be a bit quieter – he's perfectly self-aware. And, of course, quiet it was not.

Sheffield Wednesday offered a route to the Premier League in August 1997, completing a part-exchange deal worth £4.5m with Dutch wideman Regi Blinker. The striker's maiden campaign was successful, too: save for a glorious FA Cup red card against Watford – two yellows in the space of seconds, for protesting a throw-in – he wound up as the Owls' top scorer with 14 goals, one of which came in an outstanding home win against title-chasing Manchester United.

But does anyone outside of Sheffield really remember that? No. There's only one episode that gets repeated from Di Canio's tenure at Hillsborough – and it earned him an 11-game ban. It was his final act in South Yorkshire, coming days after he'd called his own boss Danny Wilson "perhaps a little immature".

His two former Wednesday managers both had their say after the fact. "I've managed a few nutters in my time but Paolo takes the biscuit," said a, er, diplomatic Ron Atkinson. "If I've broken up one fight between Paolo

Clockwise from above Battling 'gritty' Ferguson; "This probably needs another minute"; living the Highland life

and Des Walker, I've broken up a hundred."

The man who'd signed him, meanwhile, David Pleat, merely sighed, "I don't think Paolo was one of those people who wanted to fight and hit people. He just had a kind of theatrical temperament."

But what fine theatre it was...

Do you remember the weird photoshoot you did with Benito Carbone, both eating pizza on the pitch at Hillsborough (right)?

[*Laughs*] Yes! It was, "You are from Italy! Pizza! We sell that here as well," from the photographer. After training, Benny and I took a shower and then went to the stadium for this picture. "Pretend to eat it," he said. The pizza was frozen – they heated it in the microwave, then I got the idea to bite it, but it was crap. So bad. Benny and I had a great relationship. At the beginning, he hosted me – he'd already lived there for a year, so the Italian fantasy couple was formed!

Talk us through pushing over referee Paul Alcock in September 1998. What was going through your head? Some people – Alcock included – said 11 games wasn't enough...

It was a bad thing, and I've always regretted what happened. In the beginning it's normal that you also blame others, but I realised immediately that it was me who'd done the bulls**t thing. I hadn't done what some said, though – the sports minister [Tony Banks] claimed that I was some sort of barbarian who needed to be driven out of England!

But those four months out made me think a lot. I didn't change my character, but I matured. I learned. Sometimes in our game there is competitiveness, and every now and then we give each other a little kick or a push, but we're not murderers. I was struck by that reaction and could have gone to Spain or Turkey – my wife tried to convince me, but I said, "No, no – I'm staying in England!"

I defended myself with two lawyers from Bologna without the club's support. I had to pay 50 million Lire out of my own pocket, so then told Wednesday, "I'll never come back."

LIFE BEGINS AT THIRTY

What Di Canio needed was a friendly face, someone who could massage his bruised ego and ignore it when required. Sir Alex Ferguson never tried to pretend he treated Eric Cantona the same as everyone else, and that was also the case with West Ham boss Harry Redknapp and his mercurial arrival at the start of 1999.

The vilified Di Canio signed for a cut-price £1.5m – risky on a three and a half year deal, not least aged 30, but to his new boss totally worth it. Redknapp wasn't wrong. He may have had to fix small-sided training matches to unwittingly keep Di Canio happy, but the east Londoner was rewarded with the class that made the fiery forward a Hammers icon.

West Ham finished fifth in Paolo's debut season, before the Italian top-scored during a second campaign that showcased every facet of his unpredictable genius. In February 2000, a rattled Di Canio – those pesky refs, again – demanded that Redknapp substitute him while the Hammers trailed Bradford 4-2.

"I told him to get on with the game in so many words," his old manager reflected later. He did, scoring a penalty after an infamous feud with Frank Lampard over who'd take it, before Joe Cole and Lampard himself – Di Canio the assister – wrapped up a 5-4 victory.

The following month came *that* Wimbledon goal in all its glory. As the months passed, and with Cantona long gone at Old Trafford, it's no wonder Fergie fancied another crack at grabbing a bargain...

What were your feelings about joining West Ham after the Wednesday fallout?

Harry Redknapp had great intuition. My value had depreciated and he took me for £1.5m – it was something sensational, especially considering what I produced. I will always thank Harry for the opportunity he gave me, because from then on it was always a joy; always playing with a smile.

My life in London, especially at a club like West Ham with its fans, that history, that wonder and what I carry in my heart, was really something unique. I had a desire for redemption, as a man before a professional. I didn't have to prove anything to anyone after what had happened with the referee [Alcock], but the determination, the desire to repay Harry's trust, made the difference.

As soon as I arrived at Upton Park, the fans had a tune of *La Donna E Mobile* for me. I thought, 'I have to give my best, to repay this unconditional love'. I think I represented something that had been missing for West Ham. Until that moment, they didn't really have a technical footballer based on flair and dribbling. They had John Hartson, who was such a colossus in attack, but Redknapp sold him [to Wimbledon for £7.5m] in attempting to change their game.

Your stunning Wimbledon strike in March 2000 is still repeated over and over again. Is it special to you?

The Premier League was born in 1992, and every year my goal is always among the most beautiful – if not *the* most beautiful – in the entire history of English football. I won the award for the best goal ever witnessed at Upton Park; when it closed I was there, after the win over Manchester United in May 2016. The stadium was closed and the most

Clockwise from right Gerrard thanks Di Canio for his sporting gesture; "Look lads, I'm flying"; Paolo's stunning volley helped to sink Wimbledon

beautiful goal ever seen there was mine? It was a fantastic thing.

Wimbledon was a delicate match for us, because we could still aim for Europe and they were looking to survive. The goal was actually very early; after a few minutes, the late Marc Vivien Foé – this amazing guy, my friend who I joined West Ham with – won possession in the middle and turned it out to Trevor Sinclair. Kenny Cunningham was in front of me, and my first idea was to stop the ball and then go one-on-one – but when I saw that he wasn't going to jump, I lifted one leg off the ground in a split-second.

The other had to go diagonally – it's very difficult, because you have a small moment when the ball arrives and have to hit it like a rugby ball. You can see all the marks of the ball spinning – it's wonderful. The ball hit the smallest part of the net by the post. The goalkeeper [Neil Sullivan] could do nothing about it. I immediately realised I'd done something special and unusual, from the amazement painted on the fans' faces. It was magical and has remained in history.

You received a plethora of praise and the FIFA Fair Play Award for catching the ball against Everton in December 2000, when goalkeeper Paul Gerrard went down hurt. Why did you do that?

In each of us, there's a portion of demon and some angel. Especially because of moments like that, no one has ever been able to tell me that I'm dishonest on the field. I've never taken advantage of such situations. When Gerrard went down, I was on the edge of the penalty area already shouting, "Stop! Stop!" with my hands up, even after Trevor tried to take advantage. For me, the game had to be stopped, so I caught the ball, and then I was rewarded by FIFA! Funny though, isn't it, that people massacred me for months and then I was being given that accolade from Franz Beckenbauer? [*Laughs*]

How close were you to ever signing for Manchester United? Do you regret that it didn't happen in the end?

In his book, Ferguson talked about his three regrets: one was that he couldn't bring me to United. Then he said something afterwards, when perhaps he'd drunk a little too much. [*Laughs*] He believed that if I'd been with him, maybe I could have fought to win the Ballon d'Or. I think he just wanted to emphasise the idea that I could have played in Manchester at the highest level, because I had fun and played my best matches against the biggest teams. Two Christmases in a row, he called me. My wife said, "I think he said, 'Ferguson, from Manchester United?'"

"Paolo, it's Alex," he said, in an accent that I wasn't used to hearing any more. So I said, "F**k off!" It was obviously someone making a joke of me – it sounded like a half-Bergamo accent. But he kept saying, "Paolo, this is Alex – I need to talk to you..." "Are you *sure*? Are you really Alex Ferguson?" He said, "Yes, I need you – would you come here? You can play behind Ruud van Nistelrooy."

He then went on to list some unbelievable names. For a moment I thought about it, but it really took me 30 seconds to answer. "You call me in a strange moment – it's Christmas Day and I'm here with my wife and all my family. But Alex, I need to tell you that I'm very happy at West Ham. I want to stay here, I can't betray this big family. It's a big honour for me that you called and it gives me more and more energy, but I just can't leave West Ham." He also called me the following year, but I said the same thing.

How on earth did West Ham get relegated in 2002-03? Was it a massive shock to the players as well?

Incredible, incredible... a great team. Those were the years when the new grandstand was under construction, but in the meantime we were selling Rio Ferdinand one season, Lampard the next. From there they killed me: Redknapp left and I stayed with a couple of guys, under a young coach [Glenn Roeder] who'd trained the youth team. We started well and I scored twice at Stamford Bridge, but then things began to go wrong. Roeder was leaving me out because the club didn't want to renew my contract, so I argued with him and was forced to train in my garden. I had an apple orchard and used the trees to dribble around! I didn't go back to Italy – I stayed out of respect for the fans, in case I was needed. My wife thought I was crazy.

A few days before the penultimate game, Trevor Brooking [the caretaker manager] said, "Paolo, I need you." After three months away, I came off the bench and scored the winner against Chelsea. We had to win away at Birmingham on the final day, but I was on the bench again – I came on and scored to make it 2-2, but it wasn't quite enough. I saw some fans applauding us all the same, and that really moved me. I cried because I was so sorry that I couldn't say goodbye properly and show them love. Instead, I left like that. It was a big wound, but it healed every time I returned to Upton Park. I was very lucky to have been part of that family.

DIDIER DROGBA

THE LAST DANCE

Chelsea's talismanic striker knew that the 2012 Champions League Final was his one chance to win Europe's top prize before the Blues' stars were split up. In an astonishing season of turmoil at Stamford Bridge, that waltz to glory never looked likely – and yet...

Andre Villas-Boas turned to every Chelsea player, and asked the same question. One by one, they all gave an identical answer. Until it came to Didier Drogba. The previous day, the Portuguese manager had gathered together his senior pros, after a home defeat to Liverpool – Chelsea's third in four Premier League games – left them fifth in the table. He had worked with Drogba, John Terry, Frank Lampard and Petr Cech during his days as Chelsea assistant under Jose Mourinho, and appeared to be taking on board what they said. The advice was clear, particularly from Drogba: Villas-Boas should dial back on the new philosophy that he was trying to impose. It wasn't working.

Then the boss called a team meeting and doubled down on his own tactical plans. "We have to stick to our philosophy," Villas-Boas told them, ahead of a group-stage match away at Bayer Leverkusen. "I believe this is how we will win the Champions League."

Given what Drogba and the other senior players had advised their gaffer 24 hours earlier, it felt like a betrayal; confirmation that their opinions no longer mattered; a hint that he was attempting to take the club in a different direction... without them.

The 33-year-old Drogba had been rotated in and out of the team to make way for Fernando Torres. Lampard, also 33, was another that Villas-Boas – their senior by just a few months – was rumoured to be considering for the exit door. Terry, soon to turn 31, was being investigated by police for alleged comments made to Anton Ferdinand during a recent defeat at QPR.

As he brought the team meeting to a close, Villas-Boas had one question for each player. He believed that Chelsea could win the Champions League following his philosophy, but he wanted to know if they did, too. Effectively, he was asking if they believed in him as manager.

Whether they meant it or not, everyone said yes. Apart from Drogba. "I'm sorry, coach, but I don't believe we can win it," said the striker.

Chelsea lost 2-1 to Bayer Leverkusen, the hosts' late winner jeopardising their chances of reaching the knockout phase, and Drogba decided he'd had enough. Days later, before even December had arrived, agent Thierno Seydi told the media that his client would not be signing a new one-year deal at the club. "At Didier's age, he has nothing left to prove as a player," shrugged Seydi. "He will go where he is offered the most money."

Since joining forces in 2004, Drogba and Chelsea's old guard had won three Premier League titles, three FA Cups and two League Cups. Yet the Champions League still eluded them, and now the 2011-12 season would be their eighth and final season together.

Drogba may not have had much faith in his coach, but this would be his final chance. This would be the last dance.

JULY 2004: THE PICK OF THE BUNCH

When Jose Mourinho took over as manager of Chelsea in 2004, tasked with winning the club's second league title and first in half a century, Roman Abramovich's riches gave him the pick of world football's most successful strikers. Instead, he targeted Drogba, a 26-year-old who'd never won a major trophy, had only ever played six games at Champions League level, and hadn't turned pro until he was 21.

Drogba had been forced at seven years old to leave Europe and return to Ivory Coast due to paperwork issues, having moved to France two years earlier to live with his uncle, a professional footballer with Stade Brestois. When the paperwork finally came through, Drogba didn't want to go to France again. He had felt homesick in Europe. A few years later, however, both of his parents lost their jobs as the Ivorian economy crashed, and Didier went to France for a second time.

Aged 18, he joined Le Mans in the second division as an apprentice, but a fondness for junk food meant his fitness wasn't up to scratch. "An African guy will feel strong and untouchable – it's something you have in your genes," he later told *FourFourTwo*. "The danger is that you can be blinded by that confidence. Way too often, I would do things I shouldn't, diet-wise and fitness-wise, thinking that I wasn't risking anything."

A new strict fitness regime led to injuries, before his biggest setback: a fractured ankle and fibula. At that stage, he didn't know if the club would retain him for a second season. "It was very difficult," he said, "but even when I suffered a broken leg, I still believed I'd make it to the top." Le Mans did keep Drogba, then offered him a professional deal at 21, shortly after his first-team debut.

His goalscoring record there was hardly outstanding – 15 in 72 matches – but he impressed enough to earn an £80,000 move to Guingamp in the top tier. There, Drogba blossomed. He netted 21 times in 2002-03 to convince Marseille, the club he supported as a boy, to sign him for £3.3 million.

> "CHELSEA WITHOUT MOURINHO?" DROGBA MUSED TO FFT. "I DON'T EVEN WANT TO THINK ABOUT IT"

Drogba scored on his Champions League debut against Real Madrid at the Bernabeu, then bagged a hat-trick at home to Partizan Belgrade. In the third group match, Drogba put OM ahead against Mourinho's Porto. He had gained an admirer. "One day, when I can afford you, I will sign you," Mourinho told him in the tunnel afterwards.

By the time Mourinho joined Chelsea at the end of that season, Drogba had proved he could thrive against English opposition. He scored twice against Liverpool, then added a brace against Newcastle, as Marseille reached the UEFA Cup final following their elimination from the Champions League.

A month after Mourinho's appointment, Chelsea agreed a club-record £24m deal for Drogba. When the centre-forward arrived at Farnborough Airport, he was greeted by his new boss in French. "You're a good player," said Mourinho. "But if you want to become great, you have to play for a great club like Chelsea and you have to play for me."

Drogba later told *FFT*, "The biggest thing Mourinho brought was his faith in me. When he joined Chelsea, he was given the choice of some of the biggest names in football. But he said, 'No, I don't want them. I want Drogba'."

Drogba didn't know much about Chelsea, nor their squad. "At training, I noticed a tall guy who looked so young," he revealed years later. "I assumed he was from the reserves – I thought that they'd brought him in to get a bit of experience. I asked another player who he was. They laughed and said, 'It's the captain, John Terry'."

Installed as skipper after Marcel Desailly's departure, the 23-year-old Terry and summer arrival Petr Cech, 22, helped the Londoners to concede just 15 goals – still a Premier League record – in Mourinho's first season. Terry was named PFA Player of the Year while Lampard took the Football Writers' Association award, having netted the brace at Bolton that sealed the Blues' first league title since 1955.

Drogba was the spearhead who completed the spine of Mourinho's feared team. He scored in the League Cup final victory over Liverpool, and bagged home and away against Bayern Munich as Chelsea reached the semi-finals of the Champions League.

Despite all that, Drogba had a feeling of unease, as if he hadn't completely won over the club's fanbase. He had scored 16 goals in all competitions, compared to 32 with Marseille the previous season.

He plundered another 16 as Chelsea won the Premier League title again in 2005-06, but suffered mid-season heartbreak with Ivory Coast in the Africa Cup of Nations final against Egypt, missing his penalty in the shootout as the host nation secured victory.

Back in England, his mood worsened still when he admitted, "Sometimes I dive" in a post-match interview, sparking a media storm. It hadn't been exactly what he had meant to say. "Journalists took advantage of my less-than-perfect English," he told *FFT*. "There were times when it was tough for me. Some players would have gone under."

In 2006, Drogba seriously contemplated leaving Chelsea after only two seasons. His wife helped to talk him out of it, before a pivotal moment that summer.

"The guy who convinced me to stay was Frank Lampard," said Drogba of the man who, six months earlier, had finished second in the Ballon d'Or behind Ronaldinho. "I was having a short family holiday in Marrakesh when I received a text from Frank. I didn't remember ever being texted by him during the entire two seasons I'd been at Chelsea. It said, 'Hi DD, I hope you're staying because we have to win the league together and we have to win the Champions League together'.

"Frank, JT and Petr Cech were players I had a special bond with. Receiving that text was decisive. It felt really powerful. It was proof that I was wanted. I kept that phone for a long time, just to keep that message.

"That was the day that freed me. I went on to be Premier League top scorer that season."

AUGUST 2011: BENCHED AND BEMUSED

The 2011-12 campaign was just one game old when Drogba decided that he needed to speak to Villas-Boas. Having been named on the bench on the opening day at Stoke, he wasn't happy. Drogba was introduced only for the final 15 minutes as Chelsea drew 0-0.

Drogba had been the Premier League's top scorer again in 2009-10. In partnership with Nicolas Anelka, he'd helped Chelsea collect a third league title by netting a career-high season tally of 29 league goals, and another career high of 37 in all competitions. He had scored the winner in the FA Cup final against Portsmouth, too – his seventh goal in six domestic cup finals, further bolstering his reputation as the ultimate big-game player.

In 2010-11, however, Drogba had found the net only 13 times in England and Europe. Having struggled through games for a month in mid-season, he had eventually discovered that he'd been suffering with

Above Drogba scored 11 goals in Europe in his single season with Marseille

malaria. Then Chelsea had spent £50m on Fernando Torres in January, and the partnership just hadn't worked – between then and the season's end, Torres had scored just one league goal and Drogba only two. Chelsea had finished a distant second to Manchester United, and Carlo Ancelotti was replaced by Villas-Boas.

Drogba had been optimistic about the appointment. They'd had a good relationship during Villas-Boas' spell as Jose Mourinho's assistant, staying in touch afterwards. But the dynamic was different now that the No.2 was No.1, intent on putting his own stamp on the club and refreshing an ageing squad.

It wasn't long until Drogba began to hear worrying noises. "We learned unofficially that he wanted to get rid of a few people – Ashley Cole, Lampard and me," he later wrote in his autobiography.

When Drogba was benched for Torres away at Stoke, he spoke with Villas-Boas. "He told me that as pre-season had progressed, he'd decided Nando was better at everything," wrote Drogba. "I said, 'No, I don't think so. If you want to be honest and fair, the best in pre-season was Nico [Anelka] – not Nando, not me'. I asked him to be honest with me and tell me where I stood. He avoided giving me a clear answer. That was an answer of sorts, I suppose."

The striker was left dejected as he rotated in and out of the side, while Villas-Boas tried to instil his philosophy by building attacks from the back. By October and November, things weren't going to plan.

Drogba was one of two Chelsea players sent off in the first half of their 1-0 defeat to QPR, a match marred by the confrontation between Terry and Anton Ferdinand. A police investigation followed, and Terry was charged with using racist language. The Blues then went down 5-3 at home to Arsenal, scraped past Steve Kean's Blackburn and lost at Stamford Bridge again, to Liverpool this time, while team meetings exacerbated tensions between Villas-Boas and some of his players.

With Drogba out of contract at the season's end, his agent revealed that he had rejected a new deal. The club, adhering to its policy on players aged over 30, had offered only one extra year. His future was still to be resolved, but it wouldn't be at Chelsea. "It could be the United States, Russia, Qatar or somewhere else in Asia," said his representative, Seydi.

In the Champions League, defeat at Bayer Leverkusen had left Chelsea needing a result at home to Valencia in their final group-stage tie to avoid elimination. Drogba scored twice in a 3-0 win, but had been irritated that week when Anelka and defender Alex were banned from training with the first team. Both had made transfer requests and been told that if they didn't want to be there, they could leave.

Anelka had interest from China – and soon, so did Drogba. He could leave immediately, and he was interested.

"Remember what you said about players who weren't happy? I've got an offer," he told Villas-Boas. Fearing a paucity of striking options, his manager went on the back foot and urged the Ivorian to delay a move.

Drogba did depart in January, but for the Africa Cup of Nations. It ended in another crushing disappointment. As in 2006, Drogba missed a penalty as Ivory Coast lost the final, shocked by Zambia just as they looked set for a first continental triumph in 20 years.

He returned to a club even deeper in crisis than the one he'd left. Terry had learned that his court case wouldn't be resolved until the summer; he was acquitted in July but the FA felt compelled to act in the interim and stripped him of the England captaincy, which prompted Fabio Capello to resign. And while Drogba was on international duty, his club drew with Norwich and Swansea, let a 3-0 lead slip at home to Manchester United, then produced the worst display of Villas-Boas' tenure in a feeble loss at Everton. Chelsea had won two of their last 10 league games. A team meeting turned into a row, with Ashley Cole reportedly telling the manager, "I came here to win medals and trophies – I'm never going to do that with your tactics."

"The players don't have to back my project – it's the owner who backs my project," said Villas-Boas to the press. "My authority is total because

Below Drogba's relationship with Andre Villas-Boas, summarised in a single picture

Above Lamenting the 2009 'disgrace' and earning himself another suspension

it's the owner's authority as well. Two players have departed, and more will depart in the future."

Days later, Chelsea travelled to Italy for the first leg of their Champions League last-16 tie against Napoli. Drogba started, but Cole was left out of the line-up. So was Lampard. Chelsea lost 3-1 – and it could easily have been 4-1, had Cole not produced a brilliant goal-line clearance after coming on as a substitute for his own replacement, Jose Bosingwa.

Afterwards, Lampard said his relationship with Villas-Boas had deteriorated: "From the outside, you can probably see it's not been ideal... There have been certain issues."

Few gave Chelsea any hope that they could overturn a two-goal deficit in the second leg.

MAY 2008: THE SLAP

Drogba's Champions League dream had been shattered time and again during his journey with Chelsea. Never had he felt so alone than in Moscow in 2008 – watching on from the tunnel, helpless, as glory was snatched away at the final moment.

That season, Drogba had faced the devastation of Mourinho's departure. "Chelsea without Jose Mourinho? I don't even want to think about it," he'd previously told *FFT*. When it happened, Drogba sobbed as the pair hugged to say goodbye. The striker went to see Roman Abramovich, asking why the change had been made, before casting doubt over his own future in an interview with *France Football*.

Despite the upheaval, Chelsea reached the Champions League final for the first time, under Mourinho's replacement, Avram Grant. Drogba scored twice as the Blues finally overcame Liverpool in the last four, following two previous semi-final defeats to Rafael Benitez's side – beaten by the ghost goal in 2005, then on penalties in 2007.

This time, victory included a poignant goal for Lampard, days after the death of his mother. In Moscow for the final, Drogba also battled emotional turmoil. His grandmother had been admitted to hospital and didn't have very long to live. "During the game, I couldn't concentrate," he later confessed.

Lampard equalised in the final against Manchester United, but Drogba became frustrated at being left on his own upfront, and confused when Anelka was brought on as a winger, not a strike partner. Later in extra time, Drogba snapped and slapped Nemanja Vidic. He was the first player ever to be sent off for violent conduct in a European Cup final. "The walk back to the dressing room was so incredibly long," he said. "It was horrible. I knew I was responsible for this."

By the time the shootout started, Drogba had returned to anxiously peek out from the tunnel. A year and a half after fracturing his skull in a match against Reading, Cech saved from Cristiano Ronaldo and looked set to be the hero. But without Drogba, Terry had to take the fifth penalty. He missed – and so did Anelka in sudden death. Manchester United, not Chelsea, were champions of Europe.

"I went straight back to the dressing room and sat there on my own, trying to wake up from this nightmare – realising there was nothing to wake up from and it was really happening," said Drogba. "Abramovich came in with his young son, who was nine or 10, and the boy was crying and crying. When everyone started coming back to the dressing room, a few people came over to me, asked me what happened and how I was doing. I just said, 'It's OK, it's too late, it's too late'."

It would be the first of three successive seasons that Drogba's Champions League dream ended in ignominious fashion. His desire to win the competition was so great that his emotions became uncontrollable when the chances of it actually happening were under threat.

In 2009, Chelsea were within touching distance of eliminating Pep Guardiola's Barcelona in the semi-finals to halt what is now regarded as possibly the greatest club side in history, in their finest season of all.

The Blues had already seen three penalty appeals turned down at Stamford Bridge when Andres Iniesta smashed home the stoppage-time goal that took Barça into the final. When a fourth appeal was denied in the closing seconds, Drogba flipped. He berated Norwegian referee Tom Henning Ovrebo at the final whistle before turning his attention to the television camera, screaming, "It's a disgrace! It's a disgrace! It's a f**king disgrace!" as interim boss Guus Hiddink awkwardly tried to usher him away. Drogba was later suspended by UEFA.

"It wasn't a good example for youngsters watching – I know that," Drogba told *FFT*. "I learned from what happened that night. It won't happen again, that's for sure."

The next year, Chelsea faced Mourinho's Inter in the last 16. Heading for

Below The old boys celebrate another league title in 2010

a 3-1 defeat on aggregate, Drogba was dismissed for an alleged stamp on Thiago Motta. For three years in a row, he started the following Champions League campaign with a ban.

When Chelsea lost to Manchester United in the 2010-11 quarter-finals, their hopes of winning the competition seemed to be slipping further away. For years, they'd had one of the best teams in Europe, but had never quite secured the Champions League. Now, their stars were past their peak and even their Premier League form was starting to decline. Had Chelsea missed their chance?

MARCH 2012: OLD BOYS STRIKE BACK

Before the second leg of Chelsea's last-16 meeting with Napoli in March 2012, Drogba addressed the squad.

A 1-0 defeat at West Bromwich Albion 11 days earlier had proved the last straw for Abramovich: Andre Villas-Boas no longer had the support of his club's owner. The young Portuguese manager was out, and replaced by assistant Roberto Di Matteo.

Under the new boss, senior players were quickly allowed to reassert their status in the dressing room and lead from within. "I could have left in January," Drogba told the team. "But I'm still here. Why? Because I believe we have a chance to win the Champions League. I will do everything to win it."

When Napoli arrived at Stamford Bridge, Chelsea took them by storm. The Londoners surged 3-1 up to level the tie on aggregate, and their goalscorers couldn't have been more appropriate: Drogba, Terry, Lampard. The old guard had been resurrected and had unfinished business. Drogba set up Branislav Ivanovic's winner in extra time.

The Ivorian played only two minutes of the quarter-final against Benfica, having been left out for Torres in both legs. But Drogba was appreciative of greater communication from Di Matteo, who kept him informed if he was unlikely to start – the striker had turned 34 by this stage. Most important of all, the Blues won both legs.

It earned them another semi-final with old foes Barcelona. It was a game for Drogba, who wanted revenge. Guardiola's side had 72 per cent possession in the opening leg at Stamford Bridge, and completed 743 passes to Chelsea's 169. Alexis Sanchez and Pedro hit the woodwork, and Cesc Fabregas had an effort cleared off the line as Barça fired in 24 shots. "I was playing like a midfielder, they were pressing us so much," said Drogba. "We had one chance, and one chance only."

Just before half-time, Lampard robbed Lionel Messi and started a counter-attack that ended with Drogba sweeping the ball home. Somehow, Chelsea triumphed 1-0.

Above Drogba exorcises his 12-yard demons in Munich, 2012

The return leg was more one-way traffic. Barça had another 22 shots – and this time, the Blues couldn't hold out. Sergio Busquets opened the scoring at the Camp Nou, then Terry was sent off for kneeing Sanchez in the back. When Iniesta put Barcelona ahead on aggregate, 10-man Chelsea looked doomed.

However, things turned on a sixpence when Lampard's brilliant reverse pass played in Ramires for a sumptuous chipped goal against the run of play, giving Chelsea the advantage on away goals. During half-time, they discussed reorganisation. "I can play at left-back if necessary," offered Drogba. "We don't need a striker. I'll play striker and left-back, whatever it takes."

He was in the left-back position early in the second half when his

CHOP-AND-CHANGE CHAMPIONS

Chelsea triumphed after a mid-season managerial switch, as did Bayern in 2019-20 – and this lot, too

ASTON VILLA (1982)
Ron Saunders guided Villa to their first league title in 71 years, but they were mid-table the next season when he controversially quit and joined rivals Birmingham, following a contract dispute. Assistant Tony Barton duly took over the reins and lifted the European Cup three months later.

REAL MADRID (2000)
In 2016, Zinedine Zidane replaced Rafa Benitez mid-campaign and won the Champions League; Vicente del Bosque had previously done the same. He came in for John Toshack, sacked for publicly criticising his players and refusing to apologise – "There's more chance of a pig flying over the Bernabeu," he said.

ARSENAL (1934)
It's been 88 years since a team were crowned English champions after a mid-season manager change, and it came in tragic circumstances. Herbert Chapman had led Arsenal to the title in 1933 but died of pneumonia in January 1934, with the Gunners top once again. Caretaker Joe Shaw finished the job.

WATFORD (2015)
The kings of instability, Watford had four managers in 2014-15 but still won promotion to the Premier League. After Beppe Sannino resigned five games in, Oscar Garcia stepped down with chest pains and Billy McKinlay was given only two games, Slavisa Jokanovic took the Hornets up. Then he left too.

striker's attempt at a sliding tackle brought down Fabregas for a penalty. Luck was on Drogba's side: Messi cannoned his spot-kick against the bar. "Maybe the gods were looking down on us," reflected Drogba. Barça couldn't find a way through, and substitute Torres sealed a remarkable aggregate victory for Chelsea.

Di Matteo's side knew they'd need similar tactics – and luck – in the final. They were playing Bayern Munich, in Munich. However, it didn't daunt Drogba, who'd scored home and away to beat Bayern in 2005. He headed into the European showpiece after yet another FA Cup final goal, in a victory over Liverpool.

No fewer than seven players from the two teams were suspended for the Munich final, and Chelsea found it tough without Terry, Ivanovic, Ramires and Raul Meireles. Bayern rattled in 34 shots and racked up 20 corners. Thomas Muller finally broke the deadlock in the 83rd minute. "For me, that was it," said Drogba. "Game over. The end of our dream."

At the restart, Juan Mata sensed the striker's despondency. "Didier, you have to believe," insisted the Spaniard. With two minutes remaining, Chelsea won their one and only corner of the match. Mata crossed and Drogba climbed highest at the near post, directing a bullet header into the net.

The striker had rescued Chelsea – but in extra time, he undid his hard work. Just as he had in the semi-final, Drogba conceded a penalty, by clumsily tripping Franck Ribery. The spot-kick-taker would be his former Blues club-mate, Arjen Robben. "He's a good friend, so we put psychological pressure on him," Drogba later revealed. "We said, 'Arjen, you're a Chelsea player – you can't do this! We know where you're going to shoot.'"

Cech saved Robben's penalty. The match ended 1-1, and Chelsea's dreams of winning the Champions League for the first time in their history came down to another shootout.

Drogba had experienced shootout defeats so many times before: against Manchester United in Moscow; against Egypt and Zambia in Africa Cup of Nations finals; at Liverpool in a Champions League semi-final; at home to Everton in the FA Cup; against Charlton, Burnley and Blackburn in the League Cup; against Amiens and Angouleme in the Coupe de France; and against Nantes and Chateauroux in the Coupe de la Ligue. Won three, lost 12. It was an appalling record.

Mata stepped up to take Chelsea's first penalty... and hit it straight at Manuel Neuer. It was happening again. But David Luiz kept the Londoners in it and then, just as in Moscow, Lampard took Chelsea's third penalty and scored. And, just as in Moscow, Ashley Cole took Chelsea's fourth penalty and scored. Cech saved from both Ivica Olic and Bastian Schweinsteiger, and suddenly Chelsea were back in the same position they had found themselves in four years earlier. Score their fifth penalty, and they were the European champions. But this time, Drogba – not Terry – was on the pitch to take it.

"I wasn't nervous," he later wrote. "I was really sure of myself. It was almost like an out-of-body experience. I made my run-up very short, so Neuer wouldn't have time to read it. For a brief moment, I contemplated doing a Panenka, but I came to my senses. Instead, I told myself something I've been telling myself since I was a boy: 'If you score, we win. You love being in this position'."

Drogba took two short steps and sent Neuer the wrong way, firing his penalty into the bottom corner. Chelsea were European champions at last. With his final kick for the club, Drogba had achieved everything he'd ever dreamed of.

"This was written a long time ago, but we didn't know," he said in the minutes after victory. The perfect script had been signed off with the greatest triumph of all.

For a brief moment during their frenzied celebrations on the pitch that night, Drogba, Terry, Lampard and Cech found themselves together – just as they'd been together in that thorny meeting with Villas-Boas months earlier, and together so many times over the previous eight years. "I thanked them for what they'd done, and told them it had been an honour to play with them," said Drogba.

Back in the dressing room after the trophy presentation, he addressed the cup. "Why? Why have you avoided us for such a long time?" he asked, listing years of near-misses.

"I spoke about everything we'd had to do, to finally claim this trophy as our own," he later explained. "Some told me it almost felt like a religious experience. It was my way of making peace with the cup."

If some people wondered whether Drogba might still change his mind and stay, he confirmed the inevitable after the victory parade in London. The striker gathered the squad together to inform them that he was definitely leaving, breaking down in tears as he tried to get the words out. It was the most incredible end to eight incredible years at Stamford Bridge.

Following spells with Shanghai Shenhua and Galatasaray, Drogba returned for a brief second stint at Chelsea a couple of years later, but by then, Lampard had left the club and was turning out for Manchester City. After the 2011-12 campaign, never again would Drogba, Terry, Lampard and Cech all play together for Chelsea. An era had come to a close, in the most fitting way possible. This had been their last dance.

"It was like a movie," said Drogba, as he reflected on it all. "And like the best movies, it had a happy ending."

THE MISSING CLUBS

None of our top 100 represented these Premier League teams – if you don't include Harry Kane's three matches for Norwich – but each had a star

NEIL REDFEARN

BARNSLEY

Tykes fans boasted it was just like watching Brazil when their side got promoted – Redfearn took the role of Zico, scoring double figures from midfield in their solitary Premier League season of 1997-98.

CHARLIE ADAM

BLACKPOOL

Seasiders fans were never parched for entertainment in a goal-crazy top flight campaign – the Tangerines netted as many as fifth-placed Tottenham in 2010-11, with midfielder Adam scoring 12 times.

LEWIS DUNK

BRIGHTON

The centre-back has helped secure six consecutive seasons in the top flight for the Sussex side, and also became the first Brighton player to represent England since Steve Foster in 1982. Consistency personified.

PETER WHITTINGHAM

CARDIFF

Cardiff's maiden promotion to the Premier League would never have happened without Whittingham's wand of a left foot, and he remained their linchpin in the top tier. He tragically died in 2020, aged just 35.

WILFRIED ZAHA

CRYSTAL PALACE

Across two spells at Selhurst Park, Zaha has become a Palace legend – he's consistently been the Eagles' star man in the eight years since his return from an ill-fated spell at Manchester United. Now excelling as a clinical centre-forward after years playing out wide.

STEFANO ERANIO

DERBY

When Rams supporters picked their all-time greatest XIs for the city's local newspaper, almost all of them chose the classy ex-Genoa, Milan and Italy midfielder who graced Pride Park between 1997 and 2001.

AARON MOOY

HUDDERSFIELD

The Australian's Premier League dream seemed over when he left Bolton at 19, but after a stint back Down Under, he returned seven years later to thrive on the other side of the Pennines with David Wagner's men.

GEOVANNI

HULL

The Brazilian schemer epitomised the Tigers' feelgood days, immediately after their Premier League arrival in 2008. His stunning equaliser against Arsenal quickly earned him BBC Goal of the Month that September.

MARCUS STEWART

IPSWICH

A consistent goalscorer in the Football League, the Tractor Boys' talisman then struck 19 times in his debut top-flight season in 2000-01 – only Chelsea's Jimmy Floyd Hasselbaink managed more that term.

CHRIS SUTTON

NORWICH

Capable of playing in defence as well as his more regular position upfront, Sutton steered the Canaries to third in the first Premier League campaign, then posted 25 goals in 1993-94. That summer, Blackburn forked out a British record £5m for the versatile star.

GUNNAR HALLE

OLDHAM

The Premier League's first two seasons both featured the Latics – Norwegian right-back Halle bobbled home the goal that kept them up in 1992-93 and impressed again before eventual relegation, later joining Leeds.

STEPHEN HUNT

READING

After helping the Royals bag promotion with a record 106 points, the bustling Irish wideman powered the Berkshire side to eighth in their debut Premier League campaign in 2006-07 – the club's best ever season.

BRIAN DEANE

SHEFFIELD UNITED

If a list of the greatest ever Premier League players had been compiled at 3.05pm on August 15, 1992, the Blades' icon would have been top. He nodded the league's first ever goal, against Manchester United.

MICHU

SWANSEA

The Spaniard scored twice in a 5-0 win at QPR on his Premier League bow – notching 18 goals in 2012-13. His bargain £2m fee became the yardstick by which to measure transfer value. "£18m? That's nine Michus."

JAN AAGE FJORTOFT

SWINDON

Signed following Swindon's promotion in 1993, the Norwegian netted 12 times in the top flight, including a hat-trick against Coventry. The Robins still finished bottom, shipping a century of goals at the other end.

TROY DEENEY

WATFORD

The grizzled striker smashed 47 goals in five Premier League seasons for the Hornets – in 2016, he was the subject of a £25m approach from reigning champions Leicester, but Watford wisely refused to let him leave.

ROBBIE EARLE

WIMBLEDON

Signed from Port Vale in 1991, the midfielder served Wimbledon for the entirety of their Premier League stretch – earning himself a crucial role for Jamaica at France 98, where he scored their first World Cup goal.

SAMSUNG
mobile

TITLES IN THIS SERIES

MYTHICAL CREATURES AROUND THE WORLD

MYTHICAL CREATURES WITH WINGS

MYTHICAL MONSTERS

MYTHICAL SEA CREATURES

Cavendish Square

ISBN: 9781502667335

9 781502 667335